TEHRANGELES DREAMING

FARZANEH HEMMASI

TEHRANGELES
DREAMING

INTIMACY AND IMAGINATION IN
SOUTHERN CALIFORNIA'S
IRANIAN POP MUSIC

Duke University Press · *Durham and London* · 2020

© 2020 Duke University Press
All rights reserved
Printed in the United States of America on
acid-free paper ∞
Designed by Matthew Tauch
Typeset in Portrait Text Regular and Helvetica
Neue Extended by Copperline Book Services

Library of Congress Cataloging-in-Publication Data
Names: Hemmasi, Farzaneh, [date] author.
Title: Tehrangeles dreaming : intimacy and imagination in
Southern California's Iranian pop music / Farzaneh Hemmasi.
Description: Durham : Duke University Press, 2020. |
Includes bibliographical references and index.
Identifiers: LCCN 2019041096 (print)
LCCN 2019041097 (ebook)
ISBN 9781478007906 (hardcover)
ISBN 9781478008361 (paperback)
ISBN 9781478012009 (ebook)
Subjects: LCSH: Iranians—California—Los Angeles—Music. |
Popular music—California—Los Angeles—History and
criticism. | Iranians—California—Los Angeles—Ethnic
identity. | Iranian diaspora. | Popular music—Iran—
History and criticism. | Music—Political aspects—Iran—
History—20th century.
Classification: LCC ML3477.8.L67 H46 2020 (print) |
LCC ML3477.8.L67 (ebook) | DDC 781.63089/915507949—dc23
LC record available at https://lccn.loc.gov/2019041096
LC ebook record available at https://lccn.loc.gov/2019041097

Cover art: Downtown skyline, Los Angeles, California,
c. 1990. GALA Images Archive/Alamy Stock Photo.

To my mother and father

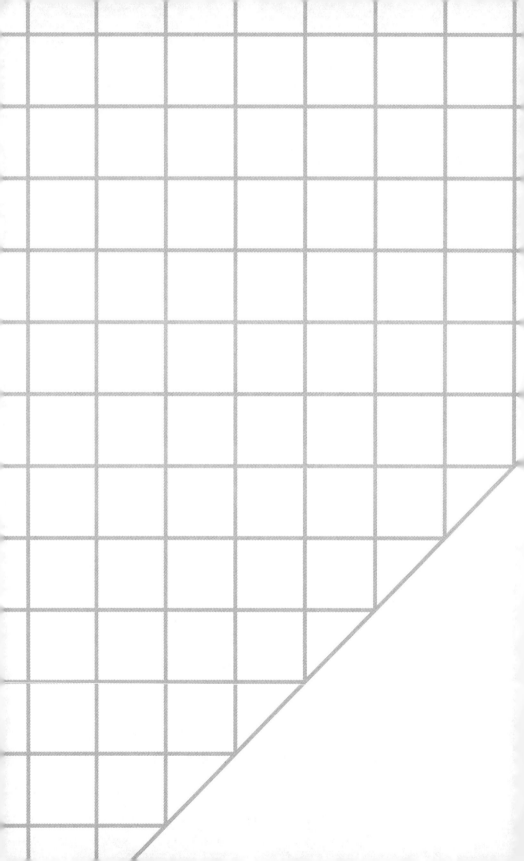

CONTENTS

ACKNOWLEDGMENTS

There is no way to fully acknowledge the contributions of research interlocutors, mentors, colleagues, friends, and family members to this book, but I will try. I do so with admiration and deep appreciation for the many, many people who inspired and influenced me. I hope they will find some small bit of themselves reflected in the following pages.

My first thanks go to Ken Wissoker for his enthusiasm about this project from first conversation to final process. The anonymous readers provided valuable recommendations that greatly improved the final product. Nina Oteria Foster was always ready to offer information and support, Kimberly Miller expertly copyedited my prose, and Liz Smith graciously shepherded the project through production.

Tehrangeles Dreaming officially began during my time in Columbia University's Department of Music. At Columbia I was taught and mentored by Ana María Ochoa Gautier, Aaron Fox, Chris Washburne,

Sandhya Shukla, Steven Feld, and Dieter Christensen. Also at Columbia I worked with Manouchehr Kasheff, Sherry Ortner, and Timothy Taylor. Each of these scholars provided a model of excellence and sources of inspiration. I thank them for their invaluable contributions to my dissertation and graduate education. Ghazzal Dabiri put me in touch with Shobeir, who generously offered his perspectives several times. William McAllister supported me with a fellowship, work space, and an interdisciplinary community in Columbia's Institute for Social and Economic Research and Policy; I was also lucky to hold a fellowship in Columbia's Middle East Institute, where I met students and faculty from across the New York area who helped put my work in broader regional perspective. Columbia University provided financial support throughout my graduate career, including a Lane Cooper Writing Fellowship, a Dissertation Completion Award, and a Herbert J. Hutner Award.

Scores of people generously shared their time and knowledge with me as I undertook research in Southern California. This book would not exist without the generosity of many individuals who took time out of their busy schedules to speak with me. Manouchehr Bibiyan, Kourosh Bibiyan, Mehrdad Pakravan, Vartan Avanessian, Jahangir Tabaraei, Rafik Avanessian, and Abbass Chamanara provided invaluable information about the business of music before the revolution in Tehran and after the revolution in Tehrangeles. Dariush Eghbali and Dr. Abbasseh Towfigh were exceptionally generous; Abbasseh has patiently answered my questions for years, and for this I am very grateful. Wonderfully informative conversations with Shahbal Shabpareh, Shahrzad Sepanlou, Babak Amini, Raha Etemadi, Zoya Zakarian, Farzin Farhadi, Nooshafarin, David Haddad, Farokh "Elton" Ahi, and Mehrdad Asemani are among those included in the book. Mahsa Zokaei gave me a taste of Iranian American life in the San Fernando Valley and beyond. I was able to undertake research in Southern California because of a PEO (Philanthropic Educational Organization) International Scholar Award, which I received through the kind nomination of Cheri De-Bruicker. Through this, together with a dissertation fellowship year from the Columbia Department of Music, I was able to assemble the resources needed to undertake research in Los Angeles.

My fieldwork began in 2006 not in Tehrangeles but in Tehranto (Toronto). With the support of the Canadian Embassy Canadian Studies Graduate Fellowship, I started a project about Iranian migrant musicians who settled in the Greater Toronto Area in the 1990s and 2000s. This work didn't make it into the final book, but in the process I met individuals who generously shared their insights, time, and connections with me, and were also instrumental to my Tehrangeles research. Chief among these are Reza Moghaddas, who put me in touch with Babak Amini, who in turn connected me to almost everyone I interviewed in Los Angeles. Reza, Setareh Delzendeh, E, and Sal were always kind to me. Kambiz Mirzaei helped me see the connections between Tehranto and Tehrangeles and shared his experiences working between these North American poles of Iranian cultural production. Arash Sobhani and Babak Khiavchi were instrumental in providing the perspectives of post-"underground" musicians. My research on the 2006 Iranian Intergalactic Music Festival in the Netherlands introduced me to a truly transnational network of musicians living in Iran and the diaspora who informed my perspectives on genre and generation, especially Arash TarantisT, Salome, Sholeh, Manny, Ramin Seyed-Emami, Melody and Safoura Safavi, and many others. In San Francisco, Ahmad Kiarostami, Lalé Welsh, Behrooz Bahmani, and Javid Jahanshah keyed me in to some of the distinctions between Northern and Southern Californian Iranian social life.

Thanks go to my fellow graduate students in New York who saw me and this project through thick and thin. In addition to my dear cohort members Niko Higgins and Morgan Luker, I count Tyler Bickford, Maria Sonevytsky, Lauren Ninoshvilli, David Novak, Jonathan Toby King, Brian Karl, and Evan Rapport as some of my closet colleagues and friends. Pardis Mahdavi generously provided me with fruitful contacts for my research in Los Angeles. Lauren, Maria, and Tyler deserve special thanks for their writing encouragement and support in the years since graduation. Tyler went over every word (at least twice), told me to get on with things when it was time, and was my biggest champion in the lengthy process of turning my research into a book. My friends in New York saw me through many stages of the writing of this book. Sam Burns, Ariana Souzis, Katie Tell, Amy Shatzkin, Nada Geha, Sarah Barrows, Casey Kelly, Beth Hayes, Laurent Auffret, Helen Georgas, Amanda Cox, Noah Leff, Jake Sherman, Shawna Wakefield, and many others were there for me again and again. Ghazal Keshavarzian connected me with friends and family in Toronto and Los Angeles who helped me very much.

Being located in New York City for so many years allowed me to access an exceptional group of scholars on the East Coast. At the City University of New York (CUNY) Grad Center, I took a course with Stephen Blum that deeply influenced how I think about Iranian music. He generously shared his insights, resources, archive, and time with me in and outside of class. Also at CUNY, I learned from and was encouraged by Mehdi Bozorgmehr, Jane Sugarman, and Ameneh Youssefzadeh. At New York University, I am grateful to Mohammad Mehdi Khorrami, who was willing to discuss research with me from my graduate student days to the final touches on the book, and to Nasser Danesh, whose Persian class was wonderful. Richard Wolf was also a mentor to me. Nahid Siamdoust generously offered me opportunities to present my work at New York University and at Yale. Afsaneh Najmabadi's response to a paper I gave at the 2014 International Society for Iranian Studies meeting inspired thoughts on women and music reflected in this book. Jason Mohaghegh shared his manuscripts and corresponded with me about silence and screams in Iranian poetry. A postdoctoral fellowship at the University of Pennsylvania in what is now called the Wolf Humanities Center was a blessing as I transitioned from graduate school to a full-time academic position at the University of Toronto. I also thank Laudan Nooshin, Mehdi Semati, Andrew Weintraub, and Bart Barendregt for their commentary on my work and their exemplary scholarship.

The University of Toronto's community of scholars and friends has been the perfect environment for this book's development and for academic life more generally. Jeff Packman, Joshua Pilzer, James Kippen, Annette Sanger, and Nasim Niknafs are the best colleagues I could ever hope for. Thanks go to Faculty of Music dean Don Mclean for his many levels of support for my research and professional development. Katie Kilroy-Marac, Sara Saljoughi, Emily Hertzman, Neda Maghbouleh, Nada Moumtaz, and Sarah Gutsche-Miller inspire me as scholars and women who do so much so well. Josh, Jim, Katie, and Emily all read chapter drafts and gave valuable feedback.

I am grateful for two fellowships from the Connaught Foundation that supported research for this book. Two grants from the University of Toronto's Jackman Humanities Institute indirectly supported the project by helping me develop on-campus forums for sharing my ideas as they developed. I have benefited from working with University of Toronto graduate students in ethnomusicology, especially Carolyn Ramzy, Yun Emily Wang, Gabriela Jimenez, Alia O'Brien, Hadi Milanloo, Hamidreza Salehyar, Nil Basdurak, Nadia Younan, Polina Dessiatnitchenko, Nate Renner, Jardena Gertler-Jaffee, Jennie Horton, Ryan Persadie, Jonathan Wu, and Sepideh Raissadat. Very special thanks to Dennis Lee for his help transcribing the musical examples that appear in the book. A well-timed course release granted by the

Faculty of Music was critical to moving forward on this project; I thank Nadia Younan and Yun Emily Wang for picking up my course on short notice while I wrote.

I am proud to be a part of the Iranian studies community at the University of Toronto, which is led by the dynamism and intellectual openness of Mohamad Tavakoli-Targhi. Mohamad, who also served on my dissertation committee, is a model of rigor, commitment, and generosity. Through Mohamad I met my dear friends Ida Meftahi at the beginning of my research, Golbarg Rekabtalaei in the middle, and Jairan Gahan toward the end. I have learned so much from each of them through our years of conversations about Iranian history, historiography, culture, literature, and more. I thank them for endless discussions, suggestions, inspirations, translations, and laughter throughout this process. Leila Pourtavaf and Shabnam Rahimi-Golkhandan offer further inspiration for what close readings of history can accomplish.

Other friends and colleagues in Toronto who have been especially important to this book are Ostad Pedram Khavarzamini and Araz Salek. Pedram patiently sat with me as we discussed and listened to numerous examples of *dāmbuli dimbol*. Kousha Nakhaei gave me space to test my ideas with the vibrant community of music lovers he has developed at Sarv Music Academy. Mehran Attaee has readily (and laughingly) accompanied me on many adventures into Iranian popular culture and beyond.

I thank my extended Iranian family in the United States and in Iran, especially Masoud, Mina, and Pegah; Saed and Elle; Susan and Ali, Kaveh and Nastaran, Naghmeh and Alireza; Aghdas and my dear departed uncle Reza; and all of my many uncles, aunts, and cousins. Pegah and I had many adventures in Iran; she was ever the patient translator and travel buddy. Thanks also to the Davanloo clan for showing me many different sides of Iranian life. A network of extended family friends taught me about the many ways of being and feeling Iranian in the United States. I ate, laughed, danced, and celebrated with the Khavanin, Bagheri, Biglary, Rezania, and Anvari families in North Dakota and Minnesota, and the Baharmand, Afshar, Motamedi/Kavosi, Bayordi, Nateghpour, Emtiaz, and Fazel/Fakheri families in Illinois.

Many thanks to my in-laws Judy and Len Linton, and David and Judith Anisfeld, for their love for me, their son, and our children throughout the many years it took to complete this project. Judy and Len housed me on many occasions as I undertook research in Southern California; their graciousness and warmth were a wonderful source of support.

My gratitude toward my parents, Harriette Hemmasi and Mohammad Hemmasi, is without limit. They have spent countless hours over the years parsing out the many ways culture and politics have affected our family, our selves, and the societies in which we now find ourselves. They have guided, supported, assisted, and inspired me in so many ways, and I am so lucky to have them as parents. I dedicate this book to them.

Words cannot express my thanks to my husband, Danny Anisfeld, who has never wavered in his love and commitment. Again and again, he has given me time, encouragement, and comfort while being an exemplar of responsibility, integrity, and fortitude. I could not ask for a better life partner. Finally, I thank my children, Soraya Io and Sandor Zal. I love you so much, and you are more to me than I could have ever imagined.

INTRODUCTION

In 2004 I traveled from Tehran to Kish, an island in the Persian Gulf just off Iran's southern coast. Since the late 1980s developers and businesspeople have transformed Kish into a free-trade zone and tourist attraction to compete with nearby Dubai. Today the island boasts fancy hotels, shopping malls, restaurants with live entertainment, and cultivated palm trees. It also maintains female-only beaches so that Iranians of both sexes can enjoy the water while upholding public-morality laws. Even so, the island has a reputation for less stringent morality enforcement than the mainland, which is crucial to attracting visitors and residents. On my visit that summer, I saw many young women sporting gauzy, brightly colored headscarves and very thin white shirts over their clothes, a contrast to the thicker overcoats and scarves women wore in Tehran.

I was sitting in the back seat of a taxi driven by a young man in his twenties when the music emanating from the stereo caught my attention. I heard a thumping *bandari* dance beat—a groove associated with the Persian Gulf—and Persian lyrics about Kish Island:

> *It's the land of fire—Kish is, Kish is, Kish is!*
> *It's where you can still be in love—Kish is, Kish is, Kish is!*
> *Its nights are blue—Kish, Kish, Kish!*
> *We won't be separated from it, will we? Kish, Kish, Kish.*[1]

Despite all its resonances with my present geographic location, I knew immediately this music was not produced in Iran. The giveaway was the lead singer's female voice. Since the establishment of the Islamic Republic of Iran, women have not been permitted to sing solo in public or have their solo singing voices recorded because of the immoral thoughts or actions they might inspire in male listeners. Instead, the lighthearted danceable pop I heard that day had made its way around the world to Kish from "Tehrangeles"—a portmanteau combining "Tehran" and "Los Angeles"—the Southern Californian home of an extensive Iranian expatriate culture industry.

Tehrangeles popular songs, music videos, and performances are spaces of desire and imagination where new, remembered, and as-yet-unrealized forms of Iranian identity and Iran itself are rehearsed. These take shape and are propelled through a transnational assemblage of media, policies, circulating representations, projections, and counterprojections that link expatriates and their home country in a long-term long-distance relationship. One example of Tehrangeles cultural producers' fabrication of an alternative Iran is the video accompanying "Kish," the song I heard in the taxi.[2] I first saw the video when I returned to Tehran; it was playing on satellite television in a family friend's living room. On the television screen, Tehrangeles vocalist Sepideh whipped her long blond hair back and forth as she danced on a Southern Californian beach, a stand-in for the Persian Gulf island's sandy shores. Moments later, she appeared in a low-cut negligee, sometimes reclining on a four-poster bed, sometimes posing in the sand as the waves lapped her body, all the while singing of a nightly dream that she'd returned to Kish. In other scenes, she was joined by a group of men and women dancing and playing instruments by a bonfire on the beach. Throughout the video, Sepideh flaunted her unfettered enjoyment of the pleasures of public singing, dancing, flirting, and fantasizing in a place that both was and was not Iran. The vocalist's imagined presence within her homeland was just as fantastical as the expatriate video version of Kish: most prominent Tehrangeles cultural producers have not visited Iran in de-

FIGURE I.1 Tehrangeles music videos' circulation into Iran brings Sepideh and her fantastical version of Kish Island into the country. Screen grab from "Kish," directed by Koji Zadori, on the DVD *Caltex Records 20 Music Videos*, Caltex Trading, Inc., 2007.

cades because they could be charged with public immorality, collaboration with opposition groups, or other crimes against the Iranian state. The music and the expatriate satellite television broadcasts that transport Sepideh's seductive performances into taxicabs and private homes are likewise prohibited within the country. Nevertheless, Tehrangeles popular culture has been an unremarkable, quotidian presence in Iran since the Iranian Revolution, entering the Iranian mediascape via cassette tapes, videocassettes, compact discs (CDs), file sharing, and the satellite dishes that, although prohibited, litter Tehran's roofs. In Tehrangeles media's transnational circulation, the sound and images propagated by Iranians in Southern California are constant reminders that counterrevolutionary ways of being are available outside the nation's borders and, through media, inside Iran as well.

Tehrangeles Dreaming explores a relatively ordinary activity—immigrant music and media production expressing longing for the homeland—in the context of its producers' extraordinary ambitions: to create globally circulating popular music and media that reach and remake Iranian culture in the realm of the imagination and on the ground. The relationship of Tehrangeles cultural production to territorial postrevolutionary Iran is characterized by a mixture of desire, opposition, distance, closeness, ambivalence, and, above all, a dynamic, productive synergy. In this book I show how Iranian expatriates in Southern California have used popular music and media to instantiate and claim enduring intimacy with their distant compatriots. Tehrangeles pop is a vehicle for homeland-diaspora connections and conflicts, and much more: it is where public forms call up intimate sentiments, memories, and urges; diasporic commerce abuts international politics; commercial pop overlaps with governmental propaganda; and freedom of expression is tempered by fears of exposure. Drawing on ethnographic research in Los Angeles, musical and textual analysis, and close attention to the music, video, and television programs that contribute to this transnational Persian-language mediascape, I argue that Iranian popular culture produced in Southern California exemplifies the manner in which culture, media, and diaspora have combined to create practices and identifications that respond to, but are not circumscribed by, the nation-state and its political transformations. These counter the revolution through both their initial refusal to disappear and their ongoing rejection of some of the revolution's central tenets: the moral purification of domestic public culture and public space, the denunciation of the deposed Pahlavi government and its cultures, the supremacy of Shiite Islam in national identity, and the rejection of Western cultural and political influence. Expatriate cultural producers interpret their products' popularity as evidence that the Islamic Republic has not fully met its citizens' needs and desires, and that they and their products may better represent "the people" than the Iranian government. "Giving the [Iranian] people what they want" is at once a business strategy and an ideological orientation that impacts how and why Tehrangeles popular culture sounds, looks, and travels the way it does.

The political potential of popular music and media is front and center in some expatriate cultural producers' actions and intentions. From their earliest days in exile, Tehrangeles performers have used popular music to respond to and intervene in Iranian national politics. This trend was inaugurated in 1979 with prerevolutionary star–turned–Tehrangeles founder Shahram Shabpareh's "Deyar" ("Homeland"), which is widely considered to be the first Persian-language pop song produced in Southern California.[3] Around the same time, fellow exile pop star Dariush Eghbali released "Vatan" ("Homeland"), an impassioned ballad that described the Iranian people after the revolution as an "imprisoned clan" and a "sacrificed tribe," and Iran as a bird with "broken" and "blood-soaked wings."[4] Tehrangeles songs and music videos depicting "Iran in ruins" (*Iran-e virān*) quickly made their way into Iran, where they contrasted sharply with the official celebration of the revolution. Both Tehrangeles's political edge and its reach into Iran have continued into the present. As this book describes, expatriate pop icons Googoosh (Faegheh Atashin) and Dariush have gone to great efforts to sing to and for the Iranian people from afar. Drawing on her prodigious talents and well-known biography of gender-based victimization, in the diaspora Googoosh has undertaken an array of politically inflected projects, including performing a song as a female version of "Iran herself" and creating a televised pop singing talent competition with the explicit goal of offering young Iranian women the opportunity to sing in public. Dariush's decades of rousing patriotic anthems, videos, and live performances have cemented his reputation as Tehrangeles's foremost "political singer" (*khānandeh-ye siyāsi*). He further combines music, media, and activism through his Ayeneh ("Mirror") Foundation, a Southern California–based nonprofit organization that uses satellite television and social media to send messages of support to Persian-speaking audiences worldwide.

The recuperation of prerevolutionary nationalist symbols and ideologies is another common way Tehrangeles cultural productions directly engage politics. Southern Californian television stations such as National Iranian Television (NITV) or Omid-e Iran ("Hope of Iran") refer to themselves and their missions in distinctly national terms, display the prerevolutionary flag, adopt pre-Islamic imagery, and even feature media personalities who speak a Persian purified of its many Arabic loanwords.[5] Skits parodying Muslim piety and insulting the Islamic Republic's leaders likewise blossomed in Los Angeles after the revolution. Tehrangeles television stations' many call-in talk show hosts can be heard openly cursing "the Islamic regime" between interviews with members of political opposition groups while branding their programs as avenues for open political expression and debate otherwise unavailable through Iranian state media.

While most Tehrangeles performers do not consider themselves activists or "political" (*siyāsi*), one of my aims in this book is to show how seemingly apolitical musicians and musical forms become entangled in the political. I have never heard anyone refer to Sepideh as a political singer, but the politics that thread through her visual, auditory, and discursive self-representation render her designation as apolitical inadequate as well. On her artist website, Sepideh describes herself as a "strong, sexy, proud, yet independent Persian woman . . . [unbound] by any taboo . . . [and] breaking away from the previously perceived Persian female image that has always been the victim throughout Iran's post-Islamic history!!!" She continues, "I am a part of all the proud and strong Persian women who . . . show the world we are not less than any man . . . !!!"[6] Sepideh's reference to women's victimization in "post-Islamic history" blames Islam for women's subordination. It also invokes a fantasy of a pre-Islamic Iranian society comparatively more favorable toward women.[7] Her self-designation as "Persian" is especially common in Tehrangeles as a way of invoking the vaguely positive imaginaries surrounding the Persian Empire, Persian carpets, and Persian cats as opposed to the threatening Islamic Republic of Iran. Finally, Sepideh describes her clothing and sexually suggestive performances—which contrast strikingly with domestic compulsory veiling laws and prohibitions on female singing—as emancipatory, taboo-breaking behaviors that speak (back) to Islam, patriarchy, and the world. Explaining her music and appearance in this way, Sepideh instructs her audiences to understand her performances in relation to cultural and political contestation even as her song lyrics and visual presentation largely steer clear of the markers of Tehrangeles nationalism described above.

Regardless of Sepideh's intentions, the singer's virtual presence in Iran stymies the state's attempts to maintain control over public morality (akhlāq-e 'omumi) and its public sphere—and is therefore a political challenge on multiple fronts. Iran's current public morality laws, outlined in the postrevolutionary Iranian Islamic Penal Code, forbid "haram [religiously prohibited] acts" that contravene "public prudency and morality." This section of the code obligates women to veil in public.[8] It further criminalizes producing and brokering "immoral media" and assigns specific punishments for "anyone who displays and shows to the public, or produces or keeps . . . advertisements, films . . . or anything . . . that violates public prudency and morality."[9] By these standards, Sepideh, her creative collaborators, those circulating the media in which she appears, and her audiences within Iran are all acting not only inappropriately but illegally. Should Sepideh ever realize her fantasy of returning to Kish, even if she comported herself appropriately once physically within the country, the vocalist could be tried for crimes against public morality. This is because, according to the code's article 7 (book 1, chapter 1), Iranian citizens can be held accountable for breaking Iranian laws while they are abroad.[10]

Those familiar with postrevolutionary Iran will be quick to note that plenty of technically illegal activities take place in private and public without consequence. Likewise, the interpretation and implementation of morality and other laws can be selective, irregular, and unpredictable. The practical, everyday, and legal delineation of the moral from the immoral, and the religiously licit (mashru') from the illicit, is context dependent and contested. Music is a shining example of official flexibility in defining the im/moral. During the revolution, Ayatollah Ruhollah Khomeini unequivocally dismissed music as sinful and distracting from reality.[11] This conceptualization of music's negative effects on listeners can be traced back through centuries of local custom and Shiite jurisprudence. However, he shortly made exceptions for revolutionary anthems and other ideologically aligned musical works (Siamdoust 2017, 87–94). In 1989, Khomeini officially changed his earlier position with a fatwa permitting "the sale of musical instruments so long as they are used for mashru' purposes." Once again, moral ambiguity was built into his conditional approval. The fatwa refers to musical instruments by the pejorative epithet *ālat-e lahv*, or "tools of frivolity," which is typically used in religious writings to malign music. This language therefore simultaneously confirms instruments' negative associations, approves their sale for "licit purposes," and leaves what constitutes a licit purpose open to interpretation.[12] The fatwa was then used to rationalize many kinds of previously off-limits musical activities. After 1989, music schools opened, concert halls hosted live performances, and musicians appeared on television—although with their "tools of frivolity" obscured behind large floral arrangements in a nod to historical prohibitions (Nooshin 2005a; Siamdoust 2017; Youssefzadeh 2000). Since the late 1990s, the Ministry of Islamic Culture and Guidance has come to grant recording, distribution, and performance permits to male performers of almost every style of music, even genres like rock and rap that were at one time disfavored because of their overtly Western associations. This dramatic shift in the status of music is an example of expediency (*maslahat*) or pragmatism supplanting rigid ideological adherence. Maslahat characterized many of Khomeini's religious-cum-policy decisions and has since become a hallmark of the mature Islamic Republic of Iran.[13]

Not everything is flexible, however. As of the time of writing, the official expansion of the moral has not extended to women's solo singing voices. Like the Islamic Penal Code's illegalization of women's uncovered hair in public, the continuing official exclusion of women's solo singing voices from public performances and recordings rests on their conceptualization as threatening to "public morality and prudency." This situation represents an obvious barrier for Sepideh's return to Iran, but it also provides an opportunity: public morality policies ironically augment the economic value and subversive potential of women's voices and their dancing, uncovered bodies.[14] Tehrangeles music and media producers are clear-eyed about the synergistic relationship of domestic prohibitions to expatriate business strategies. As Tehrangeles television producer Kourosh Bibiyan told me in 2007, expatriate satellite television stations "are not better [at attracting audiences] than [Iranian state media] except in music, because *they* cannot have . . . ten half-naked girls singing and dancing!" A similar logic of "giving the people what they want (and can't get in Iran)" applies to expatriate media personalities' and musicians' open criticism of the Iranian government, which is also curtailed in state media. Attending to Tehrangeles cultural production in its transnational context demonstrates how the Iranian mediascape has tested national, moral, and political boundaries.

The rest of this introduction lays out the contexts contributing to the formation of the Tehrangeles culture industries. I make a condensed presentation of the book's main theoretical interventions in the areas of social imaginaries, intimacy, and transnational-national politics, which are then fleshed out in the subsequent chapters. I explain the thought process behind the terms I employ to describe Tehrangeles cultural producers and productions, describe my research, and situate both my interlocutors' work and this book in a larger traffic of representations of Iranian culture and politics.

THE PREREVOLUTIONARY HISTORY
OF A POSTREVOLUTIONARY PHENOMENON

Like many diasporic and postrevolutionary cultural formations, Tehrangeles popular culture is both future oriented and deeply concerned with the past. Like other musicians and media producers who have fled revolutions—Cubans in Miami, Vietnamese in Orange County, Mainland Chinese in Taiwan after the establishment of the People's Republic of China, to name a few—the founding cohort of Iranian music and media producers in Southern California became champions of salvaged and alternative versions of national culture precisely as they met with rejection in their home country.[15] Some historical context is required to more fully appreciate which elements of prerevolutionary popular culture have become meaningful in Tehrangeles. My history will also illustrate how Tehrangeles artists and media producers understand the value of their contributions to what it means to be and feel Iranian.

The musicians and media producers who founded Tehrangeles experienced firsthand Iranian music's radically shifting moral and political position across the twentieth century. In the early part of the century, many Muslims avoided professional music making in part because of dominant, religiously derived understandings of *musiqi* (artful instrumental music), *ghanā* (artful song), and *lahv* (frivolity, diversion, amusement) as illicit activities. These beliefs coincided with a wide variety of musical and sounded performance genres that could be heard in mostly private or semiprivate settings, including the royal court, Sufi lodges, elite homes, gymnasiums (*zurkhāneh*), and coffeehouses (Chehabi 1999). The combination of Iranians traveling abroad and bringing back new ideas and the increase of foreigners and foreign media in the country stimulated the growth of urban sites of leisure like theaters and concert halls. As more Iranians publicly took part in activities beyond those explicitly approved by Shiite authorities, musical activities were increasingly incorporated into public life. In the span of a few decades, Tehran transformed from a city where music was rarely publicly heard and women wore veils on the street to a place with an active, cosmopolitan nightlife where one could take in a concert of live music, view an Indian or Egyptian movie musical, watch a female dancer onstage, and dance the tango at a local nightclub—all while drinking alcohol and mixing with members of the opposite sex (Meftahi 2017; Rekabtalaei 2018). The Allied Forces' occupation during World War II added fuel to this fire, as did the Pahlavi government's national radio broadcasts that prominently featured foreign and domestic music. For Tehrangeles cultural producers born in the 1930s and 1940s, during their childhoods music making was only just becoming a legitimate public entertainment. By their adolescence, music was widely available and more socially acceptable—at least in some quarters.

Many individuals in Tehrangeles cultural industries' founding cohort consider the 1950s to the 1970s to be the "golden age" (*dowrān-e talā'i*) of both Iranian popular music and Iran itself. It was in this period that they first entered the professional music business and, in some cases, became celebrities whose personas, musical works, and films shaped national popular culture. Musicians who were active during these decades generally delineate prerevolutionary popular music into two main categories: the populist *mardomi* (people's) genres and the sophisticated, Western-leaning, sentimental *musiqi-ye pāp* (pop music) genre of the young, aspiring cosmopolitans. Street-smart, colloquial mardomi music derived primarily from local versions of Arab popular music and the repertoires of Iranian urban popular entertainers called *motreb*. The style was associated with urban working-class cabarets and cafés and was popularized through the *filmfarsi* film genre, which commonly featured working-class characters and musical café scenes. The genres included under the mardomi umbrella tended to use Iranian and Arab instruments as well as violin, accordion, and clarinet— these played with Iranian and Arab tuning and in locally idiomatic ways.

In keeping with its imported name, musiqi-ye pāp was more Western in its musical references and performance conventions. Musiqi-ye pāp typically incorporated complicated arrangements for predominantly Western instruments; sentimental, sometimes literary lyrics; and youthful, fashionplate star vocalists. Pāp performers moved among film, television, radio, the recording studio, and the stage, sometimes performing for the royal family. Musiqi-ye pāp and mardomi were further distinguished by the fact that pāp was included on state radio and television, while mardomi was almost completely excluded. Mardomi and its stars were coded as low, vulgar, and traditional in the sense of being antimodern while, conversely, pāp stars' visual and sounded qualities manifested the glossy, cosmopolitan, sophisticated, and Western-leaning dispositions the Pahlavi state hoped to cultivate in its populace.[16]

All of this changed following the Iranian Revolution. While many in the Tehrangeles cultural industries nostalgically recall Mohammad Reza Pahlavi's reign, many others regard it as a time of political repression, pernicious foreign intervention, moral corruption, unequal distribution of wealth, and loss of authentic identity. Especially galvanized by leftists and Islamists, beginning in the 1960s anti-shah movements spread throughout Iran and culminated in the late 1970s with massive protests and a general strike that included an estimated 10 percent of the national population (Kurzman 2004, vii–viii).[17] In 1979, after months of unrest, riots, and killings, the shah admitted defeat and left the country with his family, never to return. The diverse coalition that had brought about the revolution gave way to Islamist dominance and the establishment of the Islamic Republic of Iran, a novel political system developed and led by high-ranking Shiite jurist Ayatollah Ruhollah Khomeini.

Under the "rulership of the jurisprudent" (velāyat-e faqih), the Islamic state took responsibility for safeguarding public morality according to historical, contemporary, and rapidly evolving clerical interpretations of Islamic law and local custom. In 1980 Khomeini famously compared music to opium and called for its "total elimination," a position in line with historically dominant, conventional Shiite understandings of music as immoral. Along with members of the political opposition, violent counterrevolutionaries, prostitutes, and drug dealers, celebrity vocalists were summoned to the dreaded revolutionary tribunals because, as Ayatollah Mohammad Mohammadi Gilani explained, "everyone knows that it was through these singers that we had so much moral corruption in our society."[18] High-profile musicians', actors', and media producers' contributions to popular culture were reframed as corruption and crime. There was no legitimate space for them or their work in Iran. For many of the popular musicians who fled the country either before or after their brush with revolutionary justice, the Islamic Republic's establishment marked the end of their careers within Iran and the beginning of their careers in exile.[19]

TEHRANGELES PEOPLE

The sudden influx of popular musicians and media producers into Los Angeles was critical in establishing this diasporic hub's distinctiveness, but Iranians had already been flocking to Southern California and the United States more generally throughout the prior decades. Friendly relations between the US government and the sha, (who had the American and British governments to thank for engineering the 1953 coup securing his rule) meant that from the 1950s to the end of the 1970s, there were many Americans in Iran and many Iranians in America. California was especially popular with Iranians pursuing higher education. In the 1970s, roughly fifty thousand Iranian students attended American colleges and universities, with many electing to attend the Golden State's high-quality yet affordable state universities (Shannon 2017). Some of these students and their families settled in the United States, and especially in California, establishing enough of a presence to sustain Iranian-oriented restaurants and other businesses that have lasted to this day. Some students also returned to Iran, bringing back their foreign education—and in my father's case a foreign wife as well. In 1971 my Iranian father received his doctorate from the University of Indiana; he and my Euro-American mother married in the same year. Shortly thereafter, they moved to Tehran and then to Shiraz. Both of my parents taught at what was then called Pahlavi University. I was born in Shiraz in 1975, and our social circle included many families consisting of an Iranian husband and American wife with the same basic origin story as our own.

The political unrest of the late 1970s and the eventual 1978–1979 revolution spurred the departure of thousands of Iranians and most foreigners as well. Given its already established Iranian community and a climate and mountainous landscape recalling Tehran, Los Angeles was an obvious choice for those with the means to choose where they landed. Families with connections to the monarchy, members of political opposition groups, and individuals from religious minorities persecuted under the Islamic Republic were among the first to leave Iran and settle in Los Angeles. (After leaving Iran in 1980, my family considered moving to Los Angeles as well, but because my father found an academic post in northern California, we eventually resettled there.) Today Iranians live in large numbers from San Diego to Ventura County, with especially visible populations in the western Los Angeles neighborhoods of Westwood, Beverley Hills, and Santa Monica, and throughout the towns lining Los Angeles County's San Fernando Valley. Shiite Muslims, Jews, Christians, Baha'is, and Zoroastrians are all represented in Southern California, as are Iranians of Persian, Azeri Turkish, Armenian, Assyrian, Kurdish, Arab, and other ethnicities (Bozorgmehr 1997, 2011; Kelley, Friedlander, and Colby 1993). Immediately following the revolution and the termination of Iranian and American diplomatic relations, US borders were closed to most Iranians hoping to move to or study in America. Despite these challenges, over the intervening decades Iranians have continued to enter the United States as economic migrants, asylees, refugees, and especially university students. However, the majority of individuals and families who established Iranian Southern California and the Tehrangeles media industries arrived from Pahlavi Iran.

The accidental founders of Tehrangeles pop were in California at the time of the revolution for nonpolitical reasons. Singer and songwriter Shahram Shabpareh and the vocalists Ebi, Shahrokh, and Shohreh Solati were in the United States to perform for local Iranian audiences, while music producer Vartan Avanessian was in Southern California on a business trip. When news of the shah's ouster and the Islamist triumph reached them, these musicians decided it was better to remain in the United States than risk repercussions for their "morally corrupting" activities. Especially in their early decades, the Tehrangeles culture industries represented the adaptation and continuation of Pahlavi music and media producers' careers and professional networks. Vartan Avanessian, Jahangir Tabaraei, and Manouchehr Bibiyan—prolific music producers with large catalogs of recordings and strong social and professional networks across the prerevolutionary domestic Iranian culture industries—were crucial to establishing the Tehrangeles music business in the 1980s. Prerevolutionary musiqi-ye pāp celebrities including Vigen Derderian, Dariush, Ebi, Shahram Shabpareh, Siavash Ghomeishi, Hassan Shamaeizadeh, Leila Foruhar, and Shohreh Solati were all in Los Angeles by the late 1980s. Singers specializing in light classical repertoire like the female vocalists Hayedeh, Mahasti, and Homeira also moved to Southern California, as did mardomi singers like Sousan and Abbas Ghaderi. Numerous well-known lyricists like Shahyar Ghanbari, Touraj

Negahban, and Zoya Zakarian who were active in the prerevolutionary industry also moved to Los Angeles, along with composers and arrangers like Manouchehr Cheshmazar, Farid Zoland, Jahanbakhsh Pazouki, and others with whom they had collaborated in Iran. Tehrangeles-based musicians also worked with their colleagues who landed in western Europe, including composer Esfandiar Monfaredzadeh and lyricist Iraj Jannatie Ataie. By the 1990s, Tehrangeles was the primary destination for aspiring Iranian pop musicians. Tehrangeles stars who first made their names in Southern California include the duo Andy and Kourosh, Moein, Faramarz Assef, Omid, Mansour, and Shakila; the prolific producer Schubert Avakian is also in this category. First-generation immigrants fleeing the revolution, and individuals like Sepideh who moved to the United States as children or teenagers during the Iran-Iraq War, are more often participants in the Iranian music industry than second-generation youth who grew up in North America.[20] There are also more men at all levels of the music and media industry, with women active primarily as vocalists and lyricists. The concentration of power in the hands of Tehrangeles's founding cohort—most of whom are now aged between fifty and ninety—has meant that this group's perspectives have been somewhat disproportionally represented in Tehrangeles media, even when younger vocalists, musicians, or spokespeople are the ones speaking or singing.

Taken as a group, Iranians in the United States have made their mark as "high-status immigrants," boasting impressive levels of academic achievement, entrepreneurship, and financial success in comparison to both many other immigrant groups and Euro-Americans as a whole (Bozorgmehr and Douglas 2011; Bozorgmehr and Sabagh 1988). The founding generation of Tehrangeles popular culture doesn't quite fit this profile: for many in this group, their greatest financial success and fame were in prerevolutionary Iran and didn't necessarily translate into the more modest conditions of the diaspora. Instead, an important stream of Tehrangeles performers' income comes from performing at wealthy Iranians' festivities, first in Los Angeles and later elsewhere in the diaspora. Entrepreneurship has been crucial to Tehrangeles music and media companies: a plethora of Iranian-owned terrestrial and internet radio stations, audiovisual production and reproduction businesses, cable and satellite television stations, nightclubs and restaurants, party and concert promoters, and other companies and individual ventures have generated the business infrastructure for this popular music's local and international distribution and performance.

Southern California's Persian-language popular music is stylistically varied, including sentimental ballads, patriotic songs about the homeland, songs about exile, covers and adaptations of prerevolutionary classic songs and genres, and lots and lots of dance music. When Iranians speak of "Tehrangeles pop" or especially *los ānjelesi* pop (pop "of Los Angeles"), they typically mean upbeat dance music performed by a soloist singing light, colloquial lyrics. This also has affective associations: Tehrangeles pop is generally thought of as music meant to enliven a social gathering and put listeners in a good mood. In Tehrangeles today, a few musicians limit themselves to the sort of prerevolutionary, smooth, Western-leaning, sentimental pop style (e.g., Ebi) while others are primarily mardomi artists (like Ahmad Azad), but many others compose and perform across genre boundaries to appeal to as large an audience as possible. Tehrangeles also has a less commonly acknowledged serious side, which is on display in certain artists' morose romantic pieces and in patriotic and "political" songs evoking Iran's present "ruin" and its future potential. Finally, one of the expatriate culture industries' greatest sources of income and material has been the creative remediation of popular music from the "golden age," roughly concurrent with Mohammad Reza Pahlavi's reign.

LOCATING TEHRANGELES

When either Iranians or non-Iranians speak of a "Little Iran" or "Little Persia" neighborhood, they are usually referring to the intersection of Ohio Avenue and Westwood Avenue, where many of the city's oldest Iranian-owned businesses are concentrated: Attari Sandwich Shop, the music store Music Box LA, Sholeh Restaurant, and Gol o Bolbol Ice Cream. Within these few blocks, visitors can purchase Iranian groceries, pick up tickets for an upcoming pop or classical concert, buy Persian-language magazines and books produced in Los Angeles and in Iran, and order a plate of rice, grilled tomato, and kebab. Other small businesses with Persian lettering advertise immigration services, beauticians, passport photos, and music lessons. Impressed by the number of Iranian establishments on this stretch of Westwood that bore the names of prerevolutionary Iranian businesses, anthropologist Fariba Adelkhah suggests that these few blocks were "une espèce de réinvention ou de reconstitution quelque peu nostalgique du Téhéran des années 1970" (a kind of reinvention or somewhat nostalgic reconstruction of 1970s Tehran; 2001, 3). If one walks north on Westwood and makes a right before Wilshire, one finds, tucked behind a public library and a park-

FIGURE I.2 A young woman models a patriotic baseball cap at Balboa Park's annual Sizdah Be Dar festival in 2007. Photograph by the author.

ing deck, the Pierce Brothers Memorial Park and Mortuary where Iranian businesspeople, artists, scholars, political figures, and pop music stars are buried alongside American celebrities including Peggy Lee, Dean Martin, and Burt Lancaster. Beverley Hills is also a kind of Iranian neighborhood marked by a high concentration of especially Jewish Iranian residents and the infamous "Persian palace" mansions built for Iranians (Maghbouleh 2017, 39–48). Jamshid "Jimmy" Delshad was mayor of Beverley Hills between 2007 and 2008, and then again between 2010 and 2011. Elsewhere in Los Angeles County, otherwise public spaces become temporarily Iranian for special events like the pre-Islamic Chaharshanbeh Suri festival on the beach in El Segundo, where people jump over fires before the New Year, or the Sizdah Be Dar festival on the thirteenth day of the New Year that brings Iranians to the San Fernando Valley's Balboa Park. Iranians also take over various large-capacity performance venues like the Gibson Amphitheater when Tehrangeles pop stars play to the local crowd.

Tehrangeles music and media businesses are neither in Westwood nor in Beverley Hills—these are several miles northwest in the more affordable and more ethnically diverse San Fernando Valley. During my fieldwork

FIGURE I.3 A stand at the Balboa Park Sizdah Be Dar festival in 2007 sells patriotic caps with a distinctly Tehrangeles bent: the lion, sword, and sun image from the prerevolutionary flag; the word "Iran"; and the winged Faravahar, a pre-Islamic Zoroastrian symbol that has become a popular secular sign of Iranian heritage. Photograph by the author.

and on subsequent visits, I would wander Westwood in the morning, have a bowl of *āsh-e reshteh* (noodle soup) at Attari, and then drive north on the 405 over the Sepulveda Pass, getting off at the Reseda or White Oak Avenue exits to meet someone at a Coffee Bean and Tea Leaf café for an interview or chat. Ventura Boulevard boasts many Iranian businesses and synagogues with Persian signage directly along the avenue and in its numerous strip malls, where they are often sandwiched in with other "ethnic" stores. I would sometimes stop at a strip mall with a Persian-language sign advertising *terāfik eskul* ("traffic school"), which also included a Himalayan restaurant and the small shop Shemshak Juice selling fresh-squeezed pomegranate juice and willow-tree water imported from Iran. Iranian entertainment businesses are more hidden. Cabaret Tehran, a major performance venue for Tehrangeles pop musicians, has a daytime alter ego as the lunch spot Mediterranean Express; its nightclub persona is unapparent until around eight in the evening, when the pink neon Persian-script Cabaret Tehran sign is

FIGURE I.4 A stand organized by monarchists at the Balboa Park Sizdah Be Dar festival features a portrait of Reza Pahlavi, son of the deposed monarch Mohammad Reza Pahlavi and his wife, Farah Diba. Photograph by the author.

turned on and crowds of nattily dressed Iranians smoking, chatting, and drinking tea fill up the patio for an evening of karaoke or a live performance by a Tehrangeles vocalist. Music and media production businesses, and the transnational networks that carry Tehrangeles products to international Iranian audiences, are even less apparent to casual observers. My visits to music company headquarters and television stations took me to unassuming business complexes near auto repair garages and donut shops that gave no hint of the colorful popular culture their tenants produced. Since the 1980s, music and television entrepreneurs have collaborated with and even opened offices close to one another—for instance, during my fieldwork the television station Jam-e Jam and the music company Avang were on the same floor of a Ventura Boulevard office building, while the music company Taraneh and the television station Omid-e Iran were in the same industrial park.

Tehrangeles artists extend their audiences beyond the local through regular international tours. Tehrangeles vocalists make frequent trips to cities in North America and western Europe with large Iranian diaspora populations, sometimes playing small clubs and sometimes major venues, as when Googoosh played Royal Albert Hall in 2013. While several million Iranians

FIGURE I.5 A 2007 advertisement for Cabaret Tehran appearing in the local Iranian periodical *Javanan (Youth) Magazine* contains a minimal amount of English. The Persian text at the top of the page reads, "When night falls, there's no place like Cabaret Tehran." The artists performing are the comedienne Houtan and the prerevolutionary-turned-Tehrangeles pop singer Sattar, "a beloved singer for three generations." *Javanan Magazine*, May 15, 2007, p. 65.

now live in the West, Tehrangeles artists' largest potential audiences are, naturally, within Iran. However, because Tehrangeles artists don't generally visit Iran, and because there are very few countries to which Iranian passport holders can travel without a (difficult-to-acquire) visa, it has taken some creativity for Tehrangeles artists to reach the domestic market. As of 2019, the only countries Iranian citizens can visit without a visa are Armenia, Dominica, Ecuador, Georgia, Haiti, Malaysia, Micronesia, Serbia, Turkey, and Venezuela.[21] Tehrangeles performers have attempted to meet Iranian residents partway by regularly staging large concerts in Turkey, Armenia, Georgia, and Malaysia as well as in a few other neighboring countries popular with Iranians, like the United Arab Emirates. These lucrative tours often take place during the Iranian New Year season, which coincides with the vernal equinox and is a national holiday. Since the mid-2010s, some Tehrangeles artists—Sepideh included—have begun performing on Iranian-oriented luxury cruises embarking from the Turkish Mediterranean. The combined costs of plane flights, hotels, and concert tickets are prohibitively expensive for average Iranians, but the events are popular and profitable enough to have kept Tehrangeles artists coming back year after year. Some Tehrangeles artists also entertain at lavish weddings; I heard tales of a very well-established Tehrangeles vocalist being paid $25,000 plus expenses to perform at an Iranian couple's wedding in Dubai.

By far the most common way in which audiences access Tehrangeles music is via mass media. During my fieldwork in the mid-2000s, satellite television broadcasts of Tehrangeles music videos and programs featuring or hosted by Tehrangeles performers were the primary transnational carriers of expatriate popular culture. These satellite television stations are free to air, meaning that they are accessible to anyone with a satellite dish pointed at the right celestial coordinates—no subscription is required. Iranians the world over own satellite dishes, including inside Iran, where they are illegal but largely tolerated. Since the mid-2000s the internet has become an increasingly important avenue for selling, advertising, and disseminating Tehrangeles popular music. Instagram is currently very popular within Iran and with Tehrangeles pop musicians; it is also one of the few foreign social media sites that are not blocked in Iran—at least at the time of writing. However, satellite television continues to be effective in reaching domestic audiences because fewer people have internet in their homes; the state's internet filters and policies of keeping internet speeds low are also factors. While filter breakers and virtual private networks are available in Iran, and while the state also uses satellite-jamming technology to attempt to block

FIGURE I.6 An online poster advertises Sepideh's 2018 international tour. The locations listed have significant Iranian migrant populations or are countries Iranians can visit without visas (here, Turkey and Georgia). Screen grab from Sepideh's official website, accessed March 20, 2019, http://sepidehmusic.com.

foreign broadcasts, overall it is less trouble to install a dish on one's roof and point it toward the Hotbird satellite orbiting Earth at thirteen degrees east. The satellite television business began in Southern California in the early 2000s and has since spread to the United Arab Emirates, Germany, Turkey, Canada, and the United Kingdom. Several Western governments have also embraced Tehrangeles and other Iranian expatriate popular culture as part of their "cultural diplomacy" initiatives. Voice of America Persian Language Service, Radio Free Europe/Radio Liberty's Radio Farda (Radio "Tomorrow"), and BBC Persian produce high-quality Persian-language television and radio broadcasts and internet programming for domestic and diasporic Iranian audiences; these include interviews, videos, and performances by Tehrangeles pop musicians.[22] Like satellite dishes, none of these media outlets are officially permitted, but they are nonetheless widely accessed in Iran.

As the foregoing account makes clear, Tehrangeles musicians and media producers and their productions are imbricated in an assemblage of private and governmental, diasporic and domestic, and commercial and political networks and conflicts. The Iranian state interprets unofficial media as part of "soft war" (*jang-e narm*) on Iranian citizens by Western and Iranian opponents seeking to foment a "velvet revolution" (*enghelāb-e makhmali*) (Naficy 2012; Price 2012; Rahimi 2015; Semati 2012; Sreberny 2013). Participating in this assemblage therefore puts Tehrangeles musicians in a precarious position vis-à-vis the Iranian state.[23] At times, Iranian officials have questioned, harassed, arrested, and criminally charged Iranians who work with or appear on these outlets, including Iranian citizens who live and work abroad

(Michaelsen 2018). A standout example is the Tehran Revolutionary Court 28's March 2017 announcement, published in domestic media, that it had sentenced Googoosh in absentia to sixteen years in prison. Her crimes were "propaganda against the Islamic Republic" and "creating centers of corruption and corrupting the public."[24] Googoosh has not set foot in Iran since her departure in 2000 and is extremely unlikely to return to Iran to serve her time, but she remains accessible to domestic audiences through foreign government and expatriate media and through concerts in neighboring countries—at least one of which was sponsored by the US government–funded Radio Farda.[25] While the Revolutionary Court sentence is best understood as symbolic, it exemplifies how Iranian expatriate popular music and musicians intertwine moral, commercial, and political concerns, and how transnationally circulating popular music produced halfway around the world becomes embroiled in tense relationships between homeland and diaspora, and state and international actors—all of whom have competing stakes in the Iranian nation.

THE DEGENERATE LOS ĀNJELESI SINGER

Like traveling Tehrangeles music and performers, stereotypes of Tehrangeles Iranians and Tehrangeles singers also circulate between the diaspora and Iran. The Los Angeles Iranian stereotype is not so different from common perceptions of "Hollywood people" and their shallow money-mindedness. "Persians" in Los Angeles are wealthy or want to be perceived as such; wear flashy, expensive clothes and jewelry; embrace surgical enhancements; drive fancy cars; and live in ostentatious mansions in exclusive neighborhoods. They are anti-intellectual, petty, and superficial. Tehrangeles Iranians have the additional dubious distinction of being obsessed with their pre-Islamic or Aryan roots and at the same time out of touch with contemporary post-revolutionary Iran. A plethora of songs, skits, television programs, and films made by Iranians elsewhere in the diaspora and in Iran play on the Tehrangeles Iranian stereotype.[26] Take, for example, "Iruni-ye LA" ("LA Iranian"), a song by the Iranian British expatriate hip-hop group Zed Bazi:

> *Dear wealthy Aunt Fati*
> *Bought a house on Hollywood Boulevard*
> *I say, "Aunt Fati, are you ready to party?*
> *I'll come to your house tonight and we'll go to Café Latin."*

She says, "Don't call at 5 o'clock because I'm at the gym
Every night I eat salad [because] I'm on a diet,
My eye color is the same as my [blue] jeans
Now, let me check out your six-pack [abdominal muscles]."

After establishing their superficiality, Zed Bazi describes Tehrangeles Iranians' confused identity:

Here [in Los Angeles] we're happy for no reason (alaki khoshim)
We wear sandals,
We want to be Western (farangi)
We want to be "Vanak kids" [a Tehran neighborhood]
We say, "West Coast, motherfucker"
Every time we stand up[27]

Since the advent of the American A&E television network's reality television show *Shahs of Sunset*, focusing on a glamorous group of young, wealthy, second-generation Jewish and Muslim Iranians cavorting around Southern California, mainstream American television audiences have had increased access to Tehrangeles stereotypes.[28]

One of the most recognizable and ridiculed figures Iranians associate with Tehrangeles is the los ānjelesi singer (*khānandeh-ye los ānjelesi*) and the music she or he performs, which is also called "los ānjelesi." *Los ānjelesi* literally means "of Los Angeles" but also indexes a host of other attributes, especially frivolity, shallowness, cheapness, superficiality, and low-quality, crass commercialism. Above all, los ānjelesi pop is dance music meant for parties. While far from everything produced by Tehrangeles artists is dance music, music with danceable rhythms was historically the most profitable and therefore the most prolific style, making the association between Tehrangeles and dance music hard to shake. Having witnessed expatriate television interviews become tense or hostile when it was suggested that a musician was los ānjelesi, I never dared to use the term for fear of offending my interlocutors. Calling a musician los ānjelesi has the added insult of inscribing an individual as "of Los Angeles" (its literal meaning) and therefore not primarily "of Iran" (*irāni*). As an example, Southern California–based vocalist and songwriter Mehrdad Asemani protested on an expatriate talk show that the los ānjelesi moniker was "made up by the Islamic Republic" to insult musicians like himself. "I'm not from Los Angeles," he angrily exclaimed. "My father's not from Los Angeles—I'm a kid . . . from Hafez Street! I fought in the war with Iraq. I wasn't born in Los Angeles!"[29] The los ānjelesi taint has also extended to me as someone misguided or ignorant enough to consider Tehrangeles pop worthy of study. Confused looks, polite avoidance, and peals of laughter are among the reactions I have received when telling Iranians my research topic. While attending a party in 2006 in Toronto at the home of an expatriate journalist, I was introduced to another well-known journalist who had recently fled Iran following the closure of the reformist press. After a few pleasantries, I told him that I would soon be heading to Los Angeles to study its Iranian music scene. He paused for a moment and then leveled a dismissive scowl at me. "So, you want to study shit-*shenāsi*?" he growled. His improvised combination of the English word "shit" with the Persian suffix for "-ology" (*shenāsi*) denigrated my research and me as well. I was, apparently, a "shit-ologist" (*shitshenās*).

Despite their postrevolutionary geographic inscription onto Southern California, the negative discourses surrounding professional performers and the upbeat party music they play have their roots in a national history of religious, elitist, and leftist prejudices against immoral and "degenerate" (*mobtazal*) entertainments and the professionals who produce them.[30] *Tehrangeles Dreaming* positions these disparaging sentiments as extensions of Iranian national changes, concepts, and politics of culture into the diaspora and back again. Today cultural elites and the postrevolutionary state tar Tehrangeles pop musicians with the same brush as their low-status professional entertainer ancestors known as *motreb*, relocating the negative legacy of the motreb, immorality, and degeneration outside of Iran and into exile. Los ānjelesi music is "bad music" (see Washburne and Derno 2004), and los ānjelesi singers are "bad people" who callously target audiences' basest desires for entertainment, titillation, and distraction. In official Islamic Republic discourse, Tehrangeles cultural producers are both immoral and *farāri*, or escapees—people who fled the country without serving time for their moral crimes. They are pathetic, faithless self-exiles who abandoned their homeland in its moment of need and are now deservedly cursed with permanent separation and irrelevance. At worst, they are agents in a soft war who "spread corruption" via expatriate media, including those funded by Western governments, treasonously attempting to undermine the state from afar. This book documents some of the main ways Tehrangeles cultural producers negotiate these charges through cultural production: creating alternative histories in which they are not villains but heroes, making politically committed music and attempting to politically mobilize transnational audiences, and arguing for dance, dance music, and levity as necessary elements of being and feeling Iranian.

One commonality shared by most individuals I interviewed for *Tehrangeles Dreaming* was their extended, open-ended, physical absence from territorial Iran. The terms of their separation were emotionally complicated and not always something we discussed; when it came up, I noted a tendency to mention fear of potential consequences were they to return.[31] Many of my older interlocutors who have been outside the country for decades used the terms *ghorbat* or *tab'id* to describe their condition. *Tab'id* translates as political exile, while the multivalent term *ghorbat* implies both the state of being away from one's home and the psychological or metaphysical experience of estrangement. Tehrangeles musicians of the founding generation are doubly estranged from postrevolutionary Iran. The first estrangement is their ideological exclusion from the nation: when the postrevolutionary government declared popular music and musicians immoral and degenerate, it also designated these individuals as obstacles to the country's new direction. Their main options were to reform, retreat, or remove themselves. Physically departing Iran and not returning for decades, or perhaps ever again, is the next level of estrangement. Unfamiliarity with postrevolutionary Iran is built into Tehrangeles's foundations. Expatriate music pioneers Shahram Shabpareh, Ebi, and Dariush all left before the Islamic Republic's consolidation and have therefore never experienced firsthand the transformed society toward which so many of their songs and videos are directed. Estrangement can occur even in encountering Iranians from postrevolutionary Iran, as revealed to me in my conversation with an elderly Tehrangeles media producer. Since the revolution, this man had resided in Los Angeles, where he made television programming aimed at both diaspora and Iran-based audiences. He had not returned to Iran in part because he feared what might happen when officials learned he was in the country. Instead, he arranged to travel to a resort in Turkey popular with Iranian tourists to see for himself "what Iranians from Iran were like." He found his luxury hotel to be as nice as anything one would find in the United States, but he was shocked that the female Iranian tourists wore headscarves as they mingled with other guests in the hotel's elegant lobby. They were outside of Iran and away from the Islamic Republic's compulsory veiling laws—why wouldn't they opt to socialize in public without wearing hijab? He dismissed my suggestions that the women might have maintained their modest covering out of piety, or that they had worn scarves in public their entire lives and might feel uncomfortable without them. No, he retorted, that wasn't it at all. They had "censored themselves" (*khod-sānsuri kardand*). Traveling to Turkey put him in physical proximity to people living in postrevolutionary Iran, but the experience did not overcome his feelings of estrangement. It may even have intensified them.

Over the years, I have begun to conceive of Tehrangeles cultural producers who remain outside of, and committed to, their homeland as "expatriates." Though this term comes with the sense of having chosen to leave one's home, and is therefore distinct from the fear, persecution, and hardships that impelled some of my interlocutors to relocate, I choose this term for its open-endedness. I am especially seduced by the aptness of its constituent parts—*ex-* (outside) and *patria* (native land)—which is the crux of Tehrangeles cultural producers' predicament and the source of some opportunities as well. I sometimes use "exile" in discussions where individuals have described their separation as permanent. I reserve "diaspora," a term not very much used by my interlocutors in Los Angeles but common in academic literature about Iranians living abroad, to refer to the totality of Iranians residing outside of Iran. Some scholars of migration prefer to employ "diaspora" for some later stage of migrant collective identity that is defined by "relations of difference" from both host and homeland societies (see Tölölyan 2007). What I find among older Tehrangeles residents, by contrast, is a population that has lived outside of Iran for decades but asserts its continuity and connection with homeland populations through an imagined transcendent Iranian culture in/and/as mass-mediated communications. I apply "diaspora" to refer to the steady Iranian out-migration to North America, an ever-growing and very diverse group of people. Finally, I use "diaspora" as "a category of practice" that is "used to make claims, to articulate projects, to formulate expectations, to mobilize energies, [and] to appeal to loyalties" (Brubaker 2005, 12).

THE MEANS AND DREAMS OF CONNECTION

Insofar as Tehrangeles cultural producers' separation from Iran is central to their experiences and self-regard, much of their work and discursive self-presentation rests on their assertion of an enduring connection to their compatriots at home. These assertions take different forms: references to large groups of devoted fans in Iran, statements that they know what the Iranian people want and how to give it to them, or even claims to influence people and political outcomes within the country through their music and media productions. *Tehrangeles Dreaming* examines expatriate imaginations of influence on, and intimacy with, their global Iranian audiences.

My decision to call these connections "imaginary" and to title the book *Tehrangeles Dreaming* is consciously double-edged. Iranians on every side of the political spectrum can be heard deriding Tehrangeles media producers for delusions of grandeur and their unverifiable claims of popularity in Iran. The "dreaming" in the book's title acknowledges that desire and fantasy are productive activities with indeterminate empirical effects. Dreams exist in an unresolved relation with the real. Dreaming also connects to my treatment of expatriate cultural producers' media work as "modern social imaginaries" (C. Taylor 2002). One of the core observations of the social imaginaries literature is that mass media and technologically mediated communications are the primary means through which we become acquainted with and feel ourselves to belong to groups whose members we may never meet (see Anderson 1983; Appadurai 1996; Axel 2002; Warner 2002). Our knowledge of these groups, and the world beyond our proximate environments, derives from the interplay between representations (especially discourse and media), their circulation, and the imaginations these representations and circulations contain and stimulate. This is equally true for the worlds and people in which we have no interest and those we learn to identify as "our own"—specific people like family members from whom we are physically separated and people we may never meet but nevertheless feel we know, like celebrities and politicians. Representation, circulation, and imagination are likewise the building blocks of powerful abstractions like society, nations, diasporas, markets, publics, the *'umma* (the totality of Muslims), the "global community," and so on, to which we can claim membership, from which we can be excluded, and that operate without much relation to us at all. When Tehrangeles cultural producers are dreaming of Iran or imagining their connections with Iranians through media production, circulation, and communication, they are contributing to these social imaginaries. At different points in the book, I relate the dialectic of physical and temporal distance and music-, media-, and communications-enabled closeness that I argue is central to Tehrangeles popular culture to some of the social imaginaries listed here—particularly nations and publics— to shed light on the struggle to gain knowledge of things and people with the vast yet always limited resources available to us. Social imaginaries may be fictional but are nevertheless the kinds of "dreams that matter" (Mittermaier 2011).

The space between the known and the imagined can be occupied by hope and possibility, but also by fear. Recurrent nightmares of surveillance, conspiracy, and insecurity are also themes in *Tehrangeles Dreaming*. These are the dark sides of social imaginaries: the comforting assertion that "we are all connected" can quickly give way to the paranoiac's overwhelming realization that "it's all connected" to unseen forces and political plots (Apter 2006, 366). Iranians have long considered paranoia a shameful national affliction, an illogical and pathological response to past events and—when employed by the state—an effective means of controlling and rallying the populace through fearmongering (Abrahamian 1993; Dadkhah 1999).[32] Rather than discount them, I take paranoia and conspiracy theories as "kind[s] of political imaginar[ies] . . . within a transnational context in an age where a surfeit of information is matched only by the difficulty of obtaining relevant information for political decision making" (Iqtidar 2014, 5). Paranoid imaginaries are a reaction to the partialness of knowledge and the untrustworthiness, inherent partiality, and biased ordering of facts according to political agendas. This is not to declare the inherent truthfulness of a notion like soft war or some expatriate Iranians' fear of governmental surveillance, but to say that, in many cases, there is evidence to support these interpretations. These perceptions become experiential reality for musicians, media producers, and state policy makers alike, and in turn shape the self-protective choices they make and their sense of what is *possible*.

Within the traffic of representations and cultural forms, I treat popular music as a privileged category of mass-mediated expressive culture with affordances that make it particularly efficacious in linking expatriates and their geographically dispersed diaspora and homeland audiences. Music's status as concrete, palpable, and historically and culturally contingent and its simultaneous diffuseness, open interpretability, and potential nonindexicality account for its flexibility. We experience music as hailing various social identifications that may be specific, yet to be articulated, or beyond articulation at all. Music producers and audiences describe music as calling into being collective forms of identification and shared experience, making these into sometimes fragmentary and fragile, and sometimes more durable, "aggregations of the affected" (Born 2011, 379). Stimulating affective responses—particularly joy (*shādi*) and sorrow (*gham*)—is a vital, and sometimes controversial, aspect of Tehrangeles musicians' labor and their role in mobilizing their audiences emotionally and politically.

Music's dual public and intimate quality is particularly important to *Tehrangeles Dreaming*. Throughout the book, I use "the intimate" and "intimacy" in two distinct yet interrelated ways. The first is the intimate as that which should be shielded from the public for propriety's sake. This understanding of intimacy overlaps with "the private" to a certain extent, but the connotations of social closeness and sexuality of "intimacy" more accurately capture my meaning. Which practices and bodies falls under the category of the intimate is not constant in Iranian modernity but relates to both individual understandings and historically shifting definitions of morality, gender, and sexuality. These change in different diasporic contexts as well. As discussed above, even as certain forms of music and certain musicians retain some stigma, the overarching change in music's moral status in Iranian modernity evinces its flexibility. The long history of Shiite custom and jurisprudence that defines lahv (frivolity), ghanā (artful song), and raqs (dance) as corrupting, immoral, and therefore prohibited was eventually overcome as postrevolutionary decision-makers gradually approved many musical forms out of pragmatism. The barriers to acceptability have proven to be higher where women and their public expression of sexuality are concerned because of their role in producing, and literally reproducing, the nation. If women are the backbone of the family, and families are the building blocks of the nation, then "women's honor is not a private [individual or familial] concern, but a public one" (Osanloo 2009, 185). Tehrangeles popular culture transgresses Iran's officially mandated moral order by making public women's uncovered bodies and singing voices, which, according to Iranian law and Islamic custom, should be revealed only to their husbands or their intimate circle (mahram—individuals a woman cannot legally marry). Mass-mediated, transnationally circulating expatriate popular music thus complicates the Iranian state's regulation of the intimate, the moral, the public sphere, and the nation's boundaries all at once.[33] It is a public form that can become intimate, and an intimate form that is readily transferable to the public (Dueck 2013; Stokes 2010).

The second way I use "the intimate" and "intimacy" is in reference to deep familiarity within a group. Here I am inspired by Michael Herzfeld's (2005) notion of cultural intimacy: the practices and structures of feeling that assure people of their common sociality. I show that while cultural intimacy is often articulated in terms of a people's enduring, transcendent predilections and traits, just what constitutes the stuff of intimacy is also historically contingent and contested. Media is crucial to the sense of intimacy and familiarity (āshenāi) that Tehrangeles cultural producers describe enjoying with their dispersed compatriots. This connects their activities and claims to an "intimate public" of the sort described by Lauren Berlant (2008) in relation to twentieth-century women's literature and popular

FIGURE I.7 Media afford distant audiences intimacy with Sepideh. Screen grab from "Kish," directed by Koji Zadori, on the DVD *Caltex Records 20 Music Videos*, Caltex Trading, Inc., 2007.

culture and by Martin Stokes (2010) in terms of twentieth-century popular music in Turkey: the circulating commercial texts that "express what is common" among a group of people, "a subjective likeness that seems to emanate from their history and their ongoing attachments and actions" (Berlant 2008, 21). The culturally intimate in Tehrangeles music and media can also appear as the open representation of shameful or unsettling social phenomena like drug addiction, nonheteronormative sexuality, or even an undignified love of dance music. Knowledge and expertise are central to my use of "intimacy," as is the labor of intimacy and affect. Tehrangeles musicians and media producers claim access to the stuff of cultural intimacy because they claim to know (and have produced) Iranian culture, because they know what people want, and because people love them. It is a circular relationship growing out of mutual, intimate knowledge and affection between themselves and their dispersed audiences.

THE CHAPTERS

The book's chapters examine several interrelated aspects of Tehrangeles music and media's offerings and follow musicians and media producers as they contend with the legacy of the "dissolute musician" stereotype and with their elective and involuntary political engagements. The book's chapters begin with examples of Tehrangeles cultural producers' political ambivalence and end with two Tehrangeles celebrities' conscious integration of the political into their expatriate personas and works.

Chapter 1 examines the discourses and politics surrounding a popular rhythmic dance groove colloquially called *dāmbuli* or *shesh-o-hasht* (six and eight). Though central to many traditional Iranian musical genres, this rhythm was restricted for about twenty years in postrevolutionary domestic musical productions because of its associations with dance and eroticism. During precisely this period, expatriate pop musicians incorporated dāmbuli into their productions to such an extent that the groove became associated with Tehrangeles itself. I draw on interviews with Tehrangeles musicians who both denigrate and celebrate dāmbuli, and with the audiences who desire it, to show how musical sound can index and elicit experiences of intimacy and shared sociality in the face of the pervasive ideologization of culture.

The creation of alternative national music histories in Tehrangeles is the subject of the following chapter. I focus on four figures in prerevolutionary popular music who relocated to Tehrangeles—music and television producer Manouchehr Bibiyan, singer and songwriter Shahram Shabpareh, and music producers Vartan Avanessian and Jahangir Tabaraei—and their efforts to create accounts of Iranian music that acknowledge their contributions to national history and culture. These figures grapple with their rejection in the revolution, and their subsequent reputation for producing socially irrelevant pop in Tehrangeles, by producing narratives in which they depict themselves as modernizers, emissaries of joy, and saviors of Iranian music itself.

Chapter 3 is about Tehrangeles performers as desirable, desiring, and dangerous subjects vis-à-vis homeland-based audiences. I link desire for return to the homeland to the erotics of expatriate media, showing how Tehrangeles popular culture revives sexually ambiguous and provocative aspects of Iranian history and transmits them back into the country. The chapter presents three scenarios of expatriate return to Iran: the literal return and subsequent imprisonment of gay male dancer and choreographer Mohammad Khordadian, a fictional film documenting a trip to Iran by a sexually ambiguous Tehrangeles vocalist, and the experiences of straight female vocalist Shahrzad Sepanlou negotiating her sexualized image as perceived by Iran-based audiences. I argue that these accounts together offer a complex picture of expatriates' representation of "sex in public" (Berlant and Warner 1998), which, in violating the nation's moral purity and geographic boundaries, confounds Tehrangeles performers and the Iranian state alike.

The last two chapters zero in on two expatriate musical celebrities and their claims to represent and reach the nation from exile. Here I think

through how Tehrangeles cultural producers conceive of their political responsibilities and potentials in relation to Iran-based audiences. Chapter 4
shows how prerevolutionary female pop diva Googoosh and her collaborators use her personal history of victimization as a provocative metaphor for
national suffering. To particularize the cultural and historical resonances of
voice-related terminology in Googoosh's repertoire, the chapter begins with
a short history of voice and romantically and politically motivated complaint in twentieth-century Iranian sung poetry. I then turn to a discussion of diaspora Iranians' metaphorization of Googoosh during her twenty-
year period of postrevolutionary "silence," and Googoosh's own adoption
of these metaphors in her subsequent postrevolutionary comeback. In the
diaspora, Googoosh uses her outsized voice and persona to perform as the
Iranian nation "herself." Because the female voice is the most restricted musical medium in Iran, the very act of representing "Iran as a singing woman"
is laden with political challenges and opportunities. Documentary film,
music videos, songs, concerts, interviews, and her eponymous televised talent competition are among the media through which Googoosh "sings the
nation's tears."

Charismatic male pop icon Dariush Eghbali is the subject of chapter 5.
The chapter tracks Dariush's transformation from the drug-addicted "sultan of sadness" to a postrecovery "messenger of hope" as it explores his
unique combination of transnational, media-based political and humanitarian activism. As I show, Dariush works at the intersection of sentimentality, nationalism, and the principles of the American recovery movement
to mobilize a notion of "shared suffering." Relating Dariush's attempts to
transform Iran and Iranians from afar to Khomeini's long-distance mass-
mediated reach into Iran during his decades of exile, the chapter investigates the combined political affordances of charismatic celebrity and expatriate media. Dariush's patriotic songs and videos, the media productions of
his nonprofit Ayeneh (Mirror) Foundation (focused on addiction recovery),
and his live concerts are analyzed in relation to the intimate publics they
attempt to produce. This chapter incorporates my ambivalent reactions to
Dariush's performances and media to draw attention to the complexity of
his reputation among diverse Iranian audiences. This also serves to bring
readers into my affective experience of his celebrity and works.

The final chapter offers perspectives on what has changed and what has
remained stable in Tehran-Tehrangeles relations over the forty years that
have passed since the coterminous establishment of Islamic Republic of
Iran and the Southern Californian expatriate industries.

THE POLITICS OF IRANIAN POPULAR
MUSIC SCHOLARSHIP

Postrevolutionary music scholarship published within Iran typically avoids socially and politically sensitive topics. This can be explained in part by the historical and analytical bent of domestic music scholarship and many Iranian musicologists' performance backgrounds. But some of politics' relative absence is an effect of domestic scholars sticking to less potentially inflammatory topics as a means of navigating their local context. By contrast, studies of Iranian popular music published outside of Iran, most of which are authored by diasporic Iranians, tend to privilege politics above other topics. The limiting aspects of postrevolutionary Iranian music policy, and the "resistant" potentials of popular music, especially, have received the bulk of scholarly attention. This resembles the Tehrangeles tendency to view the homeland primarily in terms of repression and deprivation and overlook other aspects of life in the Islamic Republic of Iran. The titles of articles and books on Iranian popular music clearly manifest this inclination. Postrevolutionary popular music is a key player in a process of state and citizen "subversion and counter-subversion" (Nooshin 2005a); Tehran's soundscape is a politically "contested space" (Siamdoust 2015), while postrevolutionary music is the "soundtrack of the revolution" (Siamdoust 2017); and the songs of unofficial rock musicians are "reverberations of dissent" (Robertson 2012). The scholarship on female vocalists also follows this pattern, regardless of genre: women vocalists are "singing in a theocracy" (Youssefzadeh 2004) and must "carve a space in post-revolutionary Iran" (Mozafari 2012) to represent their own and others' "marginalized voices" (Nooshin 2011). I, too, have contributed to this trend by describing Tehrangeles pop as a "transnational public beyond," and in many ways opposed to, "the Islamic state" (Hemmasi 2011); by depicting prerevolutionary domestic popular music as "intimat[ing] dissent" (Hemmasi 2013); and by discussing the "political metaphorization" of female pop icon Googoosh's sounded and silent voice (Hemmasi 2017a, 2017b). *Tehrangeles Dreaming* also contributes to this trend.

This dynamic is part and parcel of the larger postrevolutionary politicization of music, diaspora-homeland interactions, and the Islamic Republic of Iran's fraught international relations. Writing of both diasporic and non-Iranian music scholars, Laudan Nooshin (2017) notes a troubling tendency to "fetishize" Iranian popular music as "resistance." In Tehrangeles pop itself, in my account of it, and in most of the case studies listed above, what is being resisted is the Islamic Republic and not, say, Western imperialism, any of Iran's many rivals, or the US government's current Iranian sanctions or ban on Iranian visitors. Because members of the Iranian opposition and Western observers of both conservative and liberal persuasions have seized on accounts of popular "defiance" against the Iranian state as indications of its latent instability, "resistant" musicians and the scholars who write about them run the risk of underscoring simplistic, harmful characterizations of Iranians and Iranian society. At best, these pile on to Iran's already dismal international reputation, while, at worst, they can be interpreted as justifications for foreign intervention.[34] Some expatriate musicians may embrace externally led regime change, as may some scholars; my informed guess is that many, many more do not. To focus on academics: regardless of our awareness or intentions regarding these potentialities, the fact that Iranian intelligence officers have at times questioned, arrested, and imprisoned diasporic scholars of Iran (supposedly) for their research and publishing activities has led some of us to self-censor or avoid returning to the country. Scholars and scholarship are therefore enmeshed in similar imaginaries of power and paranoia as Tehrangeles cultural producers. Taken in whole, this situation is evidence of a widespread perception that circulating representations of Iran and Iranians—be they scholarly, journalistic, or artistic—are politically productive and disruptive in powerful and unpredictable ways. Just how, when, and where such representations become impactful depends on the context and interpretation at least as much as (but probably more than) the intent. This is precisely the situation *Tehrangeles Dreaming* investigates with regard to expatriate music and media producers, and it likewise informs the conditions from which my scholarship emerges.

All of this is to say that I am cognizant of the need to "carve a space" (Mozafari 2012) for Iranian musicians that is not entirely defined by politics. I also recognize the importance of this to my interlocutors as well as the larger spectrum of Muslim and Middle Eastern cultural producers and media workers with whom they will unavoidably be compared. But the pervasiveness of the contrasting political imaginaries and political conditions with which Tehrangeles musicians and music scholars contend means that to suppress political contestation and conditions in my account would be to tell half—or less—of the story. *Tehrangeles Dreaming* attempts to face head-on the challenges and opportunities that come with the pervasiveness of politics in Iranian musicians' and media producers' work alongside the politics of representing them at all.

The research for this book began in 2005 as part of my studies in ethnomusicology. It is also the product of my years of engagement with Tehrangeles pop in the company of my Iranian American family and friends, and with family in Iran, most of whom reside in Tehran and Kashan. My mother is Euro-American, and I grew up in the United States in mostly non-Iranian environments, but this didn't seem to prevent my interlocutors from identifying me as Iranian American. They typically treated me as if I understood something of the context and content of their music, and often referred to "our culture" (*farhang-e mā*) or to "we Iranians" (*mā Irāni-hā*). The fact that when I began my doctoral research I was young and spoke accented, grammatically incorrect Persian reminded my interlocutors of their children, grandchildren, or other Iranian American youth they knew. A few of my older interviewees said they were driven to speak with me out of a desire to secure their legacy in Iranian music and were eager to educate me about their contributions to "our history." I was comfortable speaking with men who were part of the same generational cohort as my father and uncles and with whom I could occupy the attentive, admiring "good [Iranian] girl" (*dokhtar-e khub*) role—a lucky coincidence since this generation happened to be the power-holding group during my fieldwork. My comparatively far fewer conversations with women, in turn, inevitably included discussions of gender-based discrimination and their accordingly limited creative roles, both because this was important to their creative work and because they rightly surmised I could relate to their stories as a fellow Iranian woman. I could also relate to the sense of profound loss of homeland that suffused my interlocutors' work and perspectives. My parents and I left Iran in 1980 in the months between the Islamic Republic's establishment and the beginning of the Iran-Iraq War. We departed with just two suitcases, abruptly abandoning our house, family, friends, and former lives. Though I was a few months shy of my fifth birthday when we left, I have vibrant memories of my early childhood in Shiraz and visits to my relatives in Tehran. I have also experienced long periods of separation from Iran. My points of connection to this book's subjects, then, are culturally and biographically based.

Even so, during my research I was also an outsider with limited access to the inner workings of the Tehrangeles music and media scene. I had not spent significant time in Southern California before my fieldwork research period and didn't have social or familial connections to industry members. My interactions in Tehrangeles were further conditioned by the fact that I was "studying up." While being a graduate student and then postdoctoral fellow at two different Ivy League universities meant that I was not exactly short on cultural capital, many of my interlocutors' male gender, celebrity, international professional connections, advanced age, and—in some cases—wealth, placed them "above" me. Formal interviews made by appointment were my main access to busy musicians, music producers, and media workers.[35] The Tehrangeles popular culture industry is small and densely interrelated, and its members share decades of memories, good times, business dealings, broken promises, and contentious legal battles, some of which were hinted at but not related to me in detail. There were many aspects of interpersonal relationships and business dealings that I knew would never be shared with me and, even when they were, that I would never commit to paper.

Firsthand experience in postrevolutionary Iran was another distinction between me and my interlocutors. I had traveled to Iran only three times since my family and I relocated to the United States, but even this minimal time spent in Iran meant that, ironically, I had more recent exposure to "our [postrevolutionary] homeland" than some of my Tehrangeles interlocutors, most of whom had left in the 1970s or 1980s and never returned. The Iranian side of my family is diverse in terms of education, religiosity, and socioeconomic status. Short visits to family and friends in Tehran, Karaj, Kashan, Sari, Khazarshahr, Shiraz, Mashhad, Isfahan, and Kish Island, and time spent with elite Tehranis, my so-called "traditional" relatives in Karaj and Kashan, and other people who fit neither of these descriptions afforded me extremely limited, but still illuminating, exposure to a variety of perspectives and lifestyles.[36] These short trips provided a useful counter to the common Tehrangeles trope of postrevolutionary Iran as a wasteland and/or prison, while also showing me that expatriate popular culture had a palpable presence in the country.

In Tehrangeles I was usually speaking with media professionals who were skilled at telling their own stories and managing their public personae. I therefore considered our face-to-face conversations as part of a continuum of their careers of publicly representing themselves, their work, and their position in Iranian culture and history—and not necessarily as "less mediated" or "more authentic" exchanges.[37] I complemented interviews with celebrities and professionals with conversations and casual time spent with multiple generations of Iranians in Southern California at concerts, in music stores and bookstores, in restaurants, and in other informal situations. I went to parties with Iranian American youth who had never been to Iran but identified as Iranian or Persian; I also hung out with groups of Iranian doctoral students close to my own age who had recently arrived in the United States. Across these groups, I learned I could count on almost everyone's awareness of Tehrangeles popular culture: it infiltrated many Iranians' lives in the 1980s, 1990s, and 2000s, regardless of where they grew up or what their stated musical preferences were.

I also attended performances by Tehrangeles musicians in Southern California and in Toronto (where I now live), and consumed lots and lots of media produced in Tehrangeles and media about Tehrangeles produced by Iranians living elsewhere. In the book, I have placed Tehrangeles media producers' statements that appeared in Persian-language media alongside quotations from interviews I conducted, checking my interpretations, translations, and assumptions with individuals outside of the immediate circle of Tehrangeles. Retrospectively, I came to recognize this approach as what anthropologist Louisa Schein (2012, 205–206) has called "ethnotextual" research. My continuous engagement with Iranian diasporic music producers and consumers as both a researcher and a fellow diasporic Iranian made "situated interpretation" the obvious (and only) way to apprehend these texts and experiences. The interpretations in the chapters are "from a site of [personal and] ethnographic entanglement with those whose subject positions allow a more seamless identification" with the media in question and "locat[e texts and their interpretation] within a wider play of cultural [and political] signification that exceeds" any single text in isolation (Schein 2012, 206).

Following my most intensive period of sustained fieldwork in Los Angeles in 2007, I have returned to Southern California almost every summer for the past decade, visiting and revisiting people and sites, attending concerts, tracking changes in the Iranian neighborhoods in Westwood and the strip malls of the San Fernando Valley, and contacting new people as well. More recent trips have included graveyards and barely functioning businesses in the cultural industry network. Members of the prerevolutionary to Tehrangeles generation are beginning to pass on; the famous singer Mahasti died in Los Angeles in 2007 when I was doing my fieldwork; the singers Hayedeh, Sousan, and Vigen and the lyricist Touraj Negahban also died in Southern California some years earlier. Some companies are slowing down or changing hands; their business strategies must shift to compete with products from Iran and elsewhere in the diaspora. All in all, Tehrangeles no longer has the international significance it once did. As such, this account is—as all ethnographies are—a history, told in a moment about a particular group of people and the conditions in which they have operated. I suppose the book is an argument against the critics of Tehrangeles and even some Tehrangeles cultural producers' own view that their music and contributions are not lasting (*mundegār nistand*), that this cultural formation has offered nothing besides a bit of distraction from the seriousness of revolution, war, economic hardship, and displacement. What I hope to show instead are the multiple levels on which Tehrangeles popular culture intersects with and preserves history, mobilizes affect and intimacy, and engenders conversation and sociality across transnational Iranian space.

THE CAPITAL OF 6/8

If Tehrangeles dance pop could be summed up in a
single sound, it would likely be the rollicking, danceable
groove known colloquially as *shesh-o-hasht* (six and eight, or
the time signature 6/8) or by the onomatopoeia *dāmbuli dimbol.*
Played on a *tonbak* goblet drum, with samples that evoke the acoustic
tonbak sound, on a trap set, or with electronic percussion, this groove
has provided the rhythmic foundation for decades of Tehrangeles dance
music. Though associated with Tehrangeles, the groove did not originate
in Southern California. It is instead "traditionally" Iranian: it is endemic to
classical and motrebi dance pieces called *reng*; it accompanies nursery
rhymes, chants and games, the light classical metered song called
tasnif, and the nineteenth- and early twentieth-century improvisatory theater genre called *ruhowzi*; and it forms the rhythmic
base of much prerevolutionary, urban, mass-mediated
mardomi (people's) popular music that drew on these
sources. It is also the sonic stimulus for a repertoire
of solo dance moves concentrated on the face,

neck, shoulders, arms, hands, and hips. Shesh-o-hasht landed in Los Angeles because of the revolution: the rhythm was not permitted in domestic music productions for about two decades.[1] Theories as to why shesh-o-hasht was singled out include its sensuality and its provocation to dance, as dancing was likewise restricted after the revolution, and also the rhythm's associations with comedy, happiness, and celebration, which were considered inappropriate during the revolution and the Iran-Iraq War. But shesh-o-hasht was not so easily dispatched. As it was prohibited in the homeland, this deeply popular rhythm thumped on in Tehrangeles and quickly made its way back to Iran via clandestinely circulated audio- and videocassettes. It was not until Shadmehr Aghili's 1999 album *Dehāti* (*Villager*, Fars Navā) that a shesh-o-hasht pop song was officially approved and released in Iran. By then, the groove had already come to be associated with Southern California. As reported by ethnomusicologist Jean During (2005, 382), some Iranians took to jokingly calling this new domestic pop "losānjelesi [*sic*] made in Iran."

It would be one thing if Tehrangeles cultural producers had proudly claimed shesh-o-hasht as their own, but in fact many Iranian musicians and cultural producers in Southern California have a deeply ambivalent, even negative perspective on the rhythm and its centrality in Tehrangeles. Take prerevolutionary lyricist and singer Shahyar Ghanbari, who, in an interview with a diasporic news website, explained that he didn't perform much in Los Angeles despite having resided there for years. This was because he didn't consider Southern Californian Iranian audiences capable of appreciating his music. "I live in . . . the capital of shesh-o-hasht," he explained. "Shesh-o-hasht is not to blame, its performance, melodies, and lyrics [in Tehrangeles pop] are trivial (*pish pā oftādeh*)." He warned that Iranian children raised in Los Angeles were in danger of falling into the same mind-set as their parents. If they listened to "the worst shesh-o-hasht all day," they would turn "shesh-o-hasht-ish" (*shesh-o-hashti*), presumably like the Los Angeles Iranian audiences he wanted to avoid.[2]

The main task of this chapter is to explore the economic value and cultural and political degradation of the shesh-o-hasht groove. I argue that shesh-o-hasht sonically and somatically taps into long-standing debates about how being properly, modernly Iranian should sound—and feel. Examining discourse about shesh-o-hasht in tandem with musical examples, I show how Tehrangeles performers consider the rhythm to be a desire and response inherent in Iranian bodies regardless of where they are in the world. This is an ambivalent observation: for some, the groove's durability is a source of pleasure, pride, and reassurance—as well as a source of income. For others, the groove is something that Iranians should let go of but that still stubbornly remains. Why, they ask, is there *so much* shesh-o-hasht coming out of Tehrangeles? I explore this question by relating the conditions of shesh-o-hasht's efflorescence in Tehrangeles, as well as its historical uses and associations within Iran, to show how professional musicians turn to shesh-o-hasht as a reliable stimulus of dance and happy sociality and, therefore, of their economic livelihoods. Examining statements by shesh-o-hasht supporters and cynics, I consider the politics and cultural values of affect—particularly unwarranted joy—and their mapping onto Tehrangeles, the postrevolutionary "capital of 6/8."[3]

I argue that like Michael Herzfeld's (2005) notion of national "cultural intimacy," the practices and attitudes around shesh-o-hasht establish a sense of common sociality among cultural insiders but are also the source of rueful embarrassment. Herzfeld's paradigmatic example is a supposedly Greek national characteristic of breaking dinner plates when excited. Here we might picture Zorba the Greek whirling about in a fit of emotion and smashing ceramic plates to smithereens. This, writes Herzfeld, is precisely the kind of behavior some Greeks will deny ever taking part in because of its embarrassing, irrational excessiveness, its complicated relation to self-stereotypes, and the modernist national-official projections of the incompatibility of such emotional performances with the rational-critical comportment necessary to become "truly modern"—according to the Greek state. Yet sometimes Greek people *do* break plates, and these plate-breaking moments can be the very ones that remind and reassure people of their Greekness, a visceral experience that Herzfeld's interlocutors discursively connected to ideas of tradition and authenticity, expressed through essentialized statements of what being Greek means. The Iranian case offers parallels in the historical marginalization of the professional musicians called *motreb* (literally, "producers of joy"), whose repertoire heavily featured the shesh-o-hasht groove and who, because of their unmodern, debauched, and vulgar associations, were restricted from prerevolutionary state radio and television. Among shesh-o-hasht's detractors in the diaspora, the rhythm's erotic associations—the reason behind the rhythm's postrevolutionary ban—are not as important a barrier to its acceptability as its perceived frivolity and excessiveness.

Even as I find cultural intimacy useful in illuminating the ambivalence surrounding shesh-o-hasht, the Iranian case also presents many challenges to the sense of national identification so central to Herzfeld's original argument. This is not only because of the country's shifting borders and long-standing multiethnic, multilingual, and multiconfessional population. The nation-as-container theory and method are challenged by Iranian history, particularly the revolutionary government's assertion of a novel, yet also traditionally identified social order; the massive out-migration; and the development of parallel strands of culture at a distance from territorial Iran that often identify not only as "still" Iranian but sometimes even as "true" Iranian culture. Iran's cultural transformations and contestations have had tremendous implications for how cultural practices and elements are understood, employed, rejected, and positioned in public and in private. There is thus ample reason to be suspicious of stereotypes, essentialisms, "aesthetics as iconicity of style" (Feld 1988), or other lay and scholarly claims to stable transhistorical, translocal cultural meaning or embodied response. But "distrust of essentialism in social theory should not blur our awareness of its equally pervasive presence in social life" (Herzfeld 2005, 26). Iranians invoke stereotypes and essentializing discourse as a way of referring to and discursively creating themselves and others. In Tehrangeles pop, one of these stereotypes is shesh-o-hasht's unique ability to hail diverse Iranians with a single sonic groove that enables happiness, sensuality, fun, and participation in Iranian social life in Southern California and elsewhere as well.

My invocation of shesh-o-hasht as a Tehrangeles groove builds on ethnomusicological and anthropological explorations of sonic forms' abilities to encapsulate or engender the social in culturally specific ways (see Feld 1988; Keil 1987, 1995; Meintjes 2003). Thinking of intimacy through groove helps bring to light one of the methods by which people "get into the groove" with one another: through dance, music making, and the physical-emotional-psychological entrainment that doing these things together well can entail. Dancing to and playing the shesh-o-hasht groove in Tehrangeles is a way for Iranians to "tune into" ways of being Iranian together through the transportable patterned movements and sounds that were uprooted from the territorial homeland and transplanted to Southern California.[4] Getting intimate with this groove means delving into unresolved debates, layers of historical implications, and enduring structures of feeling.

The chapter proceeds with perspectives on how Tehrangeles became "the capital of shesh-o-hasht." I make a historical claim that contemporary defensive discourses surrounding the rhythm's dominance in the diaspora do not begin with the revolution but are a continuation of twentieth-century contestations over popular culture's role in affirming or distracting from morality and political consciousness. I provide an in-depth discussion of the shesh-o-hasht dance groove and its use in Tehrangeles pop, and show that it produces and is produced by listeners and dancers who can tune in to learned bodily responses and historical contexts that they experience on the dance floor. Throughout, I demonstrate different ways Tehrangeles musicians respond to shesh-o-hasht, including rearticulating the critiques in their own terms and—most compellingly—claiming that the groove expresses a vital core of Iranian identity that politics, elitism, and moral reprobation cannot erase.

DĀMBULI AND THE POPULAR
IN THE TWENTIETH CENTURY

Understanding the chain of associations that link Tehrangeles and shesh-o-hasht in the postrevolutionary era requires some attention to the music with which it may be most associated, and the historical performers most associated with this repertoire. These are the motreb. *Motreb* comes from the Arabic root *ta-ra-ba*, which means "to move" emotionally, typically to joy; the term *motreb* means "one who gladdens." In the Iranian context, a motreb is a professional performer whose purpose is to enliven celebrations with festive entertainment. Further representing the connection between professional musicianship and the production of joyful affect is the official title of Qajar court musicians—*'amaleh-ye tarab-e khāseh*—the "private laborers of joy," with "private" referring to the fact that they belonged to the court (Amir Hosein Pourjavady, personal communication; Sarshar 2012). By the late nineteenth century, *motreb* was a general term for professional musicians and entertainers. Because Muslims of good standing did not want the stigma surrounding professional performers, motreb were often low-status Muslims or, very commonly, Jewish.[5] Motreb's associations with vice and the understanding of music as a substance necessitating control or avoidance sometimes caused problems: H. E. Chehabi (1999, 143–144) reports that in the nineteenth century, motreb hid their instruments under their cloaks as they walked in the streets to avoid being beaten by religious zealots. The joyful and sometimes dissolute performances of motreb were the conceptual and affective inverse of performances of Shiite vocal genres. The skills of Shiite vocalists, whose repertoire includes lamentations called *rowzeh*, *ta'ziyeh* passion plays, and the responsorial *nowheh*, were "saddening" rather than "gladdening." Religious performers' objective was (and is) to move their audiences to tears through pious identification with the suffering of religious martyrs.

However, the negative stereotypes of motreb are complicated by the fact that "respectable" families sometimes hired them to provide entertainment at life-cycle events and other happy occasions, while motreb also performed in less respectable environments, such as the brothels of Tehran's red-light district, Shahr-e Now (New City). In the early twentieth century, the motreb developed a distinctively negative valence that only increased over time (Meftahi 2016a, 51–52). Motreb were associated with drugs, alcohol, prostitution, and pederasty; some troupes included a boy or young man dressed in female attire (*zanpush*) or a young male-identified dancer (*bacheh raqqās*), both of whom could be available for sexual services. In contemporary parlance, the motreb is an almost mythical figure, a hired provider of musical entertainment of dubious morals who plays simplistic, vulgar music merely to earn money.

While the motreb's musical repertoire has included many different genres, since the late nineteenth century their signature rhythm has been shesh-o-hasht. Played on the goblet drum called tonbak, pieces featuring this rhythm were often meant to accompany dance at celebratory occasions and in segregated women's quarters (*andaruni*), and in the theatrical genres of *siyāh bāzi* and ruhowzi, performed by troupes consisting of comedians and musicians. These pieces frequently include hemiolas—three groups of two beats played over the main two groupings of three beats—which lends a sense of shifting between triple and duple meter.[6] However, while motreb played an important role in shesh-o-hasht's propagation, they were not the only ones playing it. This is a basic "Persian" dance rhythm found in a wide variety of nineteenth- and twentieth-century urban art music, including instrumental dance pieces (also called *reng*) and the popular precomposed songs known as *tasnif*.[7] An elitist hierarchization of musical genres and rhythms left the motreb with driving, danceable shesh-o-hasht. Motreb became seen as those who merely entertain, inspire dance, and incite lust (*shahvat*) and debauchery. While early twentieth-century art musicians also faced some obstacles to respectability, their association with Persian poetic masterpieces, mystical experience, and a complex musical system elevated their work. Among art-music purists, the most highly prized form of music has been the improvisatory sung poetic form *āvāz*, an artful vocal delivery of erudite, often esoteric poetry from the classical canon. In āvāz, the rhythm is dictated by text and vocalist—specifically the vocalist's skillful and emotive rendering of quantitatively metered lines of poetry—and not by a drummer hammering away at a repetitive shesh-o-hasht groove.[8]

From the mid-twentieth century, motreb expanded the reach of shesh-o-hasht as they transitioned to newly emerged popular media and sites of sociability, including Tehran's post-1950 commercial theaters in the Lalehzar entertainment district, cafés and cabarets in Lalehzar and elsewhere in Tehran, and the commercial cinema of filmfarsi, which featured song and dance often set in fictional versions of the performance venues in which real motreb played. As motreb were expanding their professional roles and milieu, they came under attack from multiple quarters. In the 1920s and 1930s, an Islamist press began registering objections to the "lust-inciting" (shahvat-angiz) presence of uncovered women in public, "centers of corruption" where unrelated men and women could openly socialize, and the dissolute music, dance, and debauchery that unashamedly permeated daily urban life. While "modern" (tajaddod) men and women influenced by foreign trends were more often the object of critique in these screeds than motreb themselves, social changes had brought the motreb's "corrupting" presence into new environments.

Motreb were also attacked by non-Islamist groups. Beginning in the 1920s, historians cite evidence of modernist objections to motreb performers for their "backwards" traditionality, lack of formal training, and associations with vice. Meanwhile, among leftist intellectuals and in artistic discourse, motreb became the embodiment of "degeneration," or ebtezāl, a complicated term that means "cheap and unoriginal" but also "degenerate and distracting from social issues in such a way as to depoliticize audiences." As Ida Meftahi (2016b) has shown, the rise of Marxist thought in the 1930s and 1940s introduced the ideal of "committed" art (honar-e mote'ahhed), art that could elevate society's tastes while developing audiences' political awareness and revolutionary spirit. The opposite of commitment was aesthetic degeneration, an epithet leftist art critics and theoreticians directed at the motreb, who, they claimed, poisoned the arts' consciousness-raising potential with their comedic, trite, and mollifying performances.

Regardless of these ideological and moral objections, the music motreb played, as well as new popular forms incorporating elements of motreb repertoire, was indubitably enjoyed and consumed by the urban masses. A collection of genres together called mardomi ("of the people")—the most lucrative and widely consumed mass-mediated music in mid-twentieth-century Iran—was likely responsible for offering a wide public their greatest exposure to shesh-o-hasht. Mardomi existed in contradistinction to the Western-influenced, glamorous, upwardly mobile jāz of the 1950s and 1960s and the musiqi-ye pāp style developed in the 1960s and 1970s.[9] While both jāz and pāp had imported names and imported sounds, the terms and associations surrounding mardomi music grounded it in Iranian and more generally Middle Eastern space, people, and culture. These links to the local are encapsulated in the various terms used to describe mardomi music, including "popular" or "populist" (*āmeh pasand, mardom pasand, mardomi*), or the urban sites with which it was associated: *kāfe-i* (of the cafés), *lālehzāri* (of Tehran's Lalehzar entertainment district), *kucheh-bāzāri* (of the street and bazaar), and even *shahr-e nowhi* (of Shahr-e Now, Tehran's red-light district).[10] This distinction also entailed financial ramifications: as I learned in my interviews with Manouchehr Bibiyan and Vartan Avanessian, mardomi music sold far more records than musiqi-ye pāp while its musicians were paid much less. With the exceptions of female mardomi singer Sousan and male vocalist Aghassi, Pahlavi state broadcasting policy prevented motrebi-influenced mardomi musicians from appearing on television or airing their songs on the radio because of their vulgar associations. But offstage and on, blurry lines separated the modern pop *honarmand* (artist) and the lower-status professional entertainer, especially when it came to family lineages. Top pāp celebrity Googoosh was *motreb-zādeh*, or the "child of a motreb," and spent her early life on the road with her professional entertainer father. One of her competitors, Leila Foruhar—who, like Googoosh, was a child actress—is the daughter of actor Jahangir Foruhar and his wife, Farangis, who danced professionally in cabarets and films. Celebrated prerevolutionary film composer and occasional pop songwriter Esfandiar Monfaredzadeh was one of several musicians who got his start playing in the Lalehzar theaters, while General Mohammad Shabpareh, father to pop pioneers and Tehrangeles cornerstones Shahbal and Shahram Shabpareh, owned a theater in Lalehzar—and there are many other examples.

Regardless of the regimes of acceptability and unacceptability under which musicians and broadcasters operated, in the revolutionary period popular music and musicians of "high" and "low" popular genres were collectively branded as unacceptable because of their role in propagating degeneration and lust.[11] When musicians across the popular music spectrum came together in Los Angeles, generic, class, and professional hierarchies weakened. In Southern California there was no state support or massive profits to funnel into unprofitable pet projects. Everyone was forced to sing for their supper and play what their fellow expatriates were willing to pay to hear. And this, very often, was shesh-o-hasht.

The association between shesh-o-hasht and Tehrangeles stems from the very earliest expatriate pop recording made in Southern California: Shahram Shabpareh's 1980 "Deyar" ("Homeland"), a song about loss of the homeland built around alternating Latin-tinged disco and shesh-o-hasht sections. Other songs by Shabpareh and his brother Shahbal Shabpareh would follow a similar pattern of switching between foreign and familiar rhythms, while Mohsen Namjoo's analysis of 163 of Shahram Shabpareh's songs found that 101 of these were based on shesh-o-hasht.[12] Many other Tehrangeles artists would rely almost entirely on the shesh-o-hasht groove.

Within a typical shesh-o-hasht dance song produced in Los Angeles, the groove is played on a tonbak or other hand drum or a trap set, or as a looped sample, or with some combination of these. When I have attended Cabaret Tehran, an Iranian-oriented nightclub in Encino with a house band and a changing lineup of guest vocalists, the shesh-o-hasht beat loop has been triggered by the keyboardist and simultaneously played on the trap set by a live percussionist. One night at Safir Mediterranean Restaurant, another Iranian cabaret a few miles away from Cabaret Tehran on Ventura Boulevard, I observed a similar mix of recorded and live percussion rhythms: the keyboardist backing San Francisco–based prerevolutionary mardomi singer Jamal Vafaei cranked up the shesh-o-hasht beat to deafening levels, completely overpowering an elderly tonbak player beside him onstage.

Though there is a bit of variation in tempo, ornamentation, and articulation, the rhythmic patterns commonly referred to as shesh-o-hasht fall in a narrow range of variations on a basic formula. In analyses by Iranian and non-Iranian scholars, it is typically transcribed in compound duple meter. The interest and sense of motion come from the pull between the typically stressed first and fifth beats, which divide the cycle unevenly into four plus two beats and make it *lang* (limping, a concept related to *aksak* in Turkish music).[13] Percussionists in the motreb tradition or emulating this style play the rhythm with a great deal of license in terms of stroke and note duration, and particularly on the final pulse beginning on beat five.

Some Iranian musicians argue that 6/8 is a wholly inappropriate description of the groove. One objection is that *shesh-o-hasht* is a grammatically incorrect rendering of 6/8 (it should be *shesh-hashtom*, "six-eighths"). While prerevolutionary and expatriate songwriter, bandleader, singer, and percussionist Shahbal Shabpareh told me that he felt the groove in "six fragments," he insisted that it be called dāmbuli instead of shesh-o-hasht. Leba-

EXAMPLE I.1 The most common way of notating the shesh-o-hasht or dāmbuli groove. Transcription by Dennis Lee.

nese American percussionist David Haddad, one of the most sought-after drummers for Tehrangeles recording sessions and performance tours, told me he hears and plays the beat as 12/8. Another objection to this name is that it is obviously inaccurate in those performances where the extended sense of time pulls it beyond the even divisions of compound duple meter. In our conversations and music-listening sessions, Toronto-based tonbak master Pedram Khavarzamini made the case that especially in older recordings with a strong motrebi feel, the groove is a fast 3+2+2+3 (10/8). In terms of proportionality, this strongly resembles a common regional rhythmic cycle known in Arabic and Turkish as *jurjina* (or *curcurna*). When sped up even more, he commented, jurjina "sounds like 6/8," perhaps because the 6/8 version retains jurjina's ratios of short to long beats (2+1+1+2). Khavarzamini's theory was that as Iranians became more accustomed to the regular meters common to Western music, their performances of dāmbuli turned into 6/8. Today most shesh-o-hasht songs are firmly in compound duple meter, making the shesh-o-hasht moniker slightly less inaccurate but perpetuating an oddly foreign name for a rhythm so densely woven into Iranian popular culture.

While Khavarzamini believed this transformation occurred gradually over the course of the twentieth century, there is reason to believe that shesh-o-hasht's arrival in California was a turning point in its standardization and squaring off. This is at least partially attributable to Farokh "Elton" Ahi, who was a major force in producing Shabpareh's "Deyar." Ahi arrived in the United States well before the revolution, attended the University of Southern California, and became a professional disco DJ, songwriter, engineer, and producer in the American and European music and film industries. He is one of the only regular contributors to Tehrangeles pop to have a successful career in the mainstream American entertainment industry.[14] After his pioneering work with Shabpareh, he went on to write and produce scores of other songs for Tehrangeles artists from the 1980s to the present. In a phone conversation, Ahi claimed to have invented a new form of shesh-o-hasht that "combines 6/8 and 2/4, so that you can hear the 2/4 in the 6/8." He did this by adding a kick drum to the groove's first and fourth beats, which emulates disco and EDM's conventional "four-on-the-floor" rhythmic base. He also added a snare drum to the fourth and fifth beats, which underscores shesh-o-hasht's characteristic rhythmic pattern.[15] As Ahi described it, this alteration had associative as well as sonic effects: he called his shesh-o-hasht "classy" and considered it "completely different" from the older "street" motrebi style.

In my observations, music that foregrounds the shesh-o-hasht groove reliably incites Iranians to perform versions of what Anthony Shay (2000) calls "solo improvised Iranian dance." This is a movement style that includes intricate, circular motions in the hands and wrists held out on extended arms; gently shimmying or rolling shoulders; articulated neck and head movements; a relatively stable lower body; and shifting of the body weight to alternating feet. The face is also part of the performance: skilled performers might undulate their eyebrows, smile, and flirtatiously catch an onlooker's eyes. As a child and teenager in the United States, I learned to perform these movements in social gatherings with friends and family members while dancing to Tehrangeles dance pop sung by Andy, Hassan Shamaeizadeh, Leila Foruhar, Jalal Hemmati, and Shahram Shabpareh. My experience matched that of many other children in Iran and in the diaspora who, guided and cheered on by their friends and relatives with the chant "[Name] must dance," were pushed into the middle of the living room to perform and praised when they demonstrated competency (or, in my case, effort). While not all Iranian families regularly incorporate solo improvised dance in their social gatherings—indeed, many don't—even children who do not dance at home are exposed to dance and dance music via visits to other people's homes and through Iranian media. Through life-long exposure, the rhythm has become part of a "musical habitus," "bodily imprinting a set of musical expectations and familiarities over time" (Yano 2002, 91). Some musicians even refer to the groove as "mother's milk" (*shir-e mādar*) (Farhat 1990, 115; Shay 2000, 84). Shesh-o-hasht sometimes seems to move listeners in involuntary, humorous ways. When I have given formal academic talks that incorporate shesh-o-hasht-laden Tehrangeles pop, at the sound of the first full cycle of the groove at least one Iranian audience member (and usually more) has smiled excitedly, adopted a coquettish facial expression (sometimes disarmingly directed at me), nodded his head in time to the beat, snapped her fingers, or stretched out his arms and twirled his wrists. The unexpected sound interjects a moment of playfulness and levity into what would otherwise be a serious scholarly proceeding.

EXAMPLE 1.2 "Farzaneh must dance!" A rhythmic chant used to encourage individuals to dance. Transcription by Dennis Lee.

Far - zā - neh   bā - yad   be - raq - seh

Though the percussion line on its own is identifiable as shesh-o-hasht, the drum provides only one part of the "interlocking composite of rhythmic entities" (Iyer 2002, 398) that contributes to the groove. Dance and sung or chanted text also add complexity and provide openings for participation, entrainment, and "participatory discrepancies" (Keil 1987). On the first and fourth pulses of the groove, dancers tend to move their feet or shift their weight from left to right (or front to back), which puts their movements in tension with the percussion pattern's emphasis of the fifth pulse. In many Tehrangeles pop songs, this effect is complemented by a bass line and additional percussion that strongly articulates beats one and four. The rhythmic setting of Persian-language texts also contributes to the groove. As in much music of central Asia and the Middle East, in Iranian popular, art, and folk music poetic meters and the rhythms of language provide the inspiration for vocal, instrumental, and percussion rhythms. In art music based on classical verse, these rhythms tend to be the quantitative poetic meters of 'aruz, but in the motrebi and other popular repertoire, lyrics are typically rendered in repeating and alternating iambs (short-long syllable pairing) and trochees (long-short syllable pairing). Sung or chanted, iambs and trochees are rhythmic cells that align or contrast with the shesh-o-hasht groove.[16]

The music-text-rhythm interaction can be observed in songwriter Manouchehr Cheshmazar and lyricist Paksima's 2004 song "Arousak" ("Doll"), as performed by Tehrangeles vocalist Andy.[17] The piece has a narrow melodic ambitus, a simple harmonic accompaniment, and straightforward lyrics organized in a regular rhyming verse-chorus structure praising the beloved's beauty over the shesh-o-hasht groove. The simple text resembles a children's rhyme in its content, rhythmic organization, and innocence:

'Arusaki 'arusaki / to khoshgel o bā namaki
Vāse del-e 'āsheqam taki
Vāse del-e 'āsheqam taki

EXAMPLE 1.3 The opening lines of "Arousak" ("Doll"), performed by Andy Madadian, music by Manouchehr Cheshmazar, lyrics by Paksima. Cherokee Music Group, 2004. Transcription by Dennis Lee.

You're a doll, you're a doll / you are pretty and cute
You're the only one for my enamored heart
You're the only one for my enamored heart

The text setting alternates among trochees, iambs, and even note values for the syllables so that their placement does not always align with the percussion. As in many other Tehrangeles dance songs, an open high-hat on beat five emphasizes the contrast with the underlying bass drum on beats one and four, complicating what might otherwise sound like a strong duple feel.

When moving to this piece, a person competent in solo improvised Iranian dance might shift her weight between her feet in a right-left-right [pause] / left-right-left [pause] pattern over the percussion line and move her shoulders back and forth on beats one and four, thus setting her physical movements in pleasurable tension with the percussion emphasis on beat five.

Tehrangeles dance pop is good-times music. This association contributes affective and contextual synonyms for shesh-o-hasht and other Iranian dance music: "happy music" (*musiqi-ye shād, shādemāni*) and "party music" (*musiqi-ye majlesi*). In the sprawling multicultural city of Los Angeles, social dance is a central part of events that bring Iranian families, friends, and communities into contact with each other. Weddings, bar and bat mitzvahs, private gatherings, public festivities, concerts, and club nights are important venues for interacting in groups and spaces temporarily filled with Iranian sounds, most notably Iranian dance music that animates Iranian bodies with the shesh-o-hasht rhythm. While in postrevolutionary Iran mixed-sex social dance is necessarily restricted to private parties and infrequently makes its way into public space, in the diaspora social dance has developed a place outside the home. Since the 1970s, live pop music concerts and Iranian-oriented public parties and nightclubs have provided spaces for intra-Iranian socializing beyond family and friend circles. Flyers for weekly, monthly, or themed dance parties are available at Iranian-oriented grocery, book, and music stores, and Iranian concert and party promoters stage annual dance-oriented parties for the vernal New Year (Nowruz), the winter solstice holiday Shab-e Yalda, the autumn festival Mehregan, massive events in Las Vegas over the Christmas holidays, and even larger Nowruz parties in Dubai and Antalya. Outside of jokes and poems, in terms of sheer numbers of participants, social dance is perhaps the most widely practiced category of Iranian expressive culture in the American diaspora. Unlike jokes and poems, no linguistic competence is required, which allows second-generation Iranians to participate. In my own case, I could dance passably to Tehrangeles pop long before I could understand the lyrics. Dance is an activity in which Iranians participate from childhood into late adulthood as families as well as in social settings more defined by age group. In 2007 I attended the annual El Segundo Beach celebration of Chaharshanbeh Suri (Flaming Wednesday), held on the eve of the last Wednesday of the year, in which celebrants leap over bonfires to purify themselves before the New Year. While large fires and acrobatic leaps were part of the appeal, my attention was also drawn to the deafening Iranian dance music that streamed out of cars on the jammed narrow road leading from the highway to the beach, and then the thumping pop coming from the three DJs whose sound systems were lined up down the beach for about a mile. Like family parties in homes or weddings, this was an all-ages affair: grandmothers and toddlers were among those celebrating late into the night with loud music. People were gathered around bonfires and, equally, the giant speakers, bouncing and twisting to the music that defined this stretch of California coastline as temporarily Iranian.

Dance is also visible in Iranian organizations and public displays of North American Iranian identity. In many North American cities, regional dances and Iranian "national" dance (*raqs-e melli*) are taught formally at studios by choreographers and performers who also create pieces for semiprofessional dance ensembles.[18] Three well-known Iranian dancers living in Los Angeles—Jamileh (a famous prerevolutionary performer), Rouhi Savoji (also well known before the revolution), and Mohammad Khordadian—performed regularly in Southern California in the 1980s and 1990s and have created instructional dance videotapes. Khordadian and Savoji also opened their own dance schools. In Southern California and elsewhere in the United States and Canada, professional and amateur dancers choreograph routines for groups associated with Iranian cultural organizations or Iranian university student associations and perform these publicly for Iranian and, less frequently, non-Iranian audiences.[19]

However, for its detractors—including Iranians who live in Southern California as well as other parts of the diaspora—the centrality of dancing and partying in Tehrangeles is interpreted as evidence of the vulgarity and triviality endemic to the Tehrangeles cultural industries or the overall Los Angeles Iranian population. Calling for "death to 6/8" (*marg bar 6/8*), California Bay Area resident Behrooz Bahmani's review of Tehrangeles pop stars Leila Foruhar and Mansour's 2005 albums plainly disparages the Los Angeles music industry in rhythmic terms: "Ah, fuck it. I am sick of 6/8. What was a hot bouncy beat in '78 has steadily become a drill straight into my brain, and I'm sorry but I just can't take it anymore! When are we going to be honest with the outmoded LA machine, the un-namables [*sic*] regurgitating the crap musical diarrhea they force us to buy?"[20] Like for Shahyar Ghanbari above, Bahmani's problem is not with 6/8; he objects instead to the lack of creativity and change. Seattle-based guitarist and music producer Babak Khiavchi, who preferred not to release his music through Tehrangeles outlets, also described his problem with Los Angeles via rhythm but attributed it to the audiences rather than the music industry. As he put it to me in an email exchange in 2005, "You know how the LA crowd is . . . it's all 6/8 dance, dance, dance all the time, just to give them the excuse to strut their stuff and show off their new 'silly-cones.'" Putting together rhythm, dance, Los Angeles, and "'silly-cones'"—an allusion to silicone

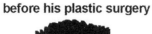

L.A. persian pop singer

before his plastic surgery	after his plastic surgery

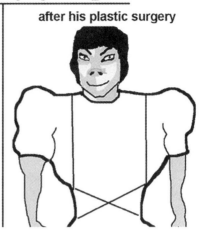

L.A. persian pop singer

before her plastic surgery	after her plastic surgery

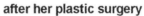

FIGURE 1.1 Cartoonist Mahmoud illustrates the grotesque, superficial los ānjelesi singer stereotype through images of a male vocalist "before" and "after" plastic surgery. "Cartoons," Iranian.com Archives, July 27, 2005, https://iranian.com/Satire /Cartoon/2005/July/pop2.html?site=archive. Used with the permission of the artist.

FIGURE 1.2 A los ānjelesi singer sports her new "silly-cones," to use Babak Khiavchi's phrase. "Cartoons," Iranian.com Archives, July 27, 2005, https://iranian.com/Satire Cartoon/2005/July/pop1.html?site=archive. Used with the permission of the artist.

آبرو ریزی

رقص ایرونی افراد چهل سال به بالا
در مهمونی و عروسی ها ..

حالا اگه مجبوری برقصی دیگه چشم و ابرو بالا
ننداز و ماچ نفرست ...

mahmoud, iranian.com

FIGURE 1.3 *"Āberurizi* (losing face, dishonor). People forty years of age and up dancing Iranian-style at parties and weddings . . . Now if you really must dance, at least don't move your eyes and eyebrows about or blow kisses . . ." Cartoonist Mahmoud's depiction of dancing as undignified behavior accords with the disdain for shesh-o-hashti dance music. Screen grab from "Cartoons," Iranian.com Archives, May 26, 2006, https:// iranian.com/Satire /Cartoon/2006/May /raghs.html?site=archive. Used with the permission of the artist.

breast implants and Los Angeles Iranians' stereotypical cosmetic surgery fetish—created a distinct picture of superficiality anchored to location and musical sound.

Putting intradiasporic debates momentarily aside, the centrality of dance and dance music is also one of the cultural elements and practices that most signifies Iranian Southern California's distinction from postrevolutionary Iranian official culture—at least on the surface. The shesh-o-hasht dance music pouring out of Tehrangeles contributed to the city's caricatural reputation for hedonism, triviality, and depoliticization: when "degeneration" and its propagators were purged from territorial Iran, they took root in Los Angeles. This view is matched by a parallel inverse caricature of postrevolutionary Iran as the seat of humorless piety, ideological rigor, and what Asef Bayat (2007) punningly calls "anti-fun-damentalism," where Shiite commemorative practices and revolutionary zeal combined to form a national "'culture of sadness' (*farhang-e gham*)" or "'culture of mourning' (*farhang-e 'azādāri*)" (Khosravi 2008, 49; see also Siamdoust 2017). While the Islamic Republic's leaders and international representatives were somber clerics, some of Los Angeles's most visible and audible envoys were popular musicians. When cabarets and nightclubs were shuttered in Iran after the revolution and dancing was banned in public, these institutions and activities became important ways for Iranians in the diaspora to congregate. And as the popular music industry was closed in Iran, it reemerged in Los Angeles as one of the most highly developed sectors of expatriate cultural production. Whether one considers these developments or characterizations positive or negative depends on which parts of the many circulating discourses of affect and morality one privileges: Tehrangeles popular culture producers are the saviors of happiness or just *alaki-khosh* (happy without a legitimate reason); the Islamic Republic's state culture is respectably somber and piously sorrowful, or so overbearing that it has attempted to squeeze the joy out of its citizens. None of these stereotypes tells the whole story, nor do they reflect the ways both Tehrangeles and the public culture within Iran have changed since the 1980s, but they remain meaningful as competing essentialisms that musicians and audiences position themselves with and against.

TEHRANGELES'S "LABORERS OF JOY"

In a meeting in 2007 with Mehrdad Pakravan, head of the Los Angeles–based record label Caltex Records, I asked how he perceived Tehrangeles pop music in relation to prerevolutionary pop. He answered, "In Iran, music was for listening to. In LA, it was for dancing." He added a moment later, "In LA, in the 1980s, it was all *vatan* (homeland) and shesh-o-hasht." The homeland focus made sense to me, but why, when there was so much to mourn, would artists churn out happy dance music? It wasn't that expatriate artists made upbeat dance music because they wanted to, longtime music producer Vartan Avanessian told me. Making party music was a financial necessity and a response to the demand: this was what their new expatriate patrons required for their festive events. It was the prevalence of quickly produced, commercially driven dance music in the industry's earliest days that led outsiders to characterize the entirety of Tehrangeles music in this light, Avanessian told me:

[In the 1980s] so many singers were trying to gain work in parties, weddings, bar and bat mitzvah, and Jewish parties [sic], so they could go to gigs, they tried to sing musiqi-ye shād ["happy music"] so that it would become popular. . . . They didn't stop and reflect to say, "So, what can we make so that it can be listened to [forever]?" . . . It came to have this name, los ānjelesi. . . . The conditions of that time led the singers to make this kind of music. . . . The term stuck, and los ānjelesi came to mean low-quality music. In my opinion, it wasn't low quality, but that's what people kept calling it.

Musicians who ended up in Southern California were not new to gigging: performing in cabarets and entertaining at weddings and private events were part of most prerevolutionary professional musicians' income, along with fees for appearances on radio or television and one-time payments for recordings (royalties were not awarded). In Tehrangeles, gigging became even more important because expatriate production and dissemination networks were so ill formed and unprofitable. Eventually Los Angeles music companies put together compilation cassettes and CDs of "dance" or "happy" music for parties, and specialized Iranian DJs would play their own selections of dance hits to enliven parties.

The market demand for dance pop was such that even musicians I spoke with who preferred to make music in other styles were financially discouraged from doing so. One lyricist living in Toronto who specialized in romantic ballads told me about his trip to Los Angeles in the early 2000s to shop his record to Tehrangeles labels. Though a music company owner he met told him she liked his work, she refused to produce his album unless it contained at least four dance songs because, according to her, it was the only way she could guarantee the record would make money. Dance music's salability was also confirmed by Caltex Records owner Pakravan, who plainly stated that it was impossible for him to provide contracts to more experimental, nondance music albums because he couldn't be assured they would turn a profit. The demand to produce and perform music for parties meant that musicians were required to play music they sometimes referred to as khāltur.[21] Part of the early twentieth-century motrebi jargon and still in use among musicians today, khāltur, or musiqi-ye khālturi, refers to the light repertoire musicians play to make ends meet, the entertaining dance music appropriate for parties but not, these musicians believed, for much else. Discussing his weekly gig playing trap set for the house band at a Tehrangeles nightclub, a drummer who specialized in jazz dismissed my questions about the shesh-o-hasht he played every night, regarding it as unworthy of scholarly attention. It was all khāltur, he said, as were the weddings and bar and bat mitzvahs he was compelled to play for the money. Tehrangeles musicians felt themselves required to meet their audience's desires and expectations for shesh-o-hasht. This music was popular in the sense of serving the people: musicians played at their patrons' pleasure, and their experiments with other forms of art were neither appreciated nor compensated.

If working Tehrangeles musicians were mere servants of popular taste, then this meant that popular taste—the people—were ultimately responsible for Tehrangeles's lack of musical diversity and creativity. This slippery causality is highlighted in a statement by Raha Etemadi, a lyricist and television personality who was the rare case of a second-generation Iranian participant in expatriate popular culture. In a 2007 interview at the San Fernando Valley offices of the internet company Bebin.tv, where Etemadi then worked, he explained that while he found many Tehrangeles music videos and songs to be illogical and low quality, this was because the people making them felt they couldn't fully express themselves and still reach "the simpleminded average listener." He presented the following scenario as an illustration: "A guy comes into [a music store to] buy a CD, and he says, 'CD-e jadid chi chi umadeh?' (What new CDs have come in?) [If] you show him something that is meaningful or deep . . . he says, 'No, no, what about that one?' So, you show him another called *The World Is Beautiful*, and he says, 'Yeah, yeah, I'll take that one! Oh yeah, shesh-o-hasht!'" I laughed in recognition of both the stereotypical "simpleminded listeners" other musicians had described to me and the interaction that Etemadi described, which I had observed in different versions on nearly every one of my visits to Iranian music stores in Los Angeles and Toronto: a customer would approach the front counter and ask the store proprietor to play excerpts of the newest albums, which the customer then approved or rejected based on thirty seconds of listening. Etemadi portrayed the "simpleminded average listener" as uninterested in the most profound or "meaningful" new music as he invoked long-standing associations between frivolity and lack of personal depth, and then linked them specifically to Iranian dance music bearing the shesh-o-hasht groove. For Etemadi and many others, it was ultimately audiences that were holding artists hostage through their intellectual, aesthetic, and emotional lack of development and through their incessant demands for "feel-good" Iranian dance music.

Given the pressures on Tehrangeles musicians and the affective dimensions of their performances, I came to see their connection to an archaic

FIGURE 1.4 Replete with butterflies, a unicorn, a waterfall, and a rainbow, the cover of Morteza's *Donyā-ye rangi (Colorful World)* album displays the kind of rosy picture that some Tehrangeles pop musicians disdain as trivial. Morteza, *Donyā-ye rangi (Colorful World)*, Caltex Records, 2002.

term for musician: *laborer of joy* (*'amaleh-ye tarab*). This formulation recognizes Tehrangeles dance music performance and production as "affective labor," or "work intended to produce or modify people's emotional experiences" (Hofman 2015, 31). The stereotypical *los ānjelesi* musician's labor is the sonic representation and instigation of joy: the circulation of affect in musical form. More controversially, to refer to Tehrangeles musicians as laborers of joy is also an acknowledgment of their historical and generic connections to the nineteenth- to mid-twentieth-century figure of the motreb. The word *motreb*, taken literally, means "one who brings about joy." In terms of musicians' professional function, the trace of shame, and elements of the repertoire—particularly the shesh-o-hasht beat endemic to motrebi repertoire—the term *motreb* is quite apt, if even more insulting to Tehrangeles musicians than the *los ānjelesi* moniker. To call Tehrangeles musicians "laborers of joy" is simultaneously to recognize the affective dimensions of their artistry and to recognize that art as *work*. This may be dirty or dishonorable work in the eyes of some Iranians—even including some musicians themselves—but it is valuable, even vital, to Iranian social life.

PROFESSIONAL "DIMBOLOGISTS": SHAHBAL SHABPAREH AND THE BLACK CATS

During my research in Tehrangeles, the person who came closest to embracing shesh-o-hasht was Shahbal Shabpareh, the elder brother of Shahram Shabpareh. Though less famous than Shahram, Shahbal is a cornerstone of the Los Angeles Iranian music industry.[22] The brothers began their involvement in Iranian pop in the 1960s as part of the Black Cats, which Shahbal re-created in Tehrangeles in the 1990s as what he has called "Black Cats in exile" (personal communication). The Southern Californian iteration of the Black Cats released nine albums between 1992 and 2014 and was for years one of the best-known Tehrangeles pop groups—indeed one of the only groups in a market dominated by solo singers. The group's combination of skillful pop songwriting, light lyrics, well-produced videos, and high production values was important to their success, as was their changing lineup of attractive, youthful front men. In Los Angeles as in Iran, the Black Cats have included many different singers and musicians, several of whom have gone on to begin their own successful solo careers in the Iranian music industry. In addition to his work with the Black Cats, Shahbal has also acted as a sort of pop music impresario, organizing other musical ensembles of young musicians, writing songs for them, and promoting them along with the Black Cats on tours and albums.[23] Shahbal was very active; he told me that on the day after our interview in 2007 he would be embarking on a world tour that would take the Black Cats to Vancouver, Dubai, Oberhausen, and Goa, among other cities. In Goa he said he expected a crowd of twenty thousand, while in Oberhausen he expected ten thousand to thirteen thousand. These numbers would be especially impressive given that the Black Cats are almost exclusively known by Iranian and Persian-speaking audiences. In the 2000s, the group also regularly played in England, the Netherlands, and Kuala Lumpur, which, like Dubai and Goa, hosts many Iranian residents and tourists.

When I interviewed Shahbal, he was in his late sixties, his distinctive raspy voice a contrast to his unlined face, dark hair, and youthful style of dress. He greeted me in his high-rise apartment in Westwood dressed in a formfitting black T-shirt and black jeans, with several turquoise stones of different sizes on leather cords worn around his neck. His home was appointed in a style common to the Iranian bourgeoisie in both Iran and the United States: Louis XIV–style furniture covered in damask and brocade shared space with a baby grand piano, and an electric samovar sat in the kitchen. Perched on a solitary pedestal near the front door was a framed studio photograph of Mohammad Reza Pahlavi in military dress at the height of his power, his glimmering medals offset by his stern visage. The portrait was positioned so that one would always see it when leaving the house, the shah's confident gaze meeting one's own. Shahbal described himself as enjoying a vibrant career when he lived in "Persia" (throughout the interview he refrained from using the name Iran). He was not an independent star like his brother, but he had the Black Cats group and steady work as a timbales player in "five different government agencies," including radio and television. When the revolution came, he remained in Iran, eventually leaving for London. It was not until the late 1980s that he joined his brother in Los Angeles, where he too began playing in Iranian-oriented nightclubs.

Though Shahbal's demeanor in our interview was quite modest, in public forums he has also made forthright claims about his influence on Iranian popular music, especially in bringing Western popular music to Iran and in developing new musical styles that combined the local and foreign.[24] In prerevolutionary Iran, he told me, the Black Cats had pioneered a new style of Iranian popular music called *rock dāmbuli*, his term for the way many Black Cats' songs switch between 4/4 rock or pop rhythms and Iranian 6/8 rhythms and back again. He proudly said he used this technique "on every album."[25] He suggested I could hear rock dāmbuli in action in the Black Cats song "Rang o reng" ("Colors and Dance Music"), which appeared on the 1993 album *Fever* (Caltex Records). I had heard this tune many times as a teenager at family parties, where it was better known by the song's giggle-inducing vocal hook: "Pishi pishi mau mau" (Kitty, kitty, meow, meow).

The song begins with a reggae-inspired instrumental accompaniment with the characteristic upbeat keyboard chordal hits but then switches to a rock beat as the lyrics reference the prerevolutionary Black Cats' covers of the Beatles: "We play rock, rock and roll! 'Yeah, yeah, yeah—she loves me—yeah, yeah, yeah!'" Another abrupt switch takes the song into Iranian dāmbuli, which the Black Cats claim to have mastered as well: "We also play 'Iruni' well / Dāmbul o dimbol / Dāmbul o dimbol." The band then transposes the originally duple meter "Pishi pishi mau mau" vocal hook into shesh-o-hasht, "Iranianizing" it and playing up the hemiola in the lyrics' setting versus the tonbak groove. Having demonstrated their flexibility and proficiency in these various forms, the band returns to the song's opening reggae beat and fades out.

EXAMPLE 1.4 The rhythmic duple meter refrain "Pishi pishi mau mau" (Kitty, kitty, meow, meow) from the Black Cats' 1993 song "Rang o reng" ("Colors and Dance Music") (*Fever*, Caltex Records). Transcription by Dennis Lee.

EXAMPLE 1.5 "We also know how to play Iranian-style!" The "pishi" refrain set to the dāmbuli groove. Transcription by Dennis Lee.

In our interview, Shahbal pointed out the lines from the "Iruni" section of the song that represent a debate over the dāmbuli beat. These reference a well-known motrebi reng "Baba Karam" that has been remade many times in Tehrangeles:

> *Let go of that dāmbul o dimbol, man! It's not us!*
> *It's in our blood and veins; "Baba Karam" isn't separate from us!*[26]

He then explained what the lyrics meant in more detail:

> [In my concerts,] I say, "We have to take pride in our music, in our rhythm." Dāmbuli is our music! When you talk about salsa, Spanish [*sic*] really take pride. When you say American country, [Americans] really take pride. . . . So, OUR music is dāmbuli! When we play, [he sounded out the rhythm] *ram beli ram*—EVERYBODY [dances]! . . . This is our blood. And I think we have some kind of a responsibility to keep our tradition. Our musical traditions [have] this rhythm. And it is living in every Per-

sian body—especially in young girls. . . . When they hear this rhythm, see how they move! . . . As a Persian musician, it is my honor and my pride to keep this rhythm in my music. And wherever I go, I say, "*I* play dāmbuli! *You* cannot play dāmbuli." I can say it to jazz people, the greatest musicians. You want to play it, here, sit and play *dombak* (tonbak). You will never play [as well] as I [do], because it is not in your blood.[27]

When I had heard this song as a teenager, I had assumed that the reference to dāmbuli was like the "Pishi pishi mau mau" hook—playful and not serious at all. As Shahbal spoke, I was taken aback at hearing a derisive slang term used sincerely as a call to respect Iranian dance music. Shahbal acknowledged his unusual stance by commenting that "people call [the rhythm and music that contains it] dāmbuli to bring it down, but I call it dāmbuli to really honor it."[28] I was surprised again two years later to encounter another prominent example of Shahbal's positive attitude: the Black Cats' 2009 album, entitled *Dimbology* (Caltex Records), on which seven of eight songs use dāmbuli dance rhythms. The idea that Shahbal could be a skillful "dimbologist" was rather silly, yet it spoke to his call to respect dāmbuli music and his group as specialists in a widely enjoyed, if frequently denigrated, aspect of Iranian culture. Even more striking was how Shahbal connected Iranian desires for dāmbuli to tradition and a biocultural desire "living in every Persian body." He spoke of dāmbuli "in our veins," "in the blood," and "right under the skin," an "itch" that needed to be scratched.

In the moment, I was tempted to write off Shahbal's explanation as an excuse for why he kept repeating the same musical formula for years on end. At the same time, I also recognized his portrayal of the seemingly involuntary response this distinctive groove generated in many Iranian listeners. When I thought back to the notion of shesh-o-hasht as "mother's milk," the rhythm appeared to me as the milk of the Motherland (*mām-e vatan*)—the comforting, nourishing, affirming sustenance, and a literal form of sustaining culture that had in turn provided the Shabpareh brothers and so many others in Los Angeles with their livelihoods. When Shahbal stated that his audiences needed to respect the rhythm and, by extension, him and his music, he was placing himself in the category of cultural preservationists working against the pretension and elitism that prevented some Iranians from admitting that they, too, loved to dance to dāmbuli.

He explained, "Some people, they want to show off differently, but down deep in their hearts, when they're alone and no one else is around, they move to this music, this [dāmbuli] rhythm, more than any other. You watch them, and all of a sudden, their butt is moving!" This extended to Iranian Americans who were born abroad and those who grew up in Iran as well. "You play this dāmbuli rhythm on a CD for your sister, who was born [in the United States]. You play it and see what she does. [She dances. But she says,] 'What is this Persian music?? I hate it!' But then they dance. And when you come back in the room, *thwiiiiiik*!! [He mimed someone abruptly pulling a needle off a record to stop the music so no one would hear what they were listening to.]" Once again, Shahbal invoked the physical response that defied concerns with social or religious mores: "in their hearts," all Iranians' "butts" want to move when they hear that dāmbuli beat. It was this maligned groove that moved them "more than any other." Shabpareh never mentioned the postrevolutionary ban on shesh-o-hasht, perhaps because it was irrelevant to his career in Southern California but maybe also because the policies were only the most recent iteration of a historically and culturally embedded ambivalence toward this groove, its practitioners, and the feelings they stimulated in listeners. Along with the rhythm itself, these associations had trailed professional musicians into the diaspora. Shabpareh claimed access to and adeptness in deploying the "culturally intimate" materials of rhythm and dance, and pointed to the "rueful self-recognition" manifest in the embodied response that Iranians experienced, even in spite of themselves, when hearing his "dimbological" music.

As he has called for people to respect dāmbuli—and therefore his own dāmbuli-propelled music and career—Shahbal is also insistent that he and his band be recognized for their artistic abilities beyond the narrow parameters of Iranian dance music. Over their many years of existence in exile, the Black Cats' opus has included rap, R&B, straight-ahead 1990s pop (à la Michael Jackson), Latin beats, and reggaeton—the lead song on *Dimbology*, called "Faghat tou [Only You] (Dimbology Opus 2009)," even opens with the beginning phrases of Beethoven's Fifth Symphony. This cosmopolitanism is a testament to the diversity of influences available in Southern California as well as representing the legacy of Shabpareh and his generation's prerevolutionary careers, when musical borrowing and experimentation was important to popular music generally and especially to the Black Cats' own rock-influenced beginnings. This refusal to be pigeonholed as "Iranian only"—or as "shesh-o-hashti" or "dāmbuli only"—came through in the group's 2006 song "Los Angeles" on the album *Scream of the Cats* (Caltex Records). The band's then–front man, a French Iranian R&B singer named KamyR, makes this clear in the chorus:

KamyR:	Am I a *bandari* singer?
Chorus:	Ain't no way!
K:	Am I a dāmbuli singer?
C:	Ain't no way!
K:	Am I a *gherti* singer?
C:	Ain't no way!
K:	I'm just a funky singer!

Rejecting the suggestion that he is only a singer of dāmbuli or bandari—the latter a gloss for southern Iranian coastal rhythms also popular in Tehrangeles —or that he is gherti (tawdry, flamboyant), KamyR asserts that he's "just a funky singer," one comfortable in any number of (African American– influenced) musical styles. Yet the fact remains that the Black Cats and KamyR (who has moved on to a solo career) play to majority-Iranian audiences who, at least in Shahbal's estimation, primarily turn to Tehrangeles pop to scratch their shesh-o-hasht itch.

SHESH-O-HASHT IS DEAD, LONG LIVE SHESH-O-HASHT

G. J. Breyley and Sasan Fatemi suggest that "the terms motrebi and losān-jelesi [*sic*] can be reclaimed as 'neutral' descriptions of music that has enlivened and sustained Iranian communities over the last century" (2016, 143). My analysis aligns with Breyley and Fatemi's appraisal of Tehrangeles pop's enlivening and sustaining functions but stops short at their suggestion of the possibility of "reclaiming" motrebi or los ānjelesi. This chapter has showed instead why Tehrangeles's founding generation has yet to embrace these terms as descriptions for themselves or their work: *los ānjelesi* and *motrebi* link professional "happy" musical entertaining with what some listeners and even some musicians consider vulgar, disreputable affective labor. Shahbal Shabpareh's concerted efforts to recast dāmbuli music and the word itself as positive, honorable, inalienable aspects of Iranian culture and Iranian physicality stand in contrast to ongoing prejudices. He argues that playing dāmbuli in the diaspora is culturally and monetarily valuable work that connects Iranians with visceral, pleasurable, and sometimes discomfiting aspects of their heritage and their bodies. The livelihoods of the Shabpareh brothers, Jalal Hemmati, Andy, and all their shesh-o-hasht-playing colleagues have depended on their ability to generate culturally intimate experiences for social gatherings and life-cycle events, which in turn relies on their knowledge of what physically and affectively moves their audiences. Especially in the postrevolutionary diaspora, where familiarity, comfort, and the assurances of stable meanings that cultural intimacy implies were all in short supply, Tehrangeles musicians were called on to provide these grooves again and again, a role that provided some measure of financial return but comparatively less room for experimentation. What some perceive to be the excessive repetition of an already repetitive groove has turned cultural intimacy into cliché and trapped the professional Tehrangeles performer in the los ānjelesi stereotype.

The affective qualities of dāmbuli-filled dance music are also meaningful in the context of the postrevolutionary politicization of affect and expressive culture. While critics of shesh-o-hasht dance music assert its anti-intellectual, uncreative, and depoliticizing effects, Tehrangeles's promotion of dance and dance music acquires a political undertone when taken in tandem with the postrevolutionary state's moral guidelines for Iranians' physical comportment and bodily discipline that include restricting public sensuality and dance. In this light, Shahbal's and others' invocations of pervasive, nationally identified bodily responses with the Iranian groove appear as counterdiscourses and counteressentialisms to the revolutionary state's version of Iranian culture, while suggesting that dance music producers understand the inherent needs and desires of the Iranian people for joy and sensuality in recognizably Iranian cultural forms. In this light, the thumping groove is a larger pronouncement that the Los Angeles culture industries make on so many levels: Iranian culture, Iranian needs, and Iranian desires are more expansive and diverse than the present Iranian state can accommodate, and that cultural producers in Los Angeles can uniquely respond to these needs and desires.

Today shesh-o-hasht no longer dominates Tehrangeles to the extent it once did. As of 2007, Caltex Record owner Mehrdad Pakravan observed that "4/4 [was] replacing 6/8" on many Iranian pop albums produced in Los Angeles. Duple meter trance, house, hip-hop, reggaeton, and Arabic pop styles became more popular on Tehrangeles albums in the 2000s, and the number of songs using characteristically Iranian dance rhythms diminished, both among younger artists and among the prerevolutionary pop musicians who have continued in Los Angeles. While this may appear to signal the triumph of those individuals who, as in "Rang o reng," want musicians to "let go of that dāmbul o dimbol" in favor of more globally current styles, another likely influence is the legal popular music produced in Iran since 1997. Perhaps because of early limitations on dance music and motrebi musical elements, the licit domestic pop of the mid-2000s drew more on 4/4 trance and house styles and therefore, rhythmically, sounds quite Western. This creates yet more possibilities regarding what musical elements signal Iranian identity; the mainstream official homeland pop has moved on from shesh-o-hasht, whether for reasons of fashion, elitism, continuing restrictions, or other factors.

But the Los Angeles industry tells only part of shesh-o-hasht's continuing story. Starting in the mid-2000s, official, unofficial, *and* diasporic pop music produced outside of Los Angeles has refashioned and indeed reclaimed dāmbuli dance beats. Music reviewer Pourya E. points to Iran-based underground dance music producer Bahador Kharazmi's 2004 single, a remake of Shahram Shabpareh's prerevolutionary song "Tu in zamuneh" ("In These Times"), as the first prominent example of "Persian trance," so identified because it uses a dāmbuli-esque rhythmic pattern while retaining trance's distinctive instrumental timbres and song structure. Art rock band 127's 2007 album "Khal Punk" (a play on *khāltur*) includes numerous songs in a *charand-gui* (rhyming nonsense) style over a shesh-o-hasht beat that unmistakably index motrebi repertoire. In 2008 and 2009 respectively, two unofficial musicians in Iran named Amir Tataloo and Sasy Mankan created an internet sensation with a run of MP3s that combined hip-hop, R&B-style vocals, and 6/8 dance beats in styles that show the continued melding of contemporary dance music trends and Tehrangeles/motrebi pop styles. Mankan took so much ownership over "608" that he called one of his songs "609," a play on a sexual innuendo but also a claim that he took the groove to a new level. Facing official harassment for musical activities conducted without a permit, Mankan has since moved to Los Angeles, where he has performed live with the Black Cats and had a shesh-o-hasht hit with his online single "Vāy cheghadr mastam man" ("Whoa, I'm So Drunk"). Whether they are bowing to the necessity of appealing to what is apparently an essential Iranian desire, or whether they gladly embrace the shesh-o-hasht rhythm as part of their heritage, recent releases show that officially approved musicians now also pump out the dāmbuli beats. Whatever one attributes these rhythms' continuity to, the dāmbuli groove's refusal to die signals its enduring appeal and its ongoing relevance to how Iranians want to feel.

IRANIAN POPULAR
MUSIC AND HISTORY
VIEWS FROM
TEHRANGELES

In *Literature and Race in Los Angeles*, Julian Murphet
writes, "The greatest difficulty in coming to terms with
Los Angeles will always be seeing it as such; not for a lack
of representations, but because of their contradictory plenitude"
(2001, 8). Something similar can be said for Tehrangeles. Since the
1980s, Iranians in Los Angeles have been prolific producers of media representing their own experience, memories of prerevolutionary Iran, predictions for the homeland's future, and revisiting of twentieth-century history.
This chapter focuses on expatriate narratives of Iranian popular music history. Creating historical narratives is always a fraught process, and especially so in the aftermath of revolution when a new regime attempts
to wipe away all signs of its predecessors. Established tenets of national identity, systems of governance, social hierarchies, cultural signs, and prior historical narratives go on the revolutionary chopping block, disassembled and pushed to
the side to make way for a new order. From this perspective, prominent prerevolutionary popular

musicians, many of whom worked in the Pahlavi state-supported national media and governmental institutions, were on the wrong side of history. Regardless of their personal politics, the postrevolutionary rejection of popular music meant there was no place for them or their work within the country, nor in its official history, except as representatives of the nation's dissolute past. As highly skilled, heavily resourced, networked elites with the desire and means to begin again in exile, the prerevolutionary cohort of media and music producers who established Tehrangeles have taken it upon themselves to create their own versions of history in which they play starring roles. These roles include those of musical modernizers, preservers of Iranian music in the face of attempted revolutionary destruction, and standard-bearers who have managed to rebuild in exile despite their loss of status. Aware that negative assessments of their pre- and postrevolutionary cultural production come from many quarters—cultural elitists, official state discourse and policy, younger generations of music fans—Tehrangeles musicians also recognize that they are both aging and less relevant to Iranian audiences than in prior decades, factors that have added a sense of urgency to creating records of their achievements for posterity.

The major medium for circulating this history is the expatriate television talk show. These shows typically comprise interviews between celebrity hosts and popular musicians who discuss entertaining events and political intrigues from the prerevolutionary era. They are a mainstay of Tehrangeles television. Broadcast locally and on satellite television, and then uploaded to YouTube and other sites, these programs constitute an electronic oral archive separate from the national archives in Iran or elsewhere, and contain stories those physical repositories may or may not include. Expatriates have been engaging in journalistic and more formal oral historical projects since the 1980s; multiple iterations of the same recollections by the same individuals, produced in different locations and by different expatriate institutions, are in circulation. Pioneering expatriate television channel Jam-e Jam conducted some of the first interviews, and many other past and present Tehrangeles-based stations followed suit; expatriate journalists working with BBC Persian and Voice of America have taken up oral history as well.[1] Most recently, expatriate television stations based in London and Dubai have solicited recollections from prerevolutionary-turned-expatriate musicians. Within these layers of historical accounts, accounts that can now themselves be historicized, the "contradictory plentitude" is astounding. Much is contested, little is confirmed, and resolution is out of reach.

It was in this environment that I sought to collect yet more oral historical accounts from the prerevolutionary generation of Tehrangeles musicians and media producers through which I hoped to contextualize the industry's past and present. Scholars often employ oral history to "give a voice to the voiceless [and] a narrative to the story-less" (Abrams 2010, 154), or to empower "individuals or social groups through the process of remembering and reinterpreting the past" (Perks and Thomson 2006, ix). In my case, oral history took on different functions and results. The well-known, sometimes quite wealthy individuals with whom I spoke in Tehrangeles were already empowered, albeit within their largely expatriate Iranian social and professional networks. Many of my interlocutors were accustomed to being interviewed, had a strong sense of their own importance, and had already rehearsed and recorded their stories within the entertainment media context many times. The interviews that I used to craft this chapter—my own personal interviews as well as interviews culled from expatriate media—were with men in their sixties and seventies who had been at the top of their industry for many decades and were used to being treated as authorities. The women I spoke with in Tehrangeles neither held nor claimed to hold authority in the present or in the past, and were also largely left out of expatriate media oral histories of the prerevolutionary and early postmigration music industry. As a diasporic female graduate student–turned–professor promising to write their stories into an English-language academic book, I represented a different kind of audience and introduced a different set of relationships into the familiar process of investigating the past. However, I did not find that this necessarily led my interlocutors to provide me with any different information and perspectives than what they had already given in prior programs. In one case, my interviewee directed me to his media appearances as a more authoritative account than our face-to-face interaction. Even when I managed to meet celebrities and speak with them at some length, the face-to-face interview could hardly be said to be unmediated—instead, it was conducted in the presence of existing and future media representations in circulation. In many conversations I had a sense of physically absent but nevertheless palpable and long-standing interpersonal and political conflicts about an individual's legacy, or about whether prerevolutionary or Tehrangeles pop should have a role in Iranian music history and, if so, what that role should entail. At stake was whether Tehrangeles musicians and media producers could be proud of what they had managed to accomplish for their local communities or for Iranians at home.

The affordances and obstacles of mass media are one of the major issues of this chapter. For Tehrangeles media producers, media are like the Iranian poetic representation of love: they are *dard o darmān*—the pain and its remedy all in one. Recording and broadcast media were critical to Tehrangeles media producers' ability to set up their businesses in exile, allowing them to not only record new material but reproduce prerevolutionary music, film, and television, which has been a stable part of Tehrangeles companies' output for years. Their inability to prevent others from reproducing those same media has meant the death of the object-oriented music business model, but, then again, it has afforded Tehrangeles pop entry into territorial Iran, where it cannot legally be sold. Media in the service of archiving history represent another thorny issue: Tehrangeles media producers have turned especially to television to forward their own narratives of prerevolutionary and postmigration music history, but they must also contend with competing narratives generated both within Tehrangeles and without. The proliferation of media—and, therefore, accounts—highlights the fact that no unitary story can be told. As much as I once hoped that my research would yield the materials for an authoritative history of Iranian popular music within Iran and in Los Angeles, attempting such a task would be both less truthful and, I think, less interesting than this chapter's ultimate form: an account of history, legacy, and their mass-mediated representation and preservation as problems with which Tehrangeles music and media producers are very much engaged. These are problems I also face in attempting to faithfully document these producers' accounts in their messy, unresolved, and unresolvable "contradictory plenitude."

What follows are three views on the history of Iranian popular music before the revolution and in Tehrangeles. I assembled these narratives from four men who have been involved in the music business since the 1950s and 1960s. Their various ethnoreligious backgrounds are representative of the cosmopolitanism of the prerevolutionary music industry and the high concentration of religious minorities in Los Angeles. I begin with Jewish prerevolutionary music producer and postmigration television producer Manouchehr Bibiyan, who discusses his attempts to create a "modern," respectable role for musicians at a time when many Muslims considered music to be sinful. Bibiyan discusses the challenges of working with government agencies in the politicized atmosphere of the decades leading up the revolution. Not content to leave the documentation of Iranian popular music history to others, Bibiyan has also embarked on an ambitious oral history project of his own contained on his personal website. I show how his efforts to publicly present his recollections are directly related to his understanding of the revisionist tendencies within Tehrangeles. The chapter then turns to Muslim pop singer and songwriter Shahram Shabpareh, the accidental "founder of Tehrangeles" whose postmigration career producing upbeat dance music laid the groundwork for the expatriate music industry and, his supporters argue, disseminated a vital if underappreciated source of joy to war-torn 1980s Iran. I close with observations from prerevolutionary and postmigration music producers Jahangir Tabaraei and Vartan Avanessian (an Armenian Christian), who together run the Tehrangeles music label Taraneh Records. Avanessian speaks plainly of his company's challenge to remain relevant and profitable as Tehrangeles has lost its position as the "standard-bearer of Iranian music" and as he and his colleagues struggle to keep abreast of technological and generational changes in the expatriate music industry at large. Each provides a perspective on a different period of Iranian music history and from the standpoint of a different professional role. They also exhibit varying attitudes toward their personal legacies and the role of prerevolutionary and postmigration Tehrangeles music's place in Iran's musical heritage. Their accounts (and others' accounts of them) are resolutely partial in the sense of being part of a larger whole that is inaccessible from the perspective of an individual's recollection, and partial also in the sense of bias.

MANOUCHEHR BIBIYAN AND THE FRAGILITY
OF IRANIAN MUSIC HISTORY

The individual in Los Angeles I encountered with the longest memory of Iranian popular music and the most invested in its preservation was Manouchehr Bibiyan. In 1981 Bibiyan opened Jam-e Jam, the first Persian-language television station in Los Angeles. He is recognized as one of Tehrangeles's founders. But this was very much Bibiyan's second career: he first made his mark in the prerevolutionary Iranian cultural industries as a music producer and executive. In his capacity as founder of the Apollon record label, which he ran for nearly twenty-five years between 1945 and 1979, Bibiyan claims to have produced and released over six thousand songs in every major musical style with some of the most famous and prolific figures of the period. According to Houman Sarshar's interview with Bibiyan for the Iranian Jewish Oral History Project (now housed at the University of California, Los Angeles), in the 1970s "Āpolon [sic] was selling an average of twenty-five thousand units per day via nearly two thousand record stores throughout the country and others abroad." It was the largest music production company in Iran, and Bibiyan was "the most influential recording executive in Persia [*sic*] prior to 1979" (quoted in Sarshar 2012). Bibiyan fled Iran in the late 1970s, landing first in Israel (where he had lived as a teenager) and then moving to Los Angeles by 1979. Along with establishing Jam-e Jam, Bibiyan opened a company called Pars Video that was to become the chief reproducer and distributor of prerevolutionary film and video in the diaspora. He later sold Pars Video as well as the masters of his prerevolutionary recordings that he had brought out of Iran. The masters went to Mehrdad Pakravan's Caltex Records.

Bibiyan may have given up the legal rights to the music he had such a hand in creating—the rights to which would be difficult to determine and enforce in any case, given the vagaries of Iranian copyright law—but when I met him in 2007 and again in 2013, he claimed ownership over his experiences and memories, as well as a strong sense of authority. In recent years, Bibiyan has focused on preserving his memories and contributions to Iranian culture. In 2010 he self-published Persian and English versions of a book called *Secrets of the Iranian Revolution: Jaam-e Jam Television's Open Forum*, a collection of edited transcripts from interviews on his Jam-e Jam television interview program. In 2012 Bibiyan gave twenty-one hour-long interviews with local expatriate journalist Alireza Meybodi recounting his work in the prerevolutionary popular music industry. These aired on Pars TV and are archived on his personal website along with many photographs of himself with notable figures of prerevolutionary popular music in their prime.

Making Iranian Music "Modern"

I first met Bibiyan in 2007 for a formal interview in the offices of his television station. These were located in a nondescript stucco office building on Ventura Boulevard in Los Angeles's San Fernando Valley, the same location where I had met his son Kourosh the day before. Bibiyan the elder spoke to me from behind his large wooden desk; I was seated across from him with a television airing Jam-e Jam's broadcast. It was positioned in his line of sight, directly behind me. For the duration of our interview, I heard a steady stream of prerevolutionary pop hits emanating from the television set while many of the singers and entertainers of the bygone age of which we spoke danced across the screen. Bibiyan spoke for over an hour with barely a question from me, his eyes flickering between my face and the television as he narrated the story of the music that filled the room.

Before venturing into our previously agreed-on topic of conversation—

his work with Apollon—Bibiyan began the interview with an unprompted discussion of the role of Iranian Jews in preserving and developing musical traditions in Iranian history. Jews had saved Iranian music over the centuries, he said, by moving musical practice into their communities when the political-religious tides of Muslim society periodically turned against such "sin."[2] He went on to describe the ways he and his Muslim and Christian colleagues in the music industry had created songs that are now beloved parts of Iranian collective memory. With their precise attention to quality, systemization of musical production, and close relationship with the state and state media, they helped raise the status of musicians from lowly *dombaki* (a dismissive term for a drummer) to "artists" (*honarmandān*). "We [Iranians] didn't have any [music] that people could feel proud of. Why not? Because it was [considered] forbidden—it wasn't good to go into music. Before, if [Muslim] people's parents figured out that they were playing any sort of music, they said, 'This is a huge sin,' that they've played zarb, or *tār* [long-necked lute], or *santur* [hammered box zither], or whatever. But then after this revolution [in music], it became *art*. It became something to be proud of." In his narrative, Bibiyan and his colleagues in the music industry enacted a fundamental transformation in Iranian culture that the Iranian revolution and its reassertion of Islamic bias against music had undone. Through his television station's recirculation of a mediated vision of an Iran long gone as well as his interviews with me and other researchers, he presented himself as occupying a similar role as his Jewish forebears, continuing to keep the best music of his era alive in the face of Muslim prejudices.

Bibiyan played an important role in creating jāz and musiqi-ye pāp. He described his decision to begin working in the music industry and with Westernized popular music as inspired by travel abroad and exposure to foreign music that he preferred.[3] Like many Iranian Jews, Bibiyan's family had moved to Israel in the early 1940s. He was a teenager at the time and an avid music fan; while in Israel, he encountered a wide variety of foreign popular music that he loved. However, the family's personal life and economic prospects were better in Iran, and so they returned. When he came back to Tehran in 1945, he had a strong desire to "create a new form of popular music." His first business venture in music was putting on "tea dances" (*tehdāns-hā*), or afternoon dance parties, at which he and a friend would play the latest records—"all cha-chas and tangos"—from western Europe and the United States. This cosmopolitan sonic space was also a place for male and female multiconfessional social intermingling, a twentieth-century phenomenon in urban Iran. Along with a mix of men from Muslim, Christian, and Jewish backgrounds, "mostly Jewish and Armenian girls would attend. The Muslim girls, when they dared to come, arrived in a chador that they put into their handbags before entering the room," he recalled. In Bibiyan's understanding, Jewish and Christian Iranians didn't face the same obstacles as their Shiite peers in engaging in foreign and "modern" leisure pursuits.

Not content to merely play and sell foreign discs, Bibiyan described wanting to create something in which modern Iranians could see themselves, especially young people of his own generation. His first major act as a music producer was recording the suave, handsome, and cosmopolitan Armenian Iranian crooner and guitar player Vigen Derderian. Strikingly handsome with his sharply tailored Western suits and perfectly coiffed pompadour, Vigen was an early embodiment of a new, sophisticated, and very modern kind of professional entertainer. His signature full-throated crooning vocal style, which was foreign to Iranian vocal aesthetics (Nooshin 2005a), and his acoustic guitar playing were both novelties in Iranian musical performance. Vigen's music was termed *jāz* but had little to do with the African American musical form for which it was named. Iranian jāz was gentle, lilting, and sentimental; used a plethora of Western musical instruments; and avoided most Iranian modal or rhythmic markers. Vigen's song "Mahtāb" ("Moonlight"), a gentle cha-cha with completely Western instrumentation, harmonization, and romantic lyrics, was one of the first jāz hits.[4]

Bibiyan's company did not limit itself to the "modern" Westernized sounds of jāz: in fact, most of the company's profits came from the distinctly local and "unmodern" mardomi music. Though mardomi music and the cafés in which it was performed were regularly featured in the popular filmfarsi genre, it was stricken from state broadcasts because of its low-class associations and coarse content. Nevertheless, mardomi music recordings were hugely popular, inexpensive to produce, and therefore lucrative. But mardomi musicians were not appropriate candidates for the musical transformation Bibiyan envisioned. As he put it,

> We tried to bring some of those [mardomi] singers closer to our generation—and we recorded all of that. But we didn't get involved in their poetry and music because this was the music of the people. And if I did [get involved], people would get upset. Like Sousan [a famous mardomi singer popular in the 1970s who later moved to Southern California], who sang, "Oh my heart! A butcher's knife in my heart!"—we couldn't control this and tell them not to sing it. . . . Plus, it was so inexpensive to

produce—the poems were cheap, and the performers were cheap—that it didn't matter.

Instead, he "used the financial gains from mardomi music to support musiqi-ye pāp," which had a much smaller audience and took many more resources to produce and promote. Bibiyan's pragmatic approach to popular culture extended to his recording of some religious music, including Hayedeh's "'Ali Guyam" ("I Say 'Ali"), a praise song to the Prophet Mohammad's nephew, a central figure in Shiism. Just as he did not interfere with mardomi lyrics, he and his colleagues "didn't get involved in religion—it was a Muslim country, [people] loved 'Ali, so "'Ali Guyam' was released so people could enjoy their religion."[5]

Musiqi-ye pāp was Bibiyan's pride and joy, a genre he described himself as directly responsible for creating. Musiqi-ye pāp contained more Iranian and non-Western musical influences than jāz; many songs were based on versions of Iranian modes played in equal temperament. Some songwriters and arrangers also included the Iranian tonbak goblet drum playing understated varieties of the 6/8 dance rhythms common to many forms of the Iranian folk and entertainment genres. Beyond these few indigenous musical characteristics and the nearly exclusive use of the Persian language, it was musiqi-ye pāp's variability and flashy adoption of contemporary trends and musical styles that emerged as its defining qualities. Its composers drew inspiration from an immense variety of predominantly European and Latin American popular music sources, which they combined in novel ways, often using several of these within the scope of a single composition. Musiqi-ye pāp's stars were its glamorous young vocalists who—attired in the latest Western fashions—appeared on state television and radio, often acted in feature films, and performed on urban cabaret stages.

One of Bibiyan's main points to me in our interviews as well as his televised conversations with Meybodi was the vital importance of the producer's role in creating prerevolutionary popular music. Audiences weren't aware of producers' important contributions, unlike those of the singer, lyricist, songwriter, and even arrangers who were credited on record and cassette covers and in music video texts. Bibiyan took pride in his creative control over the production process: he described to me a model in which he would arrange for certain songwriters and lyricists to create a piece, which he would then try out with different singers with whom he had contracts, experimenting until he found the perfect hit sound. "It seems like making this music should have been easy, but it wasn't," Bibiyan explained. His tasks as a hands-on producer were many: locating singers, songwriters, lyricists and—most difficult to procure in Iran—professional arrangers who could create sophisticated arrangements for large ensembles of non-Iranian music (Varuzhan was a prolific arranger; the Guadaloupean Erik Arconte, whom Bibiyan "brought from France," was another). Another trying but crucial aspect of his job was grooming the occasionally unruly singers into professionals who would embarrass neither him nor themselves in public. Some talented but dissolute vocalists had behaved unbecomingly and even violently in public when intoxicated. Bibiyan described this as completely unacceptable behavior for his artists, who had to act respectably if they were to appear on national radio and television or perform for official events or at dignitaries' and royals' private parties. Bibiyan's responsibilities also entailed negotiating relationships with the state employees who controlled the national airwaves and monitored songs for style and content, a task that also sometimes required him to be in contact with SAVAK, the notorious secret police. "I had to work with all the organizations of the government," he told me, "and I had to be strong so I could stand up to all the singers." This position meant carefully navigating an increasingly politicized environment in which nothing was immune from charges of subversion. Though some of this music—including "Pariyā" ("Fairies"), a song he produced about which I wrote an article (Hemmasi 2013)—contained subtle political critiques of life under the Pahlavi government, Bibiyan emphasized that he had never been interested in being involved in politics. "I wanted to distance myself from this kind of work," he said, because he didn't see any reason to rock the boat. Ultimately, no one could avoid the revolution, and he, like many others, felt compelled to leave Iran.

"They Are Erasing History!"

Though Bibiyan has not been to Iran since he left the country in 1978, the debates and political contests of the revolutionary era linger in his work in the diaspora and, most recently, in his efforts to create an authoritative account of prerevolutionary music history. This is a project to which Bibiyan has contributed considerable time and resources. His personal website, manouchehrbibiyan.com, contains twenty-one hours of his recollections, interspersed with anecdotes from Bibiyan's colleagues from the prerevolutionary years that confirm his accounts. The interviews also include songs and images of albums, business contracts, and other memorabilia from Bibiyan's personal archive. The interviews themselves are archived on his website,

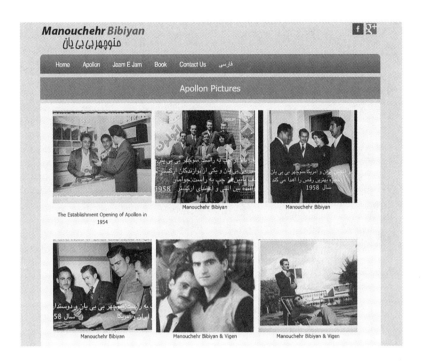

FIGURE 2.1 Manouchehr Bibiyan's online photo archive of his career with Apollon Records. Note the photographs of Bibiyan and jāz superstar Vigen Derderian. Screenshot from Manouchehr Bibiyan's personal website, accessed June 26, 2007, http://www.manouchehrbibiyan.com/apollon-pics-en.html.

along with numerous photographs, videos, and descriptions of his music and television productions; his book, *Secrets of the Iranian Revolution*; and a page of videos entitled "Iranian Jews in the West" culled from Jam-e Jam footage. Bibiyan's music-related activities make up the highest percentage of the materials on the website and provide evidence of years of personal and professional relationships with many Iranian musical greats. The Apollon pages, which relate to his prerevolutionary music label, contain photographs of him with numerous celebrities in Iranian music: in one picture, a youthful, smiling, mustachioed Bibiyan affectionately rests his head on Vigen's shoulder as the two regard the camera; another shows him behind a large desk with vocalist Ramesh at his side. Other photos—many shot after his move to Los Angeles, in the Jam-e Jam studios or in his home— depict Bibiyan socializing with vocalists Hayedeh, Mahasti, and Golpayegani; the lyricist Homa Mirafshar; the Tehrangeles media personality and

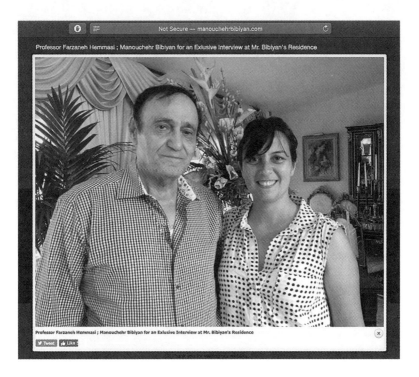

FIGURE 2.2 Bibiyan documents his associations with Tehrangeles musicians and music researchers—including the author—in his online archive. Screenshot from Manouchehr Bibiyan's personal website, accessed June 13, 2019, http://www.manouchehrbibiyan.com/apollon-pics-en.html.

music producer Alireza Amir Ghassemi; and many, many others. One of the last pictures is captioned "Professor Farzaneh Hemmasi and Manouchehr Bibiyan" and is a photograph of the two of us standing in front of the baby grand piano in his living room.

This photograph was taken in 2013, on my second round of visits to Bibiyan in his elegant home in the hills of Encino. I parked my rental car in his shady cul-de-sac and rang the bell on the automatic gate on the wrought-iron fence surrounding the house. His wife graciously ushered me into the sunken living room, where Bibiyan sat, nattily attired in a brightly colored striped dress shirt with cuff links. I was glad that I had thought to wear a dress—even more so when I realized our photograph together was to become another entry in his public archive. His wife came back into the room and offered us tea in tiny glass cups from a golden tray. He opened our conversation by reading to me from a handwritten note the names of composers and lyricists I had not included in my 2013 article about his work on "Pariyā." He was concerned that I had not adequately recognized these important individuals' contributions and wanted me to correct this oversight in the future so that they would become part of the historical record. I thanked him and said I would make sure to include these in my further accounts.[6] While he was willing to answer my historical questions in person, he repeatedly directed me to his website, and particularly his interviews with Meybodi, where I could find all the details I sought.

I was curious to learn more about Bibiyan's impulse to make an authoritative record of his memories. Explaining by way of example, Bibiyan became impassioned as he recounted an incident on a locally produced expatriate television program in which he witnessed "history being erased." A leftist songwriter and a lyricist who both lived in Tehrangeles were recalling that SAVAK agents had coerced them into creating a new version of a song they had already released. The reason for the intervention was that the agents perceived the lyrics to be inappropriate. Bibiyan, the song's producer and likewise a witness to this event as it unfolded, saw the songwriter and lyricist as propagating a gross mischaracterization of historical events on television that he feared audiences would take as the truth. In Bibiyan's understanding, these men were exaggerating SAVAK's intervention in order to paint themselves as heroes resisting the Pahlavi regime. "I called [the television station] right in the middle of the program. I said, 'I'm alive and you are making up history?'" Now joining the on-air conversation via phone, Bibiyan then recounted how he and the head of the National Radio had had a polite conversation in which the official asked him to direct these very artists to make a new version of the song with the offensive words replaced. No agents had arrested anyone or used force, nor had they even prevented the original song from circulating. Bibiyan was enraged as he recalled the episode. "[Prerevolutionary musicians living in Southern California] think that they can puff themselves up, that this is greatness? NO! 'You are erasing our history (Dāri tarikh ro az bein mibari)!' . . . I said this on TV. . . . No one [on the program] said anything [in reply]. Because it is *me* saying it. . . . I am [recording my memories so that they] can remain in the future, so that something *correct* can remain. Not these *lies*." Bibiyan then told me that he was taking the time to speak to me so that I could participate in setting the record straight.

This account highlights the stakes in prerevolutionary music history in Southern California. Even decades after the revolution, individuals' prerevolutionary political affiliations are still a contested issue. Secular partisans of the Pahlavis, the varieties of Marxists and leftists who opposed the Pahlavis, supporters of the exiled paramilitary Mujaheddin-e Khalq Organization (MKO), and others all have different accounts of who resisted or bolstered the Pahlavi regime and who helped Ayatollah Ruhollah Khomeini and his followers come to power. In this light, the question of whether the Pahlavi state's intervention in music production was or was not coercive is not merely about accuracy but is part of a decades-long contestation over whether the Pahlavi regime was excessively repressive—and, by extension, whether the revolution was justified. The issue of whether individuals cooperated with or contested SAVAK's interference in popular music is part of a larger set of concerns over collaboration, resistance, and loyalty to one's principles. Bibiyan wanted to convey that working with the state to change lyrics was the price of doing business, but leftist vocalists, songwriters, and lyricists active in this period have tended to describe the process as censorship and highlight their perseverance in the face of official disapproval.[7]

Another frustration is the layering of historical narratives in a crowded media sphere. Bibiyan revisited the story of the changed song in his oral history interviews with Meybodi, but the names, dates, and colleague testimonies that Bibiyan provided as corroborating evidence can only do so much to establish his version of events. For all his efforts to create, archive, and make public an authoritative account, there is nothing to prevent other accounts from circulating or gaining prominence. The ease with which expatriate media producers can produce and disseminate content on television and online is both the cause of his worry and an opportunity for intervention: he counters what he perceives to be misrepresentations with his own representations, and hopes that his website and authority will gain attention and force. I include Bibiyan's suggestion that I could validate and publicize his recollections as a reminder of my own imbrication in the process of producing authoritative accounts. My hesitation to do so may frustrate him even further: I have redacted the title of the song and the names of the individuals involved in the historical event described above because I cannot confirm or deny anyone's recollection of the events. For my part, I embrace the impossibility of providing an airtight, authenticated account to highlight the fragmentary, layered memories mobilized in productions of expatriate memory that sustain long-standing national political contests in transnational media.

Shabāneh (*Nightly*) is the name of a Persian-language talk show produced in Los Angeles on the Channel One satellite television station and hosted by expatriate television personality Shahram Homayun. On Homayun's desk always stands the prerevolutionary flag bearing the lion, sun, and sword—a marker of his rejection of the Islamic Republic of Iran and his continued affection for the Pahlavi era. On a program that aired in 2013, Homayun introduced his guest, Shahram Shabpareh, the first and likely most prolific Southern California–based Iranian pop singer and songwriter, as if he were arguing a case on the worthiness of his subject. Before the interview began, Homayun laid out what he believed to be Shabpareh's greatest contributions to Iranian culture. First was the high quality of Shabpareh's expatriate opus, which Homayun described as a rebuke to all who dismiss Tehrangeles pop as unenduring or unworthy of preservation. Another of Shabpareh's inspiring attributes was his patriotism—here, his faithfulness to the prerevolutionary regime. During the Iran hostage crisis, a period of open hostility and violence toward Iranians in America, Shabpareh rode his Harley-Davidson motorcycle around Los Angeles without a helmet and proudly waved a large prerevolutionary flag, displaying his identity and his affiliation with the prerevolutionary regime for all to see. Finally, Homayun lauded Shabpareh as "the founder of Tehrangeles"—the first individual to produce new Persian-language music in Southern California after the revolution and the person who laid the groundwork for other expatriate musicians when they arrived from Iran. His argument established, Homayun turned his gaze to the bearded, shaggy-haired, wide-grinning, straight-talking Shabpareh, who, in his characteristic humble and approachable style, graciously accepted his friend's flattery and spent the next hour expanding on Homayun's questions about his career.[8]

Homayun's somewhat defensive introduction of Shabpareh is indicative of the ambivalence about the cultural value of Tehrangeles pop and its producers. During my youth and throughout my research in Los Angeles, I heard from Iranians young and old that music from Tehrangeles "mundegār nist"—it doesn't last. It was disposable music, made for a moment's enjoyment on the dance floor, and then forgotten when the next new songs were released. The comparison to the prerevolutionary pop canon was sometimes articulated and almost always implied: those classics from the golden age of Iranian music endured. Though Shabpareh began his musical career in prerevolutionary Iran, the songs he wrote and performed after migrating to Southern California are more numerous than his few 1970s hits and, from my observations in the diaspora and in Iran, are among the few Tehrangeles songs that are constants on party playlists across the social spectrum. While most of Shabpareh's opus is unambiguously and unapologetically dance music produced in Los Angeles and therefore falls under the los ānjelesi category, multiple generations of fans seem to value him above other Tehrangeles musicians for his pop songwriting skills, folksy lyrics, and down-to-earth, unassuming persona. He has toured Iranian diasporic cities for decades and is still in demand as a wedding entertainer.

Like so many of his generation who moved to Los Angeles from Iran, Shabpareh and his elder brother Shahbal also made important contributions to popular music in prerevolutionary Iran. The Shabpareh brothers began performing covers of the Beatles and American R&B—often adjusted to Iranian dance rhythms—as teenagers in a beat band called the Rebels. They then developed the pop group the Black Cats, which released a few recordings but was mostly active as a live band at Tehran's Couchinie restaurant and disco. Shahram broke off from the group and became a solo artist and songwriter. His compositions continued to blend Western pop music styles with Iranian mardomi urban popular music styles featuring colloquial lyrics and the dāmbuli Iranian dance groove discussed in chapter 1. One of his standout hits from the 1970s was "Vāy vāy" ("Woe, Woe," also known as "I'u in zamuneh," or "In These Times"), a song whose short verses, Tehrani slang pronunciation, Latin and Iranian music influences, repetitive chorus, and upbeat energy characterized much of his subsequent work. Like many of his contemporaries in musiqi-ye pāp, the high-energy Shabpareh was a familiar presence on state radio and television; he also acted in a feature film. He drew on this multimedia career in the diaspora, where music and television would continue to be intertwined.

Shabpareh's role in establishing Tehrangeles was, per his own description, an accident. In 1977 Shabpareh was in the United States on a tour of several Iranian nightclubs in New York and Southern California. He was invited to do a residency at Cabaret Tehran, a nightclub then located in Burbank (it has since moved to Encino) that catered to Southern California's already substantial Iranian population. As the revolution grew violent and Islamists began their ascendance, Shabpareh's father called him from Iran and begged him to remain abroad for his own safety. Devastated but fearing for his life, Shabpareh agreed and never returned. He and Ebi, a be-

FIGURE 2.3 Expatriate television is a platform for consolidation and circulation of alternative (trans)national histories. Here, Shahram Shabpareh reflects on his Southern Californian career on the London-based Iranian satellite television station Manoto 1 program *Dar Tab'id* (*In Exile*). "Shahram Shabpareh: Dar Tab'id" [Shahram Shabpareh: In Exile], Manoto 1, reproduced by Iran Live-TV on Daily Motion, accessed August 12, 2016, http://www.dailymotion.com/video/x11qzs6_dar-tabeed-shahram -shabpare_shortfilms.

loved prerevolutionary singer who was also stranded in the United States, moved into a hotel within walking distance from Cabaret Tehran and began performing there five nights a week. Shabpareh recalled these difficult days in an interview on the Manoto 1 television show *Dar Tab'id* (*In Exile*) devoted to his career in Southern California: "This was a big change from [what Ebi and I had experienced] in Iran. [In Iran,] we each had our own things, we had our own managers, we had money. . . . [Once in Los Angeles] we had to walk down the street, go to this place and put on our performance outfits—we only had two!—perform, and go home again, night after night. Maybe it sounds easy (*sādeh*) to you, but it was difficult for us."[9] Shabpareh's recollection of hardship is knowingly circumscribed. He is aware that his experience of loss may "sound easy" to others—and especially compared to the experiences of those who served in prison, fought in the war with Iraq, or lived as refugees—but he also wants his listeners to understand the comparative humbleness of his circumstances in Los Angeles compared to the relative status and wealth he and his peers had experienced in Iran.

The "Icon of Happiness"

Shabpareh's fortunes changed with the release of his first song in the United States, "Deyar" ("Homeland"). Unlike many members of the pre- and postmigration music industries, who specialized in only one aspect of musical production, Shabpareh was skilled in singing, writing songs, and composing lyrics. "Deyar" captured Shabpareh's isolation and hopelessness in Southern California in the upbeat dance style at which he excelled. Set in a minor key, "Deyar" alternates between Latin-tinged, four-on-the-floor verses and a chorus set to a markedly urban Iranian dance music arrangement underscored by the dāmbuli rhythm. The song derives its distinctive sound from both Shabpareh's previous works and his collaboration with two other Iranians in Southern California. These were fellow expatriate prerevolutionary composer, arranger, and producer Manouchehr Cheshmazar, who had also come to California and decided not to return during the revolution, and Farokh "Elton" Ahi, who was already a professionally established American disco DJ and producer by the time Cheshmazar and Shabpareh arrived. Shabpareh's vocals were accompanied by synthesizer, electric bass, drum machine, and acoustic percussion, along with live strings and horns played by musicians Ahi knew through his personal contacts in the Iranian community and his work with legendary disco label Casablanca Records.

Shabpareh's lyrics express the pain of separation from Iran. Here are the lyrics of the fourth verse and the chorus:

> *(steady 4/4 Latin/disco beat)*
> *My lips smile "Alas," full of the wretchedness of my heart*
> *My heart's song has become wailing and grief*
> *My heart is full of sorrow—I want to cry out (faryād)*
> *Oh God, how I miss beautiful Tehran*
>
> *Chorus (abrupt change to dāmbuli groove)*
> *Oh, what a condition I'm in*
> *I long for [my] country*
> *In this country of exile*
> *I only have God*

Shabpareh's composition is complex, containing contrasting musical indices and a bifurcated musical arrangement. Its chorus points toward sounds of "home" with its spare chordal accompaniment and the rollicking dāmbuli beat common to motrebi and upbeat mardomi dance music, while its verses turn toward "here" via disco and its constituent cosmopolitan Latin and African American elements. This is not to say that disco represented the unfamiliar or even necessarily the foreign—Shahram and his generation of popular musicians were well versed in non-Iranian musical styles, as were their audiences in Iran and the diaspora, who eagerly embraced "Deyar." Rather, the separation between sections bears a structural similarity to the separation from Iran that Shabpareh and his fellow exiles experienced. The song expresses a kind of tense overlay of affective states: it is the kind of song one could easily play at a party to inspire dance while it also plainly expresses the agony and alienation of exile. In the video for "Deyar," Shabpareh acts out this tension, snapping his fingers and shaking his shoulders to the rousing beat with the occasional hint of a smile on his face while singing emotively of "sorrow," "wretchedness," "crying," "wailing," and "grief." The scenes of the video are similarly bifurcated. In some moments Shabpareh sings standing in front of a typical Southern Californian backdrop: a white stucco wall covered with pink bougainvillea blossoms. The other footage is areal scenes of rural and urban Iran appropriated from the documentary film *The Lovers' Wind* (dir. Albert Lamorrise, [Iranian] Ministry of Arts and Culture, Tolid Films, 1978), a common source in expatriate television in the 1980s (see Naficy 1993).

This initial example of Tehrangeles pop set the standard for much of the music that would follow. Shabpareh combined these attributes in "Deyar" and in a number of songs following the same basic formula, while compositions by subsequent Tehrangeles artists focused more on upbeat, playful dance pop on romantic themes, and slow or midtempo serious songs about the homeland or exile.[10] "Deyar" also jumpstarted Shabpareh's postmigration career as a live entertainer. He recalled in *Dar Tab'id*, "With God as my witness, within two weeks after 'Deyar' was released, I was booked to play fifteen to twenty weddings a month." Performing at cabarets and private parties had also been a part of vocalists' professional activities in Iran, but it became even more important in exile, where income from live gigs outstripped the financial returns on record sales.

Profiting from the sale of physical albums was a challenge because the size of the buying audience in the diaspora was so small and there were no established distribution networks. The ease with which cassette tapes could be copied, and LPs and 45s copied to cassette, also cut into potential sales. But pirated Tehrangeles media also made their way throughout the diaspora and into Iran, which helped Shabpareh and then other Tehrangeles-based artists gain entrance to dispersed households, social events, and

FIGURE 2.4 Shahram Shabpareh displays his allegiance to Los Angeles in head-to-toe Los Angeles Lakers gear. Cassette cover of Shahram Shabpareh's album *Shāgerd-e Avval* (*Top Student*, 1990) from Taraneh Records' archive. Photograph by the author.

stores. Shabpareh recalls that a few weeks after "Deyar" had been released in Southern California, a friend called from Iran and played him the song over the phone. "I don't know how it got there!" he exclaimed.

One of the opening questions of the chapter was whether to consider Tehrangeles pop as something foreign and inappropriate for inclusion in the Iranian cultural heritage. While the term "heritage" is loaded with suggestions of inherent and incontrovertible value, the term "history" might be more appropriate and less controversially applied here. Among Tehrangeles dance music producers, Shabpareh's productions are, in my experience, more frequently cited as a valuable part of the national history and, more important, valued for expressing what needed to be expressed in Iranian social life during the dark years of revolution and war: the combination of pain and joy. Homayun's introduction of Shabpareh on his television show included just such a dramatic testimonial:

> The revolution occurred. Terror reigned across the country. People were terrified, wounded, [and] worried. It was the 16th of Farvardin, 1358 [April 5, 1979]. It was Sizdah Bedar [the thirteenth day of the New Year,

when people go out of doors and picnic]. Like everyone else, I went out of the city to a garden and suddenly I noticed that all around me, people were listening to music, music that had come from Los Angeles. No one could believe it. And this music had a drama [and] a happiness that were brought together in one package. It sought to memorialize that tribulation (*balā*ʻ), that disaster (*mosibat*) that had befallen the Iranian nation. And on top of this, it lifted the spirits.

Homayun's recollections position "Deyar" in Iran as a kind of miracle of survival and circulation—"no one could believe" that this music could be produced in California, or that it had made it all the way around the world into the country.

Because Homayun is a member of Shabpareh's generation and a long-time friend, his praise for Shabpareh is less surprising than that of Mohsen Namjoo. Namjoo, who was born in 1976, is a musical innovator whose sharp, politically inflected lyrics, unique combination of Iranian classical music with Western blues and rock, and charismatic stage presence have garnered him much popularity within Iran and in the diaspora (Siamdoust 2017, 182–208; Steward 2017). Namjoo was sentenced in absentia to five years in prison for his sacrilegious musical setting of a verse of the Quran, and he has lived outside of Iran since 2007. Widely celebrated in the Western and expatriate Iranian press and enjoying the support of international networks of Iranian artists and academics in the diaspora, Namjoo has not only performed widely and recorded numerous albums but also held fellowships at Stanford and Brown Universities, appeared in documentaries, and written a book.

While a fellow at Brown, Namjoo delivered a lecture on Shabpareh's music. Namjoo spoke at length on his analysis of "163 [of Shabpareh's] songs," of which "101 were in the 6/8 rhythm." Shabpareh was the "icon of happiness," Namjoo said, but this did not comport well with either the rarity of joy in Iranian expressive culture or the disdain for happy pop music among Iranian intellectuals. "We don't have many public festivals for expressing happiness in Iranian culture," he commented. "Our festivals abound in sadness and mourning (*ʿazādāri*)." He argued for the profundity of happiness, especially in the context of his generation's difficult childhood in 1980s Iran, through one of Shabpareh's best-loved songs. This was "Pariyā," a dance pop tune written by prerevolutionary-turned-expatriate songwriter, vocalist, and multi-instrumentalist Hassan Shamaeizadeh and sung by Shabpareh. Namjoo commented:

In 1980s Iran I was a kid, and Shabpareh and his generation were no longer living in Iran. Think about an ideological government that had stopped every kind of music. It came to the point that they played military music all day long, and traditional and pop music had vanished completely. Los Angeles had become for us a place from which heavenly sounds (sowt-e behesht) emerged. The entire country was being bombed by Saddam Hussein. At school, they didn't teach us anything besides ideology and aggression. There was no room for happiness. This was an eight-year period, and in this period, there was just one happy song (āhang-e shādemāni) that everyone enjoyed at parties. I'd like you to imagine this situation and understand the significance . . . the music you're about to hear had thirty-five years ago [during the revolution]. This is a simple story of someone in love.[11]

Namjoo then played "Pariyā" for his audience. This song lacked the darkness of "Deyar" and other homeland-oriented songs; it was instead a playful tune about a young man worried that the neighborhood guys would steal his girlfriend. The tinkling synthesizer hook, the dāmbuli dance beat, and nursery-rhyme simplicity made it ear candy: "Oh you who are more beautiful than the fairies / don't go out into the alleys / the neighborhood boys are thieves / they'll steal my love away." Namjoo continued, "Right now, listening to this song, even here, makes me think of the pinnacle of happiness (owj-e shādi), and can make me cry. Imagine the family that is playing this music for their guests at their daughter's wedding, and that very night their son is coming back wounded from the war and being sent to the hospital. . . . No one from this generation can imagine that time, when there was no internet, . . . how valuable this music was." In both Namjoo's and Homayun's accounts, a context of scarcity and deprivation is crucial to understanding the value of Shabpareh's music. His upbeat tunes were the antidote to "horror," "disaster," "aggression," "war," "military marches," and "ideology." Namjoo's commentary also challenges the exclusion of Shabpareh and other Tehrangeles musicians from national history merely on the grounds of their physical distance from the homeland. Their music miraculously made its way into the country as if from "heaven"; it played on rhythms, sounds, and affects that were part of Iranian cultural heritage even if declared morally and politically incorrect during the revolution and war. Homayun and Namjoo likewise argue that Shabpareh's music is worthy of preservation and respect, a counterclaim to revolutionaries' and elitists' disdain for the happiness he helped bring to a dark period.

FIGURE 2.5 Taraneh's archives include Southern Californian reproductions of prerevolutionary art and pop music as well as new Tehrangeles pop productions. Photograph by the author.

TARANEH ENTERPRISES: ADAPTATION IN EXILE

The offices of Taraneh (Song) Enterprises, Inc., sit in a nondescript office park in Reseda, California, one of the small towns that line the floor of the San Fernando Valley. In its wider neighborhood are auto body repair shops and insurance companies, intermixed with modest stucco single-family houses and low-rise apartment buildings. Taraneh is one of the first music companies (*sherkat-hā-ye musiqi*) in Southern California to commercially produce and release Iranian popular music. Its founders are Vartan Avanessian and Jahangir Tabaraei, former colleagues in the prolific prerevolutionary popular music company Avang who established Taraneh in the early 1980s after the revolution. In exile, Avanessian and Tabaraei reproduced recordings from before the revolution and recorded new material with expatriate artists in Tehrangeles. Avanessian later began a satellite television program named after his record company where he introduced, interviewed, and played videos by artists on his label. Tabaraei focused on the music company.

Taraneh is one of the most prolific Tehrangeles record labels; most well-known expatriate artists in Los Angeles have released at least one album with the company over the years. The more I learned about Avanessian and Tabaraei, the more impressed I was with their flexibility and tenacity, the ways they had found to continue operating in a challenging and changing field while still working in expatriate music. Starting over in Tehrangeles had not been easy. The atmosphere in which these materials were produced and sold was quite far from the heady days of the Pahlavi era. In the early 1980s, Avanessian recalled in a television interview, the only option for selling this material was the few Iranian grocery stores (*ba'qāl*) that had opened to serve a small but growing migrant population: "In those days, people would say, 'You can now find artistic works (*kār-e honar*) next to the cheese and yogurt.'"[12] This was one-stop shopping for the whole spectrum of Iranian sensoria that could be re-created in a limited way through commercial products in the diaspora.[13] At least one music company, Caltex Records, combined food and music into a single venture: one of the leading music producers and distributors between the 1980s and 2000s, this company is a subsidiary of Caltex Trading, a company that continues to distribute Iranian canned and dried goods to these very grocery stores. Avanessian's comments in the interview made it clear that he and his Tehrangeles compatriots faced many difficulties in re-creating themselves and Iranian popular music in exile: they did the best they could with limited resources and even less prestige. The progress was gradual. Beginning with cassettes tucked into the dairy case of Tehrangeles grocery stores, Taraneh eventually gained a small section devoted to music in these same stores. The music spread to Iranian food stores in "New York, Washington, Texas, San Francisco, San Jose" (and Chicago, the ones I visited as a teenager). He summed up in a modest fashion: "By the end of the 1980s I can say that [business] was good for those of us who had come out of our country and made a music company. This music of ours went back into Iran, and people there listened to it, enjoyed it (*lezzat mibordand*), they called us [on the phone] and thanked us. . . . [These companies] started [music] again. We can say that the original existence of Iranian entertainment is directly connected to these few companies, and it is because of these companies that music was able to [emerge after the revolution]." Avanessian's confident narrative of his prerevolutionary achievements contrasted with his humble, restrained recollections of what he and his colleagues had been able to bring about in the diaspora. He viewed his major contribution in Tehrangeles to be sustaining Iranian music through the period of its endangerment and into the present, as if this bridging role was more important than the actual products he had helped bring into being.

A similar perspective emerges in the company's mission statement as displayed on its website.[14] Like many other Tehrangeles labels, Taraneh has had a more advanced and innovative television presence than online identity. This marks the music industry's interconnections with cable and satellite television, which in turn are related to local social and business agreements between music and television producers, and to the importance of television over the internet as a means for Iranians within Iran to access music and media. Taraneh's website is not a dynamic, up-to-date representation of the company in its best light but a relic, a static portal of limited functionality for either sales or information. For all its intangibility, even the website somehow feels dusty and unused. It also contains a fascinating display of Iranian American "double consciousness" on its bilingual "About Us" page. The page's English-language section describes the company as a "major manufacturer . . . of Persian media (CD, VHS, DVD) . . . [with] a large selection of new and old Iranian music," and goes on to specify that the company can ship to most places in the world "except a few countries (i.e. Iran, due to postal restrictions)." I have wondered who these sentences are intended for—the website does not mention that Taraneh's products, like all Tehrangeles pop, are not permitted within the country. Don't most of the people who visit Taraneh's website already know that "postal restrictions" are just the tip of the iceberg?

The English section is followed by a several paragraphs in Persian that describe another identity entirely: "Taraneh . . . will not spare any effort . . . to preserve and protect Iranian music at this moment in history. We request that you, the devotees (*shiftehgān*) of music, assist us with your continuing support for the cultural heritage of our beloved country." The juxtaposition of the dry, transactional English-language description of the company with the extended, poetic, and impassioned self-description for Persian-speaking audiences reveals several key tensions. The first is the overlap between patronage and preservation. The statement merges support for the nation's cultural heritage with purchasing music from Taraneh, asking potential customers to help preserve the preservers by buying their products. But what, exactly, do Taraneh's owners suggest should be preserved? Is it the country's prerevolutionary popular music (presumably the "old Iranian music" referred to in English), which Avanessian, Tabaraei, and many others who landed in Los Angeles had a role in creating in Iran and then reproducing in the diaspora? Or does Iran's cultural heritage include new music like *los ānjelesi*?

The designation of "this period in history" (*barheh-ye zamān*) as one in which music was in peril also raises questions. Its presence on the website in 2019, forty years after the revolution and roughly twenty years after popular music was permitted within Iran, resonates with a larger Tehrangeles temporal orientation toward the revolution as the community's defining moment. The revolutionary rupture was, and continues to be, both destructive and productive. The ban on popular music and the declaration of popular music producers as propagators of corruption had deprived individuals like Avanessian and Tabaraei of their professional identities, livelihoods, dignity, and country. In exile, they shifted their professional activities to unite commerce and a cultural mission. This may once have been an effective strategy, but as the Islamic Republic enters its fourth decade and has seen the emergence of state-approved, unofficial, and expatriate popular music scenes beyond Los Angeles, Iranian pop is flourishing. Neither is the traditional object-oriented music business model selling "CDs, VHS, and DVDs" as profitable as it once was. The "digital revolution" has compounded the displacement caused by the political revolution, while the postrevolutionary state's pragmatic accommodation of popular music has destabilized Tehrangeles's founding generation once more.

"By Tooth and Nail"

Though I knew Taraneh was central to Tehrangeles pop music, and I was aware of Avanessian's and Tabaraei's contributions to prerevolutionary music, it was unclear to me how this illustrious duo were faring in the present. I hadn't noticed many new releases on the Taraneh website or on the shelves of any music stores I'd visited over the past few years. When I visited Taraneh's offices for the first time in 2007 to speak with Vartan Avanessian's brother Rafik, who was also involved in the company, he indicated that even then their company was facing financial challenges. He blamed the introduction of digital reproduction and the internet. I wondered how I could broach this topic in a later visit without appearing cheeky.

In the summer of 2014, I met Jahangir Tabaraei and Vartan Avanessian in the main office of Taraneh's suite. I sat across from a large desk behind which Tabaraei was seated. Avanessian—the more gregarious of the pair—sat closer to me at a small table on which I put my iPhone to record. Years before, I had met Rafik in the packing area near a machine that shrink-wrapped CDs in plastic. The middle room of the suite was what they called the archive: the storage area for the audio- and videocassettes,

FIGURE 2.6 From Taraneh's archives: *Ranga-rang 3 (Colorful 3)*, a 1991 Tehrangeles reproduction of prerevolutionary pop by Googoosh, Taherzadeh, Ebi, Leila Foruhar, Sattar, Shahrokh, Maziyar, and Habib. Photograph by the author.

CDs, and DVDs the company had produced and, in some cases, only repro-duced. There were prerevolutionary recordings repackaged for sale abroad, pop produced in Tehrangeles, and postrevolutionary domestic Iranian mu-sic and films, a reminder of the multidirectional circulation of media and money between the homeland and the diaspora. The brightly colored 1980s and 1990s albums were meticulously organized on rows of shelves, the fa-miliar faces of pop stars staring out from an otherwise dark room.

I had studied up for my meeting by watching three of Avanessian's in-terviews online, all of which originally aired on expatriate satellite televi-sion and were about an hour each. Like Shabpareh and Bibiyan, Avanessian was used to answering questions about the history of Iranian music before and after migration. In one of the interviews I had seen, Avanessian had described the height of the Tehrangeles industry's influence and financial success as occurring between 1990 and 2005, the period between the adop-tion of CDs by Tehrangeles music companies and the arrival of the MP3 for-mat that made CDs commercially obsolete. But what about the emergence of domestic popular music in the transnational Iranian mediascape? Hadn't this had an impact on Los Angeles sales and popularity? When I posed this

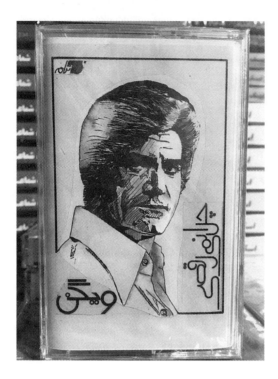

FIGURE 2.7 From Taraneh's archives: *Cherā nemiraqsi* (*Why Aren't You Dancing*, 1989) by Vigen. Photograph by the author.

question to him, Avanessian answered in the affirmative, using the term *unvar* ("that side") to refer to Iranians within Iran and *invar* ("this side") to refer to Iranians in the diaspora, but specifically in Southern California. His comments reflected how much the relationships between "the sides" had changed over the years: "I always say, the music in LA in one period, was the leader—but when Iran was allowed more freedom, well . . . it had an impact. When the music started on 'that side,' it began to damage music here (*latmeh zad*). 'This side' was overshadowed by 'that side.' . . . Even the number-one singers of LA started using lyricists and songwriters from inside Iran. . . . Dariush, Ebi, Googoosh, Sattar, Moein [are all working with songwriters within and outside Iran]. Singers from 'that side' are coming to 'this side' both for work and for concerts."

As far as his own career was concerned, Avanessian was also moving between this side and that. Along with four other figures from the Tehrangeles music industry, since 2008 he had served as a celebrity judge on Next Persian Star, a pop music talent competition produced in Dubai and Turkey by the originally Germany-based expatriate satellite television station TV Persia 1. Most of the contestants were residents of Iran who traveled to

Dubai to take part in the competition. If expatriates could no longer claim to be rescuing Iranian music from an uncertain fate, they were still able to find ways of profiting from music and entertainment media's ambivalent position within the Islamic Republic of Iran by innovating new ways to offer homeland-based audiences entertainment and opportunities they could not easily access within the country. While this entrepreneurial spirit had a less heroic cast than being the "standard-bearers" of Iranian music, it was a living, and it kept Avanessian, his expertise, and Tehrangeles Iranian music celebrities in the transnational Iranian public eye. He also made a point of telling me that most of the repertoire that young Iranian contestants performed on Next Persian Star was prerevolutionary pop classics, the songs he and his generation had developed when they lived in Iran.

What did these transformations suggest about the future of Taraneh or the Tehrangeles cultural industries more generally? I asked what a typical day at Taraneh was like now that their business had changed so much. Avanessian answered at length, comparing the old days of recording and producing with the current realities of doing business on his smartphone:

> The daily routine is that Mr. Tabaraei sits there [behind the desk] and turns on the TV, I [am busy with] Telegram, WhatsApp, Instagram. . . . You know how it is, these days everything is on your iPhone—you're in contact with the world. [Before,] anyone who wanted work, who needed something . . . would come here [to the office], sit down, and we would talk. But not anymore. Now with this [holds up phone] they send work, they get work, they can dance, they can talk. . . . Our generation is not very comfortable with this technology. And the next generation is familiar with it, so this is also a factor [in the change in business]. Imagine—before, we had to go to the studio and wait outside in the cold until it was our turn to go in and record. Now, in every home there is a studio—so easy. Imagine, when someone wanted to find a drum sound . . . [but] now there is a sample. The studio musicians, instrumentalists—they are also out of work [because of technology]. We had so many musicians who would come by every week . . . and now there are musicians who we haven't seen for maybe fifteen years. . . . *Everything* has changed. And it's good . . . you can't fight with technology and say, "Why has this come? I don't accept it!" You must move with it, and if not, you'll fall behind. It's changing so fast we won't even be able to reach its shadow, you know? But because we have put our lives into this work [pause], we both want to accept this and we don't want to accept it at all. Overall, it is better

for the company to continue to be open, we can sit here, we can have an interview with you, we have four artists we're working with—this is it. This is the end (*in ākharesh-e*), but we keep going.

After his partner's meditation on the necessity of changing with the times, Tabaraei spoke for the first time in perhaps forty-five minutes with a short but pithy interjection: "Bā chang o dandun." Literally, this means, "With claws and teeth," and is roughly equivalent to the English phrase "by tooth and nail." Tabaraei and Avanessian were holding on to all they had built with the tenacity of wild animals. Avanessian then offered me a hard candy from the bowl sitting on the table between us, and I had the distinct feeling it was time for me to go. His and Tabaraei's resigned statements felt like a natural ending point in our conversation. They were reaching the end of their story of Tehrangeles music, and whatever future direction it might take, they were aware that they would not be participating in it for much longer.

The accounts that make up this chapter offer a layered, ambivalent relationship to legacy, history, and heritage. Impelled by exile and financial necessity to reimagine themselves and their careers in Southern California, a privileged group of powerful musicians and media producers became migrant entertainers and entrepreneurs at the center of an expatriate cultural industry. It has been easier for Bibiyan, Avanessian, Tabaraei, Shabpareh, and others of this first generation of Tehrangeles music producers to proudly associate themselves with the "modern" golden age of Iranian popular music than with Iranian popular music's comparatively humble reformulation and propagation in exile. Yet even prerevolutionary musical heritage is endangered from many sides, both by its revolutionary rejection and by varying recollections and accounts disseminated in expatriate media. Audiocassettes and CDs, videocassettes and DVDs, and cable and satellite television have been critical to prerevolutionary musicians' rebirth in Southern California. Physical, broadcast, and streaming media have provided means to share and sell music, to deliver to Iranian audiences the happy "heavenly sounds" some segment of the population desired during the darkness of the war and immediate postrevolutionary period, and television interviews allow the producers to proclaim and repeat historical narratives that argue for the significance of their achievements. But media and technology are also uncontrollable: copying and downloading cut into Tehrangeles companies' profits, and new technologies develop so quickly that aging Tehrangeles producers "won't even be able to reach its shadow."

The very media that can be used to assert truth and authority are the same media that can propagate distortions and lies. Whether subsequent generations will consider Tehrangeles music worthy of preservation or whether it will be considered valuable primarily as a bridge between a period of silencing and a contemporary efflorescence is unknowable. If Tehrangeles musicians continue tenaciously, then the music and its producers may at least be remembered, and the revolution will not have obliterated them from history.

EXPATRIATE EROTICS,
HOMELAND MORALITIES

Desire for the homeland is a fundamental aspect of
Tehrangeles cultural production. This desire overlaps with
the quest for recognition, financial gain, a place in the nation's history, and a place in its heart. Desirers desire to be desired
in return: a common topic for Tehrangeles artists is their devotion
to their distant homeland, and a common way of flattering Tehrangeles
stars is to tell them how much they are loved in Iran. Speaking with an
interviewer about her 2005 concert at the Kodak Theatre in Los Angeles, prerevolutionary-turned-Tehrangeles pop vocalist Shohreh Solati related that singing in front of such a large crowd of expatriates made
her think of her dearest wish: to perform in Iran one day. Her heart
was still in Iran; the homeland was the beloved to whom she is
faithful until the end. Her interviewer replied by emphasizing his certainty that Iran-based audiences reciprocated
her feelings: "I know everyone in Iran also wishes that
you . . . and all the good singers here could go back
and perform there one day. You would certainly

have a crowd of 100,000 people. . . . People in Iran definitely want you [to return]."[1]

A more elaborate realization of passionate reunion is the animated video for expatriate singer Andy's song "Gol-e Bandar" ("Flower from the Port").[2] The video opens with an image of a banner strung over a multilane highway. It reads, "Andy Returns to Iran." Andy then parachutes from an airplane and lands in the center of a packed stadium, where he kicks a soccer ball into a goal and sets the giant crowd to screaming. He jumps onto a waiting motorcycle and zooms out of the stadium surrounded by an Iranian military escort. Andy then proceeds to ride around the country, first to Tehran's Freedom Square, then to Esfahan and Shiraz, meeting giant crowds that cheer as he passes and wave placards reading "Welcome to Iran" and "We Love You, Andy!" He concludes his tour with a huge concert in the Persian Gulf city of Abadan. He appears as a returning hero, lauded across the country, giving the people what they truly want: a reunion with their exiled idol and a chance to dance and celebrate together at a giant concert.

Expatriate portrayals of Iranian audiences' and Tehrangeles artists' mutual desire are thrown into relief by the fact that the Iranian state officially rejects Tehrangeles artists and their music. It has, at times, punished Tehrangeles celebrities who have dared to physically enter the country. The media circulation joining Tehrangeles artists to Iran-based audiences also transports unsettling los ānjelesi figures and sounds back into the idealized pious, pure homeland. This chapter argues that while expatriate artists and homeland audiences are in a physically unconsummated long-distance relationship, they are also engaged in "transnational media erotics" that disturb the nation-state's moral and geopolitical boundaries. As described by Purnima Mankekar and Louisa Schein, transnational media erotics can be found "pulsating out of iPods, flickering across television screens and computer monitors, casting flirtatious glances at us from billboards, . . . creat[ing] sensoria and generat[ing] patterns of intimacy that confound assumptions about propinquity and distance, physicality and virtuality. Through their (often discontinuous) itineraries across region and nation, mediated erotics enable forms of affect and reimagined sodalities that variously transgress and reinscribe dominant notions of community and identity" (2012, 2). Transnational media erotics "remix sex and space"; through their creation and circulation, "physical distance and proximity come to be complexly articulated in the contours of homeland desire" (Schein 2012, 228). Tehrangeles media threaten to undo the Islamic Republic of Iran's legally mandated moral order. They return to Iran its rejected prerevolutionary music and film stars along with sounds and images of unveiled women, social dance, male-female physical contact, and nonheteronormative celebrities. In this light, Tehrangeles popular culture's penetration of the homeland—especially its private spheres of homes, parties, taxicabs, and so on—is a transgression of geographic, legal, and moral boundaries that borders on sexual violation or, perhaps more accurately, violation by the sexual. When conceived as foreign and expatriate "cultural attacks" and "soft war" waged against the Iranian nation by its enemies, transnational media erotics intersect with national security concerns. Culture then becomes a weapon in the international battle to win Iranian bodies along with their hearts and minds.[3]

What this means for Tehrangeles cultural producers is that they and their work operate within multiple moral, legal, and transnational regimes, and that the consequences of this work can quickly and unpredictably escalate in stakes and intensity. In this chapter, I analyze three performers as they attempt to grapple with the unintended consequences of their Tehrangeles careers. These are the dancer Mohammad Khordadian, a fictional Tehrangeles vocalist named Maxx, and a Southern California–based female pop vocalist named Shahrzad Sepanlou. When Khordadian, a folkloric and cabaret dancer turned exercise instructor, returned to Iran in 2002, he was charged with "promoting depravity and corruption among the youth" via Tehrangeles videotapes and jailed in Evin Prison (Papan-Matin 2009, 131). I relate Khordadian's case to the comedic film *Maxx*, a fictional story of a bumbling Tehrangeles cabaret singer's return to Iran after many years and his attempts to convince Iranian officials that he is not a Western agent. I show that Maxx's and Khordadian's personas connect to the sexually ambiguous male los ānjelesi performer whose very existence troubles both the moral purification of postrevolutionary Iran and heteronormative Iranian modernity as well. Ratcheting up the ambiguity, Maxx and Khordadian also poke fun at the seriousness with which postrevolutionary cultural policy treats expatriate cultural producers. They deny their threateningness to Iranian society while also showing how desirable domestic audiences find them, their music, and their dance.

Unlike Maxx's and Khordadian's, vocalist Sepanlou's travels to Iran are solely in the realm of media-enabled fantasy. Nevertheless, she feels compelled to manage the negative associations projected onto her as an "immodest" female singer from Tehrangeles. I discuss her attempts to manage her artistic image in relation to these stereotypes and in relation to her desires to be "respectful" toward Iran-based audiences as she likewise maintains her own respectability. This requires her to carefully calibrate her dress, physical movements, and musical choices; to reckon with Iran-based audiences' approving and disapproving comments; and to interpret the impact of her on-screen behavior in terms of a morality she knows she can only partially understand and is always in danger of transgressing.

A TROUBLED HOMECOMING:
MAXX AND MOHAMMAD KHORDADIAN

The tricky circumstances faced by Los Angeles–based performers who return to Iran form the driving scenario of the massively popular 2005 Iranian comedic feature film *Maxx* (dir. Saman Moghaddam, Hedayat Film). Through the familiar figure of the Tehrangeles pop musician, the film pokes fun at exile musicians—and diasporic Iranians more generally—who are nostalgically focused on Iran but are not at all familiar with life in the Islamic Republic. The film also critiques the ideological rigidity and contradictions surrounding official approaches toward expatriate Iranians. *Maxx* was a smash hit both in Iran and in the diaspora, and as such has attracted scholarly attention for its sly political commentary and its comedic treatment of diaspora-homeland relations. As Nacim Pak-Shiraz (2013) convincingly argues, Maxx plays a role like the *siyāh* (black) trickster character common to late nineteenth- and early twentieth-century *taqlid* ("emulation") dramas and siyāh bāzi theater. The siyāh character, typically an actor in blackface playing a domestic servant or slave, makes fun of those in power while himself being an object of ridicule.[4] Pak-Shiraz then shows how we laugh not only at Maxx's ineptitude and gaucheness but at officials' paranoia in response to his lighthearted and often very silly performances. Nasrin Rahimieh regards the film as the story of "the return of the repressed," by which she means the staged confrontation of "diametrically opposed articulations of Iranianness . . . in Los Angeles and Tehran," and the resulting "repressions that undermine the stability of any given construct of the ideal Iranian" (2016, 64).[5] While valuable, these accounts overlook the fact that *Maxx* is a comedy predicated on Iran-based audiences' familiarity with Tehrangeles popular culture and its attendant stereotypes. What is also repressed and emerges on-screen is a broad-based appreciation of degenerate (ebtezāl) music and dance and the open secret of Tehrangeles popular culture's presence in domestic daily life. I argue that Maxx also indexes the historical figure of the sexually ambiguous and sometimes sexually avail-

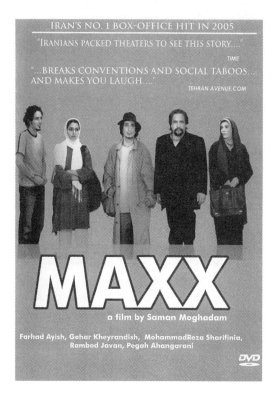

FIGURE 3.1 The cover of the North American DVD release of *Maxx* (directed by Saman Moghaddam, Hedayat Films, 2005), a domestic film parodying a Tehrangeles pop musician that also became popular in the diaspora. The title character (*center*) wears a fedora and coat.

able male performer that predates Iranian heteronormative modernity and reemerges in Tehrangeles popular culture.

Working in a half-empty cabaret one night, Maxx, our ponytailed, bandana-sporting hero, mistakenly receives an official letter of invitation from the fictional Iranian governmental Committee on Attracting Brains. The committee's mission is to encourage accomplished expatriate Iranians to return to their home country. The letter, which was intended for a classical musician with a similar name, makes its way to the Tehrangeles cabaret where Maxx works. Maxx is so out of touch with the changes in Iranian culture, politics, and language that he cannot comprehend the jargon-filled invitation when it is read to him. Through a friend's help, Maxx (mis)understands that he, a "great artist," is being invited back to Iran for a warm official welcome. He decides to play along. However, once Maxx arrives in Iran, his subterfuge slowly becomes apparent to those around him through his inappropriate performances of prerevolutionary songs and Tehrangeles-style dance pop, his use of American slang–inflected Persian, and his misuse of ideological terminology (for instance, mistaking *ghoghāsālār*, or "demagogue," for "guitar"). He is a ridiculous but endearing figure, over-come with nostalgic tears at the sight of an Iranian in-ground toilet and playing the motrebi song "Dāsh dāsh" (roughly, "Tough Guy") at a meet-ing with state officials, who initially attempt to mask their discomfort by declaring him "avant-garde." Though the plot establishes Maxx's attraction to the uptight female cultural minister Gohar, his character also shows subtle signs of nonheteronormative masculinity. These include the afore-mentioned sentimental crying, his comical overuse of terms of endearment and exclamations more typically employed by women ("Fedātun besham! Elāhi!" [I sacrifice myself to you! Oh God!]), and his repeated statements of affection for fellow Tehrangeles mardomi singer Jalal Hemmati, a real-life figure whose plucked eyebrows, perceptible makeup, flamboyant wardrobe, and penchant for singing women's repertoire has led many to whisper about his sexuality.

I understand Maxx as a composite of historical figures, circulating ste-reotypes, and real-life people and events. In terms of appearance, Maxx bears a physical similarity to Shahbal Shabpareh in the 1990s and early 2000s, when Shabpareh wore his hair in a ponytail like Maxx. This led to an embarrassing moment in my 2007 conversation with Shabpareh: when I innocently asked him if he had seen *Maxx*, he said no, but that several people had asked him whether he had acted in the title role. I consider the more relevant real-world reference to be the 2002 arrest and imprisonment of longtime Tehrangeles resident and cult figure Mohammad Khordadian, a dancer. In the 1980s and 1990s, Khordadian became a regular part of Los Angeles expatriate media as a performer and choreographer who staged a mixture of folkloric and cabaret-style dances for Persian-language television variety programs. Though Khordadian did not come out as gay until the mid-2000s, his sequined, satiny, and often revealing costumes; feminine-coded movements, such as running his fingers through imaginary tresses; and performances redolent with the provocative hip and shoulder move-ments known as *gher*, were an array of hints suggesting Khordadian's non-normative sexuality and masculinity.[6]

Iran has a long-standing association connecting professional entertain-ers, dance, dance music, and a sexuality and gender presentation that pre-dates and exceeds the modern heteronormative male identity. In urban Iran prior to the twentieth century, a nonbinary gender system ruled, and status-defined sexual relationships between adult and adolescent males were com-monplace (see Afary 2009; Najmabadi 2005, 2014). While male-female mar-riages were socially, economically, and religiously mandated, love poetry, music, visual art, literature, and historical accounts all document the position of the beardless adolescent male (*amrad*) as a central object of romantic love and erotic desire. Within the performing arts, motreb were sometimes accompanied by young male dancers attired in women's clothing called *zanpush* ("dressed as a woman") and/or young male or boy dancers called *bacheh raqqās* ("male child dancer"), who could be sexually available to customers. Song texts also described sexual desire and sexual acts between males, sometimes in graphic terms.[7] Beginning in the nineteenth century, in part inspired by contact with disapproving Europeans, Iranians began reevaluating their sexuality and the segregation of women from public life. Historian Afsaneh Najmabadi (2005) asserts that Iranians came to understand heterosexuality and a new binary (male/female) gender system as necessary to the "achievement of modernity," while open sexual relationships between younger and older males became shameful signs of "backwardness." So too did the zanpush and bacheh raqqās disappear from the nation's stages, replaced by the chaste female "angels and princesses" of the newly developed, early twentieth-century staged art form called "Iranian national dance" (Meftahi 2016a, 33–37). The "heterosexualization" of interpersonal relationships and the performing arts was, naturally, never complete, and traces of this lineage last into the present.[8] This relatively recent history of a very different ordering of gender and sexuality has been suppressed in popular memory and remains shocking to many Iranians today. I argue that it is plainly on display in expatriate culture through figures like Tehrangeles singer Jalal Hemmati and Tehrangeles actor and singer Eskandar Hojati, who perform historical ruhowzi, motrebi, and andaruni repertoire that harks back to "traditional" Iran and its submerged sexual past.[9]

Mohammad Khordadian likewise recalls this historical legacy but in a distinctly Southern Californian style. Khordadian and his mostly female dance troupe were regular fixtures on expatriate television variety programs, especially the annual Nowruz programs that were broadcast, recorded to video, and circulated widely in the diaspora and in Iran. In the 1990s he embraced the aerobics craze and recorded several instructional videos combining calisthenics with the movements of solo improvised Iranian dance. Attired in formfitting, low-cut tank tops and skintight shorts, he playfully joked and shimmied his way through routines, leading a group of male and female backup dancers. He was a lovable if often derided figure whom many Iranians knew by sight.

In 2002 Khordadian returned to Iran for the first time since the revolution to visit his ailing mother. There he was arrested by Iranian intelligence

FIGURE 3.2 Tehrangeles Mohammad Khordadian's fame has increased since his 2002 arrest for "spreading corruption" via videotape. Here Khordadian (*left*) gives journalist Behzad Bolour a dance lesson during a BBC Persian–produced television special about his life. Screen grab from "Bolur-e banafsh: Mohammad Khordadian ghesmat-e do" (*Purple Crystal* [television program]: Mohammad Khordadian part two), YouTube video, BBC Persian, June 30, 2017, https://youtu.be/Le9CNKIUIC4.

officers, detained for more than sixty days, held in solitary confinement, and eventually charged with drinking alcohol and promoting corruption among the youth.[10] Reflecting on his experience after the fact, Khordadian has maintained that he was completely taken off guard by his arrest—he never imagined that he could be charged in Iran for activities in California, or that his dancing would be considered criminal. Khordadian was eventually found guilty "on the basis of Article 7 of the Islamic Penal Code, which gives the state the authority to try crimes that have occurred entirely or partially outside the country" (Papan-Matin 2009, 131). During the trial, Khordadian never mentioned his sexual orientation, nor did those questioning him. Author Firoozeh Papan-Matin (2009, 129) attributes this to the fact that plainly identifying his homosexuality would open the case up to more serious sentencing, potentially including capital punishment. She explains that Khordadian's sexual transgressiveness was instead coded as a general charge of "promoting depravity and corruption," which could apply to his dancing, costumes, and interactions with female dancers on video. His sentence was reduced on appeal; he left the country with his male partner and resettled in Dubai, where he came out as gay and continued to perform, teach dance, and record videos.[11] He has since moved back to California.

Khordadian's case generated much attention in both the diasporic and mainstream press. In American reporting, the main issues were his arrest because of aerobics tapes, which summed up the Islamic Republic's overreaction to popular culture. The fact that he was an Iranian American dual citizen who was being charged as an Iranian also raised eyebrows; as with other subsequent arrests and detentions of dual citizens, the American government allowed Iran to handle the case, and no American agencies publicly intervened on his behalf. In the diasporic press, his arrest provided fodder for humor about what many considered to be the excessive seriousness of the charges. Much of this humor was homophobic and poked fun at the combination of Khordadian's character and Tehrangeles Iranians' ignorance of postrevolutionary Iranian laws, ideology, and the heavily Arabized official discourse in which these are encoded in official speech (see also Papan-Matin 2009, 134).[12]

Many elements of Khordadian's story also appear in *Maxx*. In the film, the imaginary los ānjelesi cabaret singer is also portrayed as unable to comprehend his behavioral and sartorial transgressions. Maxx's embrace of Western fashion, his admiration of Jalal Hemmati, and his emotional sensitivity contrast with the gruff, serious, hypermasculine, restrained male officials who are increasingly unsettled by his presence in Iran. Maxx's easily relatable manner likewise connects him to both the frivolity and the lack of pretension surrounding Khordadian and other Tehrangeles performers for whom being mardomi and supplying people with upbeat entertainment is a source of pride. Finally, as in the humor surrounding Khordadian's arrest, the film *Maxx* uses the scenario of a los ānjelesi performer in Tehran to simultaneously critique Tehrangeles and the Iranian state. This critique is most pointed not via Maxx himself but in the character of Qader, a macho, conservative, government-aligned hard-liner. Qader is hilariously hyperbolic: he coaches a soccer team whose players wear jerseys reading "Death to America" and brings protesters to Maxx's hotel to stone him while leading them in the chant "Death to Degeneration" (*marg bar ebtezāl*). Qader then attempts to force Maxx to admit that he's come from abroad as part of a foreign plot. When Qader accuses him of entering the country with the purpose of "smashing our culture," Maxx protests that he was invited, using the English word "invitation" in his reply. This incenses Qader, who launches into a stream of accusations recalling the charges leveled against Khordadian: "Look at that—there he goes—he's speaking 'American' to me. Death to America! You think we don't know who's paying you? You're paid by George Bush or that Zionist Michael Jackson or that Zionist Metallica, who pay you to corrupt our people! You spread corruption, don't you?!" Characterizing American pop musicians Michael Jackson and Metallica as Zionists who would finance Maxx's mission to spread corruption (not to mention mistaking Metallica for a single individual rather than a band), Qader's impassioned parroting of official discourse highlights its ridiculousness. Even Maxx understands this. Upon hearing these improbable but nonetheless actionable allegations, his response is incredulous and irritated—"You're kidding, right?" he asks Qader, pushing him to reconcile these outsized accusations with the hapless, sympathetic figure who sits before him. As the exchange continues, Qader loses his ability to keep up the tough-guy act: he forgets what he was saying, accidentally lets on that he's "depressed" (using the English word) because he's losing his hair, and sheepishly asks the long-haired Maxx for advice on how to prevent himself from going bald. Maxx has softened even his most ideological opponent.

Another way in which the film criticizes official sensitivity toward expatriate music and musicians is by portraying Maxx as utterly harmless. The plot shows Maxx getting into deeper and deeper trouble with governmental officials and concludes with his ejection from the country, but those characters closest to Maxx find his personality, many foibles, and sincere love for Iran amusing and even admirable—even Qader can't resist him. The film's final scenes further complicate the portrayal of Los Angeles musicians by showing their music's mass appeal despite their political or moral incorrectness. Though he has been found out by governmental officials and will soon be sent (back) into exile, Maxx timidly goes forward with presenting a large concert he has been rehearsing with a university orchestra. His female love interest introduces him to the audience as performing a program of "folklor-e Tehran"—a euphemism (though not an inaccurate one) for the motrebi/mardomi styles that Maxx loves. After performing the motrebi reng "Dāsh dāsh" with a dignified orchestral accompaniment, Maxx turns to the highlight of the night. He sings a danceable pop song called "Farār-e maghz" ("Brain Drain") with lyrics recommending that Iranians never leave the country as Maxx once did but remain at home, where they will find true happiness. "Farār-e maghz" is mobtazal in form but ideologically on target, and therefore strikes essentially the same compromise as the postrevolutionary acceptance of music for "licit purposes" (see the introduction).

This performance signals Maxx's (and perhaps the director's) acquiescence to official pressures and seems to convince the youngsters in the audience that they should take his advice. At the same time, however, Maxx's

FIGURE 3.3 Maxx's favorite singer is Jalal Hemmati, a nonheteronormatively masculine Tehrangeles mardomi vocalist that many Iranians love—and love to hate. *Lalezar*, MZM Records, 2006.

audiences are also shown knowingly demonstrating their pleasure in his music, smiling and shyly sketching the outlines of Iranian dance movements with their bodies in ways that just barely avoid crossing into inappropriate public behavior. The film concludes with further representations of transgressive enjoyment that Maxx stimulates in a splendid example of the diaspora pop-enabled cultural intimacy of shesh-o-hasht-laden dance music. As the credits roll, we hear Maxx singing the flirtatious Iranian folk song "Beneshin kenāram" ("Sit Beside Me") set in a synthesizer-heavy shesh-o-hasht dance pop arrangement. Each character appears individually, looks into the camera, and lip-synchs the words to the song. The female characters do not dance because to do so would contradict Iranian law. By contrast, each of the male figures—including the disapproving governmental officials—first slowly, and then enthusiastically, dances to the music. Qader's appearance is especially notable. He looks around to make sure he is alone and, once confident that no one can see him, shimmies rapturously. His former performance of political commitment is cast aside, and his repressed desires to dance are unleashed by Maxx's unwarranted presence in Iran. The los ānjelesi singer has put Qader in touch with a publicly unacknowledged part of himself, which he explores only when "alone," leaving the film's audience to laugh in recognition at the hypocrisy.

Through the fictional Maxx and the real-life Khordadian, the moral, heteronormative space of Iran is entered by nonheteronormative singing and dancing men from Los Angeles who seduce their Iran-based audiences with comforting and pleasurable culturally intimate music and dance. Iranians' familiarity with these figures is no secret. When Maxx claims more than once that Jalal Hemmati is his idol, no explanation is required—everyone is in on the joke, because everyone of the postrevolutionary generations has danced to Hemmati's motrebi music remade in Los Angeles—whether they admit it or not.[13] What is palpable in these stories is the erotic charge of transgression combined with the comforting familiarity of a class of performers and a class of sexual and artistic expression.

SHAHRZAD SEPANLOU: ASPIRING TO RESPECTABILITY

Female vocalist Shahrzad Sepanlou has also struggled with the eroticization of Tehrangeles, the historical and continuing stigmas surrounding female performers, and their combination in the figure of the female los ānjelesi singer. Men outnumber women in all aspects of the Tehrangeles music industry; when women are involved, they tend to serve as vocalists and sometimes as lyricists. Many Tehrangeles music videos feature a male singer surrounded by scantily clad dancing women. As expressed by satellite television producer Kourosh Bibiyan in the introduction, unveiled singing and dancing women have an important commercial function in attracting viewers to expatriate television specifically by providing them with the glimpses of female flesh they cannot get from official media. This puts pressure on video producers and musicians alike, who may not wish to make such videos but are compelled to do so. A male musician active in the Tehrangeles pop industry explained the situation this way: "If I make a dance music video with lots of talentless seminaked young girls with long legs, I don't even need to waste one hour in a [Tehrangeles] record label's office: I am signed in *half* an hour!!"

The combination of active male musicians and silent, desiring female dance corps is a tried-and-true formula in American music videos from rock to hip-hop, where women serve as props emphasizing the sexual desirability of the male vocalist (Andsager 2006, 43–44). Indeed, many if not most of the women dancing in Tehrangeles videos are not of Iranian descent or are assumed by Iranian viewers not to be Iranian. This is deduced from the dancers' physical appearance and from their inexpert performances of Iranian dance. The relative absence of Iranian women in these roles could be partially explained by the availability of professional dancers in the Los Angeles area or the exotic appeal of non-Iranian women, but Iranian women's

FIGURE 3.4 A cartoon by Mahmoud titled "Los ānjelesi singer" mocks the stereotype of an aged male Tehrangeles vocalist flanked by attractive women. The vocalists hypes the crowd using pop clichés: "Yāllā . . . everybody . . . clap, clap, clap, clap." Screenshot from Iranian.com Archives, April 5, 2005, https://iranian.com/Satire/Cartoon/2005/April/sing.html?site=archive. Used with the permission of the artist.

reluctance to perform should also be factored in here. Though dance is a common part of diasporic social life, many women are hesitant to participate in videos or become professional dancers because of familial and community pressures to avoid such activities (Shay 1999). The substitution of non-Iranian women to fulfill a role deemed inappropriate for "nice Iranian girls" bears similarity to the historical practice of Muslim Iranians hiring Jewish and Armenian entertainers because Muslims considered these professions immoral, even if the lively music provided by these performers was vital to their festive gatherings.

In the case of Iranian female vocalists, outsourcing to others is not an option. These women must contend with how to manage their physicality in promotional materials, on album covers, in music videos, and in performances. The careful negotiation of desire and desirability are critical. Like so many Tehrangeles artists, Sepanlou wants to be wanted by fans—especially those in Iran—but she seeks an artistic, affective, and cultural

FIGURE 3.5 The CD insert to singer Faramarz Assef's 2009 album depicts him enjoying the company of a diverse group of women-as-props. Faramarz Assef, *Ghashang-e Roozegar [Beautiful Days] Dance with Ecstasy*, Afra Productions.

connection that avoids the performance of sexual availability. Through her artistic choices, she works to appeal to audiences and differentiate herself from other los ānjelesi female singers by signaling her respect for and familiarity with Iran-based audiences and their expectations. She is also concerned with respecting and being true to herself, which she relates to how much she covers or uncovers her body, whether she dances, and whether or how she sings or speaks of love and the erotic. The work of monitoring herself, dealing with the pressures of the industry, and extrapolating the effects of her efforts is an especially complicated endeavor given that she does not travel to Iran and must therefore rely on perceptions and circulating imaginaries of the homeland cobbled together from media and communications with fans, friends, and family within the country. Through an analysis of her intentions in three songs—"E'terāz" ("Objection"), "Mirdāmād bulevār" ("Mirdamad Boulevard"), and "Hezār va yek shab" ("1,001 Nights")—in tandem with the Iran-based audience's reception, I show how her early career struggles represent the challenges of navigating the transnational erotics and moral regimes that mass-mediated Tehrangeles pop engages.

Shahrzad Sepanlou was born in Iran in 1972 and moved to the United States in 1985 in the middle of the Iran-Iraq War, when she was twelve years old. Her parents—her father, Mohammad Reza Sepanlou (1940–2015), and mother, Partow Nooriala, both poets—remained in Iran. She finished high school and college in Southern California and received a bachelor's degree in sociology from the University of California, Los Angeles, in 1995. She began singing professionally with a girl group called Silhouettt (spelled with three *t*'s to represent the three singers) that was produced by Shahbal Shabpareh in collaboration with composer and saxophonist Farzin Farhadi. After one album with Silhouettt, she started a solo career, and she has released five solo albums since 2000. Her solo albums contain a smooth jazz influence born out of her long-term collaboration with Farhadi; she also released a few "hot jazz"–style songs that match very much with the sound popular among expatriate and Iran-based bands in the mid-2000s to 2010s. She has studiously stayed away from shesh-o-hasht rhythms and the sounds of typical Iranian-flavored dance pop, and has worked with lyricists who write poetry, such as her father, the Toronto-based musician Kambiz Mirzaei, and Sanaz Zaresani. These stylistic and collaborative choices are important ways of separating herself from the typical los ānjelesi model of dance pop with trivial lyrics. However, she began her career in the Tehrangeles industry and has continuing artistic and professional connections to the industry, and her works have been released and broadcast through channels based in Los Angeles and elsewhere in the diaspora. She has therefore remained linked to Los Angeles in some people's minds.

In 2007 I visited Sepanlou at her well-appointed, spacious home, located in the hills that divide the city of Los Angeles from the San Fernando Valley. Her husband was working at home, and her young daughter was playing with a babysitter as we conversed for several hours, eventually moving to a small diner to continue our exchange. In comparison to many other musicians I met in Los Angeles, Sepanlou was forthcoming about her hopes, challenges, and disappointments as she worked to find satisfaction in her musical life. Perhaps this was because I, like her, was a young woman who had grown up mostly in the United States and had a sense of the conflicting expectations she held regarding her life choices and musical career. Sepanlou saw her work as a struggle on many fronts: she was fighting against dominant stereotypes, trying to find her own style, and attempting to have a musical career while being an involved wife and mother. She knew that she was dealing with representations that were beyond her control, but she also saw her work as a means for intervening in dominant Los Angeles aesthetics, politics, and portrayals of women as well as a way of reaching Iranians in Iran and in the diaspora. She discussed negotiating her desires for integrity and sincere self-presentation in artistic works with the pressures she felt from record producers, video directors, and audiences near and far, all with the specter of the dissolute los ānjelesi singer surrounding her. Sepanlou knew she had an audience in Iran because fans wrote her emails and even called her on the phone to let her know their reactions to her work (she had once given out her number on a television program, which she came to regret). In our conversation, she mentioned three songs from her first two solo albums, and discussed how encounters with fans around these songs shaped how she thought of herself and her career.

Sepanlou's first solo album was *Our Story* (1001 Productions, 2000). This included a song titled "E'terāz" ("Objection") that addressed the fraught relationships between Iranians in Iran and those in Southern California. The text was written by Zoya Zakarian, a female lyricist who was active in the prerevolutionary industry, moved to Los Angeles following the revolution, and has worked in the Tehrangeles culture industries as both a lyricist and a television host. The song title refers to diasporic Iranians' objections to homeland-based Iranians' misconceptions and judgments of them, particularly the perception that those in the diaspora have trouble-free lives or have lost their moral compass. The lyrics present mutual resentments between the homeland and diaspora populations, a very different kind of relationship from the affectionate exchange of mutual love and respect invoked by Tehrangeles artists in the examples that opened this chapter. "E'terāz" also refers to the specific pressures on young women vis-à-vis Iran-based audiences. The song opens with a statement declaring the singer's displacement, which becomes the refrain:

> *Where can I stay in this world?*
> *I'm a stranger from one end of the world to the other*

The verses relate the discomfort of being judged from afar:

> *Someone sitting from up on high*
> *Who knows nothing about my life*
> *Throws stones at exiles (ghorbat) . . .*
> *Thinking that we're sitting by the beach all day*
> *Completely unaware of life's sorrows*
> *Now they think we have lost our roots*
> *We have no pain, no sadness, and no homeland*
> *At home, asleep all day*
> *No problems besides having to mow the lawn*

The lyrics express outrage at the accusations hurled at Iranians in Los Angeles: they ignore the world's problems while getting drunk on the beach. The refrain's introductory statement of displacement frames the verse as a fabrication by those who cannot know the challenges faced by their compatriots in the diaspora: televised appearances of leisure and comfort don't account for the lyricist's and singer's deep "unsettlement" (Mankekar 2015).

The second verse objects to how Iranian women in Los Angeles are regarded by those at home:

> [This person] thinks we're a bunch of dolls
> Naked and with our heads uncovered
> Now we have no home, we have no loyalty (vafā)
> We've "broken God," we have no modesty (khodā shekastim/hayā nadārim)

The lines succinctly invoke multiple stereotypes about Iranian women in Los Angeles: they are immodest, as empty-headed as dolls, clothing-less, rootless, Godless, and country-less all at once. The video for the song is predicated on the contrast between Sepanlou's persona and the litany of unflattering descriptors she articulates. Unlike Tehrangeles female vocalists who tend to favor eye-catching and sometimes revealing outfits, she is dressed casually in a track jacket and jeans, with her body fully covered, and does not dance. She also never smiles.

I was curious whether Sepanlou had received any reaction to "E'terāz" from audiences in or outside of Iran. She replied that she had received emails from both constituencies. A person in Iran told her that they would "'listen to it every day before I go to school,'" and another thanked her "'for trying to tell us how you guys are doing.'" Some listeners from outside Iran wrote, "'That's exactly how I feel! That's it!'" she remembered. She explained her understanding of the song's impact:

> ["E'terāz"] really hit a nerve with [Iranians]. Inside and outside of Iran; even though it's coming from a woman who is speaking from outside of Iran, outside of the country, and she sort of has a bone to pick with the people inside the country, saying that you people think that we're just sitting here all day. No, I'm working [very hard], I feel like a stranger no matter where I go! But people in Iran really loved it! Because it was communicating with them! Because, what do they *see* in Iran? They turn on the [Los Angeles–based satellite] TV, and they see these [expatriate] singers standing with women with short skirts moving their butts on the beach, you know, the male singer with his shirt wide open. . . . I can't imagine what's going on in their heads back in Iran. With all . . . they have to deal with, you know, they come here and they look at this, . . . [and they think,] "Wow, these people must be having the time of their

FIGURE 3.6 Shahrzad Sepanlou performs her frustration with the los ānjelesi stereotype in the video for "E'terāz" ("Objection"). "Shahrzad Sepanlou Eteraz (Objection)," YouTube video, posted by Shahrzad Sepanlou, January 1, 2007, https://youtu.be/g9M6znkZ4hc.

lives!" This is what they're [Los Angeles musicians are] representing, in a way. And it's *not true*! I mean, sure, we have people who sit in their BMWs and they don't have to work . . . but the truth is that there are a lot of people struggling. Especially people who left when they were a little bit older. Teenagers, they have a serious identification with Iran, but they are here [in the diaspora] and have to go to high school here . . . it's really hard. You feel torn, and you're never one unit, you never feel like you belong. So ["E'terāz"] was explaining all that in a short amount of time. And both people inside and outside of Iran got it.

Sepanlou's comments point to the double-sided nature of mediated imaginaries: the succinctness of transnationally circulating, mass-mediated song is an effective communicative medium but can also produce damaging misunderstandings in distant audiences. "E'terāz" critiques the Los Angeles music industry for producing a host of unflattering and, in Sepanlou and Zakarian's view, largely inaccurate portrayals of diasporic life, while the song also talks back to those who mistakenly believe the imaginary is real. Sepanlou imagines that "E'terāz," as a song and video, could intervene in the traffic of fantasies and contribute a more accurate representation of life abroad.

Though Sepanlou rhetorically states that she "can't imagine what's going on in [audiences'] heads back in Iran," her comments reveal both that she has empirical evidence of what a few individuals think and, crucially, that imagination is very much at work on both sides of the border. The song itself is about homeland audiences' projections onto Los Angeles, while she in turn imagines homeland audiences' reactions to the song's projection of their projections. The portrayal of diaspora as hardship and alienation is important to both Zakarian and Sepanlou: leaving Iran allowed them to escape the effects of the revolution and war, but it put them in a permanently unsettled state that undergirds whatever "good life" those in the diaspora might have achieved. (Zakarian's lyrics for Googoosh's song "QQ Bang Bang," discussed in chapter 4, likewise communicate this dissatisfaction.) Suffering the negative judgments of those at home on top of their displacement adds insult to injury.

Another way in which imagination figured into Sepanlou's early work was in her conceptualization of Iranian landmarks and the country itself as part of a larger moral space. Her first album also includes "Mirdāmād bulevār," a song about memories of a well-known thoroughfare in northern Tehran. The piece is a cross-border and cross-generational collaboration: Sepanlou's poet father wrote the song from his own perspective and remained in Iran throughout the recording and release. In the vein of *she'r-e now*, or Iranian modernist New Poetry, the song lyrics are an impressionistic collection of images and disconnected lines that together hint at regret regarding Iran's present "sad era" (*in zamān-e ghamgin*) and hopes for a happier future. The midtempo, jazzy song is moody and melancholic, pierced by songwriter Farhadi's plaintive soprano saxophone interjections. Its musical and poetic style separate Sepanlou from the los ānjelesi stereotype: the song is not particularly danceable, its lyrics are about a specific place in Iran and by an Iran-based poet rather than an expatriate in Southern California, and its jazz-influenced sound is a far cry from the familiar pop and mardomi musical markers of many Tehrangeles productions.

Reflecting on this song in a 2014 televised interview with Shahbal Shabpareh in Los Angeles, Sepanlou commented that "Mirdāmād bulevār" didn't represent her experiences; she was performing the sentiments and attachments of her father's generation. Shabpareh, who is of the same generation as Sepanlou's father but left Iran in the mid-1980s, asked her whether Mirdamad was one of the streets whose names had been changed following the revolution, when Tehran's cityscape was purged of references to the monarchy, which were replaced with the names of war martyrs and religious figures. He hadn't been back to Iran and didn't know—did she? Sepanlou laughed and said that she also wasn't sure, but that it was the feeling of nostalgia inherited from her father that led her to sing the song. That neither Sepanlou nor Shabpareh knew this basic fact is telling with regard to the distance between them and the country, which exists in firsthand memories, inherited nostalgia, and snippets gathered from conversations, gossip, news, and other information exchanges, including Sepanlou's father sharing the poem with her. What matters is not Mirdamad's present name (it is still Mirdamad) but the song and poem's representation of the "immemorial land."[14]

The video for "Mirdāmād bulevār" did more bridging work by visually closing the distance between Sepanlou and Iran. In some scenes, she appears to be strolling the streets of Tehran, a trick of technology in which her moving image is superimposed over postrevolutionary footage of Mirdamad and other areas of the city. This feat was arranged in the studio, accomplishing at the editing console what couldn't be so easily undertaken off-screen.[15] While Sepanlou was not physically present in Tehran, she related to me that she made sure to dress "very conservatively" in the video in a way that would respect what she understood to be local preferences. In a scene where she appears standing by the side of the busy boulevard, she wears a turtleneck, loose jacket, and long pants. Save for the absent head covering that is required for all women in public according to Iranian law, her outfit would otherwise be acceptable on the streets of northern Tehran where Mirdamad is located. But this gesture toward Iranian law and cultural codes is also striking because it doesn't resolve the most basic issues of her song and presence's incompatibility with postrevolutionary Iran. If Sepanlou had attempted to make this video on Tehran's streets, she could have faced local restrictions on her uncovered hair and public solo female singing voice. Even though she was "conservatively" attired according to her North American standards, by official Iranian standards she was in a state of undress and thus would be subject to punishment for violating the national moral codes.[16] Yet for both Sepanlou and her Iran-based fans, this video served to cement her image as a respectful and respectable woman who sang serious songs on serious topics and avoided the immoral taint of Tehrangeles. She was a good girl, the kind of young woman you might want as a daughter or daughter-in-law, not the female dancer, or *raqqasseh*, a term virtually synonymous with immorality and prostitution.

Sepanlou felt her carefully crafted reputation threatened by her next album, particularly the song and video "Hezār va yek shab" ("1,001 Nights"). Unlike her self-produced first album, Sepanlou's second album was made with Avang Records, a Tehrangeles record company. This experience forced

Sepanlou to confront the pressures to produce a certain kind of album to sell more copies, as also expressed by other Tehrangeles musicians. She recalled, "They never tell you you need to make a commercial album, but the pressure is there. So, on [this album's] first two songs, I am being a little more, you know, fast-paced, a little happier. . . . By nature, I gravitate toward songs that . . . deal with deeper issues. I really forced myself to have more songs that were universal and lovey-dovey. So, those aren't really me—I was performing, more than anything else. . . . They were made to please the audience." In working with Avang, Sepanlou felt she had to sacrifice her personal tastes as well as her commitment to sincere self-representation. The lyrics, written by longtime (female) Tehrangeles contributor Paksima, were more romantic and less literary than her previous songs, and the album's sound was also quite different from her other work. While "Hezār va yek shab" avoids the shesh-o-hasht sound or other mardomi musical markers, it includes "Oriental" musical references and utilizes electronic dance grooves in ways that depart from typical Iranian pop sounds: augmented seconds, harmonic minor scales, and samples that emulate Middle Eastern instruments contribute to a sort of poppy "world music" amalgamation. The Oriental theme is echoed in the album's title song, which is also a play on Sepanlou's given name, the mythical storyteller:

> I'm Shahrzad [Scheherazade] the storyteller . . .
> . . . [M]y body contains the warmth of the sun . . .
> If you come, if you come,
> I'll put my head on your shoulder
> If you come, if you come,
> I'll tell you a thousand stories . . .

On top of her discomfort with the song itself, Sepanlou reflected on the song's video as a regrettable point in her career in which she "didn't follow [her] instincts." In the video, Sepanlou wears a satiny pink, floor-length evening gown with spaghetti straps that leaves her shoulders, arms, and décolletage bare. With a flower behind one ear, she sings gazing directly into the camera, her face, hair, and upper body filling up the screen. In other scenes, she dances with similarly dressed young women, moving her arms in curlicues in an impression of Iranian solo improvised dance. These are interspersed with scenes of her in silhouette with long, sheer veils draped over her arms as she twirls and spins. At the end of the video, Sepanlou, outfitted in a sleeveless shirt and formfitting trousers, dances with a crowd of men and women as if at a nightclub. She jumps and waves her arms around as she dances. Again, the camera shows her face and upper body; it doesn't focus on her breasts, abdomen, or posterior in the way that Tehrangeles videos with female dance corps often do.

After the video's release, Sepanlou was chagrined to receive negative emails and phone calls about the video from fans in and outside of Iran. She compared her appearance in the new video to "Mirdāmād bulevār": "['Mirdāmād'] is my first video, and that's what people have in their heads. I was very conservative in that video. And when I went from 'Mirdāmād' to ['Hezār va yek shab'] it was completely different. And I don't blame [audiences for their negative reactions]. I was not happy about the video." Though "E'terāz" rails against Iran-based audiences for their moralistic judgments of women in Tehrangeles, I found it interesting that Sepanlou did not protest when she herself was the object of these objections. Instead, she accepted the critique that she had crossed the line for appropriate and respectable female comportment. She placed some of the responsibility for this transgression on the director, and some on her own lack of "strength," but also abrogated her ownership of the performance by refusing to identify with the woman she portrayed in the video. "[The director was an] American woman . . . and she bullied me into wearing these outfits and doing things in the video that are not me! When you see the video, that is not me. And I let down a lot of my fans with that video. I showed a different side of me that's not me. They saw me as stronger than that, they saw me as tougher than that, that I didn't want to be sexy. I disappointed myself and my fans." The claim that this "sexy" singer was "not her" or "a different side of me that's not me" displays a kind of split female subject that I encountered several times in Tehrangeles. Once was in a meeting with a prerevolutionary dancer who told me she "wasn't what people said about [her], she was *pāk* [clean/pure/sober]." Another instance occurred with a prerevolutionary female vocalist who—very unusually in Tehrangeles—attended our interview without any makeup and called it to my attention, saying, "I only wear that makeup in videos because I have to." It was important to these women that I understand that they felt compelled to present themselves in a certain way, and that this was a prerequisite of their professions rather than an expression of their authentic desires or selves.[17]

Criticism of "Hezār va yek shab" was especially pointed from Iran-based audiences, who provided a sharp contrast to the perceptions of the American director: "[Iran-based audience members said,] 'You didn't need to do that to yourself, you didn't need to dance, acting like an LA singer.' I told the American director [their reactions], and she was shocked; she said, 'I thought you were so classy.' But I told her, we are dealing with a country with different standards.... Right or wrong, we have a certain respect for ... [she hesitated] for a 'classy woman,' we say." Sepanlou's recollections of her conversation with the American director juxtapose two distinct understandings of what constitutes a classy woman. Though we were speaking in English during the interview and Sepanlou used the same word to describe both the American director's understanding of classy and the Iranian cultural understanding "we have," the difference between these positions is part of the problem. But an Iranian "us" versus an American or Hollywood "them" also doesn't adequately capture the complexity of operating in transnational mediated moral regimes that include the postrevolutionary homeland and its multiple generations of diaspora in which one's moral and/or erotic performances are wrapped into markets, culture, and political positioning.

I find Sepanlou's story compelling for the way she succinctly describes the challenges of navigating her emplacement in layered American, Iranian, and diasporic cultural fields. While the American director had her own vision of what constituted a classy performance, perhaps informed by her work in Hollywood, Iran-based audiences communicated in no uncertain terms that Sepanlou's video performance called into question her previously respectable reputation. This prior reputation was itself constituted through the transnational circulation of carefully crafted, technologically mediated performances developed based on Sepanlou's predictions of how her dress and bodily comportment would be interpreted in relation to imagined Iranian audiences. In their creation and in their later circulation, Sepanlou's performances were produced and understood in relation to a host of cultural stereotypes made larger than life through commerce, politics, and religion: the pious, veiled woman; the seductive Hollywood starlet; the "half-naked" "modern" woman of the Pahlavi era; the excessive sexuality of los ānjelesi pop; the sincere singer who reveals her authentic self in her songs; and others.

"ARE LOS ĀNJELESI SINGERS COMING TO IRAN?"

A 2013 headline on the domestic Iranian website *Farda News* asked a provocative question: are los ānjelesi singers coming (back) to Iran?[18] The article was spurred by the surprising return of longtime Los Angeles resident Habib Mohebbian, who had a prerevolutionary pop music career, released ten albums outside of the country, and then moved back to Iran in 2009 without any official repercussions. In various reported statements, Mohebbian declared that he had committed no actions in the diaspora that would be considered illegal in Iran and had made no political statements opposing the Islamic Republic or its policies. Now that popular music had been permitted in Iran for almost twenty years, there was no reason for him not to live in his home country or even release an album there. While he was never granted the necessary permissions to release an album, which might indicate some official reluctance to fully embrace this returnee, the fact that Mohebbian was not openly harassed or made into an example provoked the question announced by the article's breathless title: was a door to Iran opening for expatriate musicians—at least those who present as cisgender heterosexual men?

The same article included a pronouncement by then minister of culture Mohammad Ali Hosseini on the permissibility of other Tehrangeles artists returning to Iran. He is reported to have said, "If the [artists in question] have no political history and have not acted against the Islamic Republic of Iran, they may return to their own country and there will be no repercussions regarding their [prior] activities." He then added an important caveat: "Anyone that has any hint (*nemād*) of los ānjelesi culture cannot be active in the country."[19] Which of Tehrangeles's many markers are most offensive to state officials at any given time? Who decides, and on what grounds? As in the real-life and fictional cases of Khordadian and Maxx, does the "immorality" of singing or dancing remain interpretable as an offshore act "against the Islamic Republic"? How deeply do the unruly erotics of Tehrangeles popular culture penetrate territorial Iran, and to what effect? None of these questions is answerable or perhaps ultimately even the most important consideration in terms of gauging whether it is safe for Tehrangeles artists to return. As the repeated triumph of pragmatism and political expediency in postrevolutionary ideological matters has shown, the fate of any particularly well-known Tehrangeles returnee is likely to be based on many factors beyond aesthetics or morality, while a degree of unpredictable and unorganized enforcement is useful for keeping Iranians at home and abroad on their toes. And yet the interpenetration of transnational Iranian imaginaries, desires, erotics, and moral regimes, and the media that carry them, also means that in some sense, Tehrangeles artists are already in Iran even while their dancing and singing bodies remain half a world away.

IRAN AS A
SINGING WOMAN

A well-preserved blonde in her late fifties wearing a silvery-blue, décolletage-revealing dress looks deeply into the camera lens. A synthesized string section swells in the background. Her carefully groomed brows furrow with pained emotion, her outstretched arms convey an exhausted supplication, and her voice almost breaks as she sings:

Do not forget me
I know that I am ruined
You are hearing my cries
I am Iran, I am Iran...[1]

If one were to imagine postrevolutionary Iran in human form, it might more likely be a turbaned, bearded cleric, not a bareheaded, revealingly dressed female pop singer. How can this woman credibly claim to represent the Iranian nation? Or, more precisely, which Iran does she perform, and for whom?

The woman in question is Faegheh Atashin, better known by her stage name Googoosh. Googoosh is Iran's most famous and beloved female pop vocalist of the twentieth and now twenty-first century. Born in 1950, the charismatic performer came to national awareness as a singer and actress on television and in films before she was ten years old; by her twenties, she was the country's primary female interpreter of musiqi-ye pāp and its biggest female celebrity. Before 1979 Googoosh appeared in over twenty-five feature films, released wildly popular songs, and was a ubiquitous presence in the popular press. Like other prominent entertainers, during the revolution Googoosh was charged with propagating moral corruption, but instead of fleeing the country like so many of her colleagues, she remained in Iran and removed herself from public life. As her prerevolutionary music industry peers established the expatriate culture industries and became ambivalently associated with Los Angeles, she remained frozen in time and remembered in the diaspora as a symbol of both the nation's "silenced" women and the Pahlavi past. Then, in 2000, Googoosh suddenly reappeared: she left Iran and embarked on a wildly successful set of performances in the diaspora, eventually settling in Southern California. Since her comeback, she has performed her best-loved repertoire, released a new corpus of albums, and courted controversy as she has embraced the symbolism that grew around her in her absence.

This chapter examines the interconnections among women, voice, nation, and nostalgia in the Iranian diaspora through the singular figure of Googoosh. Googoosh is uniquely situated to perform the national role in the diaspora because she is known for her public biography of victimization and because the official "silencing" of her and other female vocalists maps neatly onto the Tehrangeles trope of the embattled, "stifled" postrevolutionary nation. That Googoosh is a singing woman and not a singing man is crucial to the kind of representative work she has been given and now actively takes on.[2] As I have argued in the preceding chapters, Tehrangeles female vocalists transgress official Iranian morality, and therefore law, by the mere fact of their participation in the expatriate music industry. Via their music's transnational circulation into Iran, they become political regardless of their awareness or intent. Googoosh's response to this quandary has been to embrace her politicization and make politics central to her postmigration career. She has drawn on preexisting Pahlavi symbols and Tehrangeles discourses while also extending her collaborations outside of Southern California and creatively capitalizing on her unique fame. In and beyond Tehrangeles, Googoosh has fused female singing and political expression in newly audible ways.

This chapter's title is inspired by Beth Baron's *Egypt as a Woman: Nationalism, Gender, and Politics* (2005), a seminal history of female activists and female national political symbols in twentieth-century Egypt. My inquiry into Googoosh pursues many of the same questions that guide Baron's book: how Googoosh is "incorporated into the collective memory," how the icon has "become a site of collective memory," and how she has "become a symbol because [she has] already been excluded" and is also "excluded because she is a symbol" (2005, 3). Examining a diasporic documentary about Googoosh's relationship to national history, her performances of Iranian history in her video "QQ Bang Bang," and her many postmigration claims to represent the nation's voice in song and speech, I show how the icon first became the object of national metaphorization and, since her reemergence, has begun to participate in her metaphorization. To ground my questions about "how and when 'voice' becomes a salient metaphor and what is at stake in it" (Weidman 2014, 38), I assemble a brief history of vocal-political terminology in twentieth-century Iranian poetry and song and then highlight instances where Googoosh has put this terminology to use. Finally, I argue that Googoosh's career after her migration provides a window onto larger dynamics of Iranian expatriate political contestation over Iran's past and future.

THE ANGUISHED CRY IN IRANIAN POLITICS, POETRY, AND SONG

Over the course of the twentieth century and into the present, political movements for representative government, rights of expression, and political self-determination have fed—and been fed by—poetry and song lyrics that employ a terminology of voiced anguish to express political desires and discontents. The following brief history connects politically inflected Tehrangeles pop to this legacy. In so doing, I show the sound and text of Tehrangeles to be more than lighthearted love poetry over a shesh-o-hasht beat. Tehrangeles pop also resounds with cries of anger and pain.

The anguished voice in politically inflected Tehrangeles pop can be traced back to the changes to poetry and music during the Iranian Constitutional Revolution (1905–1911). During this time, poets reformulated the *ghazal* from a classical form predominantly expressing the suffering of love to a genre that could accommodate individual or collective sociopolitical discontent. Persian's rich vocabulary for anguished vocalization, which had previously been employed to communicate romantic or metaphysical longing and disappointment, was now used to cry out against social and political disappointments and injustices. A key musical example in this transformation is the famous Constitutional Revolution tasnif (metered song) "Morgh-e sahar" ("Bird of the Dawn"). This well-known song opens with the line "Bird of the dawn, cry out" ("Morgh-e sahar nāleh sar kon"), where a person speaking to a caged bird asks it to moan or cry (nāleh) against oppression (zālem).[3] A link between anguished vocalization and a demand for justice is also found in the terms dād and faryād. Dād can mean a shout or cry but, in another register, also means "justice" (for instance, a court of law is a dādgāh, or "place of justice").[4] Faryād likewise indicates a "loud voice" or "loud cry" and can also mean "to cry out for justice," whether to protest mistreatment by a beloved or abandonment by the Divine, or to demand fulfillment of an unmet obligation.[5] The language of politically inflicted suffering developed further with the twentieth-century New Poetry movement, which strongly influenced pop lyricists in the 1960s and 1970s. Mehdi Akhavan Sales's famous 1960s poem "Khāneh-am ātish gerefteh ast" ("My House Is on Fire"), also known as "Faryād," is a paradigmatic example of the political resonance of the anguished cry. In Akhavan Sales's work, and that of his leftist contemporaries working in New Poetry, the terminology of screams, shouts, cries, and silence has been interpreted in terms of the (im)possibility of expression in the repressive atmosphere following the 1953 coup.[6] The lexical and sounded dimensions of the anguished voice are brought together in musical performance, as in preeminent art-music vocalist Mohammad-Reza Shajarian's postrevolutionary performances of both "Faryād" and "Morgh-e sahar." Shajarian's iconic live performances and recordings have lent these texts a deep, pathos-filled sounded form, where singing at the top of his extensive range and using extensive passages of tahrir give the expression of anguish an intensely affecting form.[7]

Tehrangeles music and media producers have likewise made use of the rich poetic and sonic resources surrounding voice, vocalization, deprivation, and demand. In Southern California these demanding, disappointed voices were those of the revolution's "losers," who either saw their needs as unmet or viewed themselves and their way of life as being rejected by the incoming regime. Desires for the expression of marginalized viewpoints and of alternative national identifications came together in expatriate media. In the late 1970s and 1980s, Southern Californian television stations such as National Iranian Television (NITV) or Omid-e Iran (Hope of Iran) and television talk show programs like Jam-e Jam's Tribyun-e āzād (Free Tribune) combined national terminology, the pre-Islamic imagery favored by the Pahlavis, and explicit references to media as avenues for political expression and debate.[8] Seen in this light, Tehrangeles media industries were not just driven by the financial rewards of providing entertainment to their audiences but by the need to create a public sphere beyond the Iranian state (Hemmasi 2011; Naficy 1993). Musicians were also involved: singers like Shahram Shabpareh who had not previously expressed political opinions now did so, while others who already had reputations for subtly conveying political dissent in their prerevolutionary music, like Dariush and his lyricist-collaborators, then amplified their critiques in exile.

In early expatriate pop, the "voice of the people" or the "nation's voice" had become literal and figurative. When the nation's main vocalists were silenced within the country, expatriate musicians and the industry supporting them tasked themselves with singing their own suffering aloud as they simultaneously sang to, and on behalf of, those they had left behind. While the postrevolutionary restrictions on music set the conditions for both popular music and the voice's political metaphorization, expatriate pop singers, composers, and lyricists also drew on the legacy of political song and poetic tropes in crafting "political" Tehrangeles pop. As previously discussed, Shabpareh's "Deyar," Tehrangeles's very first pop song, inaugurated the trend in exile as he sang of his "heart's song" turning to "wailing" (nāleh), "weeping" (geryeh), and "outcries" (faryād). Other first-generation Tehrangeles performers also employed both vocal metaphors and vocalizations of anguish, as in exiled female vocalist Hayedeh's 1981 song "Faryād," written by composer Anoushirvan Rouhani and lyricist Karim Fakur.[9] Here Hayedeh, a classically trained vocalist who recorded pop in Tehrangeles, sings of her profoundly painful separation from friends (yārān) with many of the previously mentioned lexical and nonlexical signs of vocalized anguish. Dariush's first song in exile went further in combining vocal and musical tropes with the desire for liberation. Like many expatriate songs from the late 1970s and 1980s, "Vatan" ("Homeland")—sometimes called "Begu be Iran" ("Tell Iran")—reflects the bleak circumstances of departure and the potential impossibility of return, and depicts the country in ruins. It is also an early example of how music and voice assume importance as a metaphor for the nation itself and as a tool for national emancipation:

> Say that once again I will sing
> With all my companions
> The broken beautiful song

Say, say that I will sing with blood
With my heart and soul
The final words of deliverance
Say this to Iran, say this to Iran[10]

The song enunciates a desire for its circulation into Iran and anticipates a proxy relationship between the nation's voice in exile and exilic nationalists like Dariush.

The early pattern of expatriate popular music commenting on the homeland and registering despair, discontent, and hopes for its future transformation carried into subsequent decades of songwriting to the point that in the 1990s and 2000s, many if not most Tehrangeles artists had recorded at least one song in this vein. While the depiction of the homeland in danger or in ruins was more prevalent in the 1980s than today, for many expatriates Iran's current condition still inspires the anguished cry. Iran is woefully transformed from their lived or inherited prerevolutionary (post)memories, while its people continue to suffer from economic deprivation, environmental disaster, and human rights abuses. Forty years on, Tehrangeles artists still wail in response to their and their homeland's lamentable plight—and on behalf of its people as well.

A DAUGHTER OF PAHLAVI IRAN

Googoosh is bigger than Tehrangeles. Her strong associations with the Pahlavi era, outsized fame, high-profile concerts and media appearances, and professional collaborations stretching outside the Southern Californian Iranian diaspora combine to make her a transcendent, unofficial national icon. This image is reinforced by most of her non-Iranian media coverage, in which she is often portrayed in comparison to Euro-American pop singers—for instance, as "Iran's Beyoncé before [the] Revolution."[11] The celebrity vocalists to whom Googoosh is compared change with the times in an attempt to communicate her influence among Iranians; a report on her 2001 Wembley Stadium concert quotes a British Iranian teenager saying, "She's not just Madonna for us. . . . She's Michael Jackson and George Michael, too."[12] Rarely does this coverage address the fact that Googoosh is part of a larger generation of prerevolutionary musicians who left their home country, or that her career is facilitated by the highly developed transnational Iranian expatriate culture industries. This is not particularly surprising since, even as an artist's works and distinctive persona are typically the product of extensive if invisible collaborative relationships, celebrity vocalists are often understood by their audiences first and foremost as exceptional individuals. While I will eventually argue that seeing Googoosh as an isolate does not adequately attend to her engagement with broader Tehrangeles culture industry themes and tropes, her special position in Iranian history must also be recognized.

Perhaps the most important reason Googoosh occupies a unique place in the Iranian imagination is her dominant position in mainstream, cosmopolitan prerevolutionary Iranian popular culture and her close association with the 1960s and 1970s. Googoosh's father was a professional entertainer, and he incorporated his charismatic daughter into his acrobatics acts when she was three years old. She soon moved to acting in musical films and television programs in the burgeoning popular culture industries. She was the star of the first nationally broadcast television program when she was ten years old (Chehabi 2000, 162) and had acted in fifteen films before she was twenty. In her teens and twenties, Googoosh became a beloved singer of musiqi-ye pāp, recording a varied corpus of songs that highlighted her vocal flexibility. Some remember Googoosh's appearance as more important to her fame than her voice (Breyley 2010). Though Googoosh's female peers in light classical music, such as Mahasti (1946–2007), Hayedeh (1942–1990), and Homeira (b. 1945), were arguably more technically accomplished, Googoosh's beauty, fashion-plate image, and dancing abilities set her apart. A talented actress who had been onstage since her toddler years, Googoosh performed her songs with her face and body as much as her voice, using her large, expressive eyes, heart-shaped mouth, lithe body, and delicate hands to underscore her sung expressions. Her malleability was also manifest in her constantly changing image. Magazine covers and television appearances featured the star in a wide array of hairstyles and flamboyant attire; one week she would appear as a long-haired blond wearing jeans and a cowboy hat, the next with her signature pixie hairstyle in a bell-bottomed white sleeveless jumpsuit and long gloves. When Googoosh lopped off her hair into this short style, women all over the country copied the look, which became known as the *googooshi*. Googoosh's gift for self-transformation was also on display in her many films. Like many other actresses in Iranian popular cinema, she often played the roles of "damsel in distress" and "fallen woman." Googoosh's characters spanned the innocent ingénue, the sexually mature (and sexually active) woman, and even a cross-dressing thief named Reza in the 1976 film *Shab-e gharibān* (*Night of Strangers*, dir. Farzan Mohammad Deljou, Payam Cinematic Organization).

Googoosh was embraced by some—winning the equivalent of the Iranian Academy Award and being invited by the royal family to perform at court—and rejected by many as well. For her leftist and Islamist critics, Googoosh embodied the caricatured *gharbzadeh* ("West-stricken") woman. The gharbzadeh woman was "a propagator of the corrupt culture of the West . . . who wore 'too much' make-up, 'too short' a skirt . . . 'too low-cut' a shirt, who was 'too loose' in her relations with men, who laughed 'too loudly,' who smoked in public" (Najmabadi 1991, 65).[13] In the revolution, Googoosh's fame became a liability: she was charged with propagating corruption, her passport was revoked, and she and all other "immoral" and "immodest" women disappeared from postrevolutionary Iranian media and public life.

Revolution and regime change—those moments when public culture is swiftly dismantled, purged, and reassembled—ripen symbols of the old order for politically infused reappropriation, preservation, and historical memory practices (Berdahl 1999; Boym 2001; Bryant 2005). Following the revolution and the forcible absenting of the country's female singing stars, for many Iranians in the diaspora, Googoosh became an object of both nostalgia and political metaphorization. While revolutionaries understood the "West-stricken" woman as both a victim of modernity and an agent of the nation's corruption, Googoosh has in turn been reevaluated—and eventually reframed herself—as a victim of the revolution. Likewise, if the absence of Googoosh and her fellow female performers marked the moral purification of public culture in revolutionary Iran, that the same figures have become so important in the diaspora is an important indication of many Iranians' refusal to let go of the country's prerevolutionary history. This is perhaps especially true of Googoosh's age cohort, who grew up listening to her music and watching her film and television programs, but is also the case for their children, who have "inherited nostalgia" for the Pahlavi period from their parents (Maghbouleh 2010). For the diasporic generation that left Iran around the revolutionary period, and their offspring, the Iran coincident with the reign of Mohammad Reza Pahlavi (r. 1949–1979) represents the last version of Iran they truly knew or, in the case of the second generation (who often have had limited exposure to pre- or postrevolutionary Iran), the only Iran they understand in positive terms (Maghbouleh 2010; Naghibi 2016). The diasporic inclination to reimagine the nation and positively evaluate the Pahlavi past "in response to a deficient present world" of postrevolutionary Iran is a manifestation of the dynamic, creative, and politically provocative aspects of "nostalgia [as] critique" (Tannock 1995, 454).

Remediating the prerevolutionary films, television programs, and audio recordings of prerevolutionary female performers is a popular way of expressing nostalgia for the Pahlavi era. Googoosh has often been the subject of these efforts. Immediately following the revolution, Iranian expatriate media companies in Los Angeles compiled salvaged collections of Googoosh's films, music, and television clips. These and other prerevolutionary media were soon available internationally through emerging transnational distribution networks, which granted Iranians in the diaspora in North America and western Europe the opportunity to access this lost era via reassembled remains and grainy copies (Hemmasi 2011; Khosravi and Graham 1997). After the advent of the internet, collectors around the world uploaded rare images, newspaper clippings, recordings, and television footage in which Googoosh and other female stars featured, making the audiovisual fragments of popular 1960s and 1970s media available online and—through platforms like YouTube and Facebook—affording audiences the opportunity to comment on the past and present.

The diasporic impulse to reconstruct and renarrate Googoosh finds its most elaborate expression to date in Farhad Zamani's experimental documentary *Googoosh: Iran's Daughter* (Atash Productions, 2000). Zamani explores Googoosh's multiplicity through interviews with twenty fans, critics, colleagues, and associates as well as historians of Iran, and through carefully edited excerpts from her feature films and prerevolutionary songs. The production is broadly Iranian American rather than specific to Tehrangeles: Zamani was born in Iran and moved to New Jersey as a child following the revolution; the film was his MFA thesis project at Columbia University in New York City, and most of the interviews were recorded in Los Angeles and New York. However, the concentration of Googoosh's prerevolutionary colleagues and collaborators in Los Angeles—and the fact that Tehrangeles media companies had remastered, reproduced, and claimed ownership of Googoosh's prerevolutionary sound recordings and film and television footage—meant that the documentary was built on the people and products of the Tehrangeles cultural industries.[14] The film was released just before Googoosh's migration in 2000. While her recorded voice and image are ubiquitous, Googoosh is present in the film only in representation, through her contemporaries' memories, platitudes, and sly digs, and Zamani's painstaking selection of illustrative scenes and songs from her large corpus of films and audio recordings. Zamani's decision to highlight diverse individuals' reactions to Googoosh conveys a sense of her broad impact on Iranian society, albeit exclusively from the perspective of Iranians in the diaspora, by a director in the diaspora, and largely for a diasporic audience.[15]

One of Zamani's favorite sections of the film portrays Googoosh as Iran's abused daughter and Iran as an abused woman. Zamani first shows well-known footage of Ayatollah Ruhollah Khomeini in 1979 descending the steps of a plane when he returned from France to Tehran, followed by footage of the shah's coronation in 1967. We are then presented with a scene from one of Googoosh's first films, *Fereshteh farāri* (*Runaway Angel*, circa 1961), in which her real-life professional entertainer father, Saber Atashin, guides her through an acrobatic and contortion act for an audience of children.[16] Googoosh, who was around ten years old when the film was made, cuts an impressive yet pitiable figure: she is completely poised as her father places her on two stacked chairs that he then precariously balances on his chin, lifting her some eight feet in the air. It is impossible not to feel sorry for this painfully thin little girl whose father seems unconcerned with her safety and whose act relies so heavily on his daughter's talents. At different points in his film, Zamani repeats this scene to highlight Googoosh's victimization as emblematic of Iranian women's suffering generally. He also hoped to make a larger point about the father archetype in Iranian culture and politics. As he explained to me in an interview in 2004, the film sequentially shows "Khomeini, the shah, Googoosh's father, [and implicitly] all our fathers," a reverse-chronological progression that expressed his understanding of the roots of Iranians' political troubles regardless of gender: a history of abusive father-child relationships that is then writ large in Iranians' self-sabotaging acceptance (or selection) of abusive patriarchs as national leaders. The jump from the national to the familial and back again is illustrative of Zamani's thesis for the film and of the expatriate possession of Googoosh as "Iran's daughter." Her persona is particularly open to these kinds of intimate national metaphorizations owing to her unparalleled celebrity and her embodiment of the victimized child-woman role.

Zamani's film points to a central tension in Googoosh's relationship to twentieth-century Iran as both victim and beneficiary of the Pahlavi era. His interviews reveal that some remember Googoosh as representative of a new, modern Iranian woman who moved effortlessly between different song styles, hairstyles, and romantic partners, enjoying the new choices and mobility afforded her by the spirit of the times. This perception is complicated by the popular narratives surrounding Googoosh's early years, which suggest not that she controlled her career but that she was managed and manipulated by men: first her father, then a series of producers, songwriters, and directors, domineering and even abusive husbands, and, in Zamani's view, both the shah and Khomeini. Any perception of Googoosh's professional self-determination and personal self-expression is further undermined by the fact that she is not remembered as a woman in possession of her own voice in the agentive sense of the phrase. As was the case for most musiqi-ye pāp singers, Googoosh did not write her own lyrics. But while her male contemporaries Farhad Mehrad, Fereidun Foroughi, and Dariush gained audience respect for performing songs (written by others) containing political critiques, Googoosh did not acquire a reputation for choosing lyrics that correlated to her personal sentiments, even if she sang them with conviction. Indeed, some of the commentators in the documentary question whether she understood the political undertones of her prerevolutionary songs like "Āghā jān-e khub" ("My Dear, Wonderful Sir") and "Shekāyat" ("Complaint"), which some have interpreted as expressing support for Khomeini and criticism of life under the shah, respectively. Whether Googoosh was politically engaged or aware at the time of the revolution or later in her career is a question that has continued to haunt her.

It is precisely a narrative of lack of agency, both pre- and postrevolution, that has allowed Googoosh's personal and professional victimhood to map onto the tragic depictions of both Iranian women's postrevolutionary subjectification and the nation itself. Both narratives are intensely nostalgic and profoundly skeptical of postrevolutionary Iranian cultural and political developments. Zamani's tagline for his film is telling: "Her Silence Made Her the Voice of a Nation." This identifies Googoosh's lack of (agentive) voice as the key to her national political metaphorization. Zamani's film then illustrates his tagline's claim by showing how he and his diasporic interlocutors fill the emptiness of Googoosh's absence with their interpretations of her life, her choices, and her relationship to Iranian history. For comparison, note the contrast between Googoosh and Egyptian superstar Umm Kulthum, the most influential female vocalist of Middle Eastern modernity: Virginia Danielson's (1997) classic text on Umm Kulthum proclaims her "the voice of Egypt," while interviews from the related documentary reveal the tremendous and lasting influence that her vocal performances and political maneuvers had on Egyptians.[17] Laura Lohman's (2010) treatment of Umm Kulthum's exceptional "artistic agency" and her enduring impact on Egypt and the rest of the Arab world likewise emphasizes her power.[18] While Umm Kulthum's story is one of triumph, Googoosh's is tragic: she does not define history so much as she has been subjected to it.[19]

SINGING THE "NATION'S TEARS"

As of 2019, a woman's solo singing voice before mixed-sex audiences or on a recording is still not permitted in Iran, yet the present situation for female vocalists there is more complicated than the terms "ban" or "silence" might imply (Breyley 2013; DeBano 2005, 2009; Mozafari 2013; Nooshin 2011, 2018; Youssefzadeh 2004). For many years, women have been permitted to sing in vocal ensembles or duets with a male "co-singer" (*ham khān*), which act as an aural veil. Women-only concerts take place on a semiregular basis, concerts attended by mixed audiences are held in private spaces, women singers record in private studios, and social networks, music sellers, and the internet provide means for distribution. Today many women play musical instruments, and in greater numbers than before the revolution (Milanloo 2015). Recent reports also indicate that actresses have been singing onstage as part of theater productions, which can slip under the radar because they are performances and not recordings and therefore both more difficult to monitor and possible to change midstream. Yet the barriers to women's solo public singing qua singing when so many other musical activities have been justified indicate its symbolic import. Intimately related to the Islamic Republic's insistence on veiling, which obliges women to perform the national commitment to Islam, the insistence that the singing voice be obscured imbricates women's singing with consuming questions of national identity and its manifestation in moral comportment. This is where the moral and the political are very tightly interwoven, and where women's right to sing relates to the rights of safe public expression pursued by Iranians seeking full political participation.

The conceptual overlap between female singing or silencing and other quests for rights has made the postrevolutionary female vocalist into a potent trope, ripe for all kinds of exploration and deployment. Documentary films such as Ayat Najafi's *No Land's Song* (Chaz Productions, Hanfgarn & Ufer Film und TV Produktion, Torero Film, 2014) and Mojtaba Mirtah-masb's *Sedā-ye dovvom* (*Back Vocal*) (Kârâ Film Studio, 2004) explore the challenges female vocalists face in trying to stage concerts or record their music within Iran. One prominent art-world example is New York–based visual artist Shirin Neshat's two-screen video installation *Turbulent* (1998).

On one screen, the male singer Shoja Azari sings a song based on a Rumi love poem to a large, all-male crowd, a reference to public sex-segregated spaces. On the other screen, avant-garde vocalist Sussan Deyhim, veiled in black, sings a wordless, contorted vocalization before an empty room. More recently, the Iran-based visual artist Newsha Tavakolian has made a series of photographed portraits of (veiled) women vocalists living in Iran called *Listen* (2011); the images render the singers visible while highlighting their inaudibility. Tavakolian describes her series through a direct parallel between singing and political representation and participation: "For me a woman's voice represents a power that if you silence it, imbalances society, and makes everything deform. The project 'Listen' echoes the voices of these silenced women. I let Iranian women singers perform through my camera while the world has never heard them."[20] Again, this is not quite accurate: Iranian women singers can be heard in Iran in private settings, online, on satellite television, on homemade CDs, and outside of the country, but their strict limitation on moral-religious grounds continually reinscribes them as problematic and necessitating external control.[21]

The political metaphorization of the female singing voice was already in full swing when Googoosh decided to leave Iran and take on an outspoken role in her postmigration career. In 2000 Googoosh was granted a passport for the first time since the revolution. What sort of deal Googoosh might have made to acquire these permissions is the subject of many rumors; some have suggested that she "collaborated" with Iranian officials, a cardinal sin among many Iranians in the diaspora who are suspicious of anyone who appears to have a working relationship with state officials. Whatever the conditions, Googoosh took the opportunity to leave the country and never returned, landing first in Toronto and eventually making her way to Los Angeles, where she settled and restarted her career in exile.

Googoosh's first performances after her migration were wildly successful. She played the Air Canada Centre of Toronto, which reportedly sold out its fifteen thousand seats with tickets selling for $30 to $250 (and unofficially sold for much more). Her two concerts in Dubai in March 2001, timed to coincide with the Iranian New Year holiday, drew more than ten thousand Iranian residents to the popular Gulf destination.[22] Reports from the early concerts focused on both the star's and audiences' intense emotional experiences: articles in the Western press repeatedly described Googoosh and her fans weeping as they faced each other.[23] Likewise, a report by an Iranian attending Googoosh's concert in New York described "the tears shed by the dentist from Connecticut, the taxi driver from Queens, the teenager who left Iran when she was two and the grandmother who still speaks no English," demonstrating the breadth of Googoosh's fan base (Sabety 2001). Another report posted to Iranian.com states the powerful desire for "a sense of connectedness to the past" that drove expatriates to her concerts:

> It was as if [audiences] had made a pilgrimage to the concert to forget the last 23 years and step into a time machine back to an era when they had never heard of revolution, [the Islamic R]epublic, war, and exodus. This was true even among the young who were attending the concert. They would voice the same nostalgia even though many had not even been born in Googoosh's prime years. The young fans reflected a sense of awe and regret that they had probably picked up from their parents. In effect, many Iranians saw in Googoosh's re-emergence a connection with a time (in contrast to their present discontent) which presented content[ment] and security.[24]

Videos of these early concerts reveal that Googoosh's voice remained true to her prerevolutionary sound, touched by age but still agile and forceful, suggesting years of vocal maintenance during her extended "silence."

In her very first press conference in Toronto in 2000, Googoosh addressed a crowd of reporters in Persian, answering questions about her experiences during and following the revolution, the conditions of her emergence, and her artistic intentions now that she was finally back onstage. On the last point, she declared, "I shall sing my old songs because these are full of memories both for myself and for those who lived with my songs. . . . But . . . over these past twenty years, I have found poems that have more specific and profound meanings [than my past work]."[25] Her new album, titled *Zartosht* (*Zoroaster*, 2000), presented an unmistakably sober political agenda and vocalized subtle critique of the Islamic Republic. The album cover contributes to this perception: over a black background, Googoosh regards the camera somberly, a black "birdcage"-style netted veil covering most of her face, recalling both mourning and captivity. As advertised, a number of the new songs on this album distinguished themselves from her prerevolutionary romantic repertoire by subtly but unmistakably referring to the Iranian homeland as a barren garden in "Khāk-e asir" ("Captive Land") and as a "palm [tree] without bird or flower" in "Zartosht" ("Zoroaster"). Later in the press conference mentioned above, Googoosh described herself as lacking a "political mind-set" at the time of the revolution and suggested that the ensuing decades had made her a wiser, politically savvier woman who now intended to express herself, perhaps for the first time in her professional life. The new album's title song questioned the Islamic pro-hibition on women's singing by recalling a mythological pre-Islamic history in which music was sacred:

If I sing, it is a crime
If I don't sing, it is a crime
In the body of this good, green kingdom
Which is older than history
When could singing have become a sin
When Zoroaster planted this earth with hymns?

Singing these lines in her first concert in Toronto in front of a set resem-bling the ruins of the pre-Islamic city Persepolis solidified her symbolic invocation of ancient Iran and drew on a long-standing tactic of disasso-ciating Iran from Islam (and particularly clerical political influence) that extends throughout Iranian modernity (Tavakoli-Targhi 2001).[26] This same song also aided the pop star's transition into exile and the political meta-phorization of Googoosh's (female) voice as a medium for communicating the suffering and desires of the Iranian people as a whole:

I who became a woman with you, oh women
I will loan my voice (sedāyam) to history
And your cries (faryād), oh young men and women
Oh sacrificed land
Grant me permission
To sing your tears (geryat rā man bekhānam)

Though written while she was still in Iran, this and other early songs antici-pate her departure from Iran and performances before diasporic audiences as they draw on established tropes of voice and representation while apply-ing them to a most appropriate medium: Googoosh herself. She presents herself as having performed a metaphorical and literal transformation from a silenced to a vocal woman who not only sings for herself but also "loan[s] [her] voice to history" and projects the perspectives of less audible others. Googoosh thereby adds another layer to her polysemous character: the si-lenced songbird who escapes her cage to find freedom and lift her voice to the skies.

Googoosh's return to the limelight also meant that her newly audible opinions and perspectives came under scrutiny. As an example, during the Toronto press conference in 2000, Googoosh was asked whether the Ira-

FIGURE 4.1 Googoosh appears as if trapped or in mourning on the cover of *Zartosht* (*Zoroaster*; Kia Entertainment, 2000), her first album after twenty-one years of silence following the revolution.

nian government would allow her to return to Iran and sing. "I don't have that information," she replied, "but I do have hope that this could happen one day, because our revolution is moving towards democracy, and I am very optimistic about the future." Tehrangeles-based lyricist Zoya Zakarian remembers that Googoosh's statements caused controversy and even anger in the Los Angeles music industry. Zakarian, who had worked with Googoosh and many other musiqi-ye pāp stars in Iran and then in Los Angeles after the revolution, was at the time the host of a call-in television program in Los Angeles. She had contributed an interview to Zamani's film as a former collaborator and friend of Googoosh's, and then aired the documentary on her program. When I asked about audiences' responses to Zamani's film, Zakarian said she felt reactions were colored by how fans felt about Googoosh now that she had emerged and started articulating her perspectives. "Some would love her no matter what she did or said," she commented, "but others were angry that she didn't come out of Iran saying [the slogan] 'Down with the Islamic Republic.'" Because so many Tehrangeles media and music producers harbor deep antipathy toward the postrevolutionary government, Googoosh's statements were hard to bear; some questioned whether she might be maintaining hidden ties to government affiliates. When Googoosh appeared in the flesh from Iran after twenty years of silence, she was unrulier than she had been as a mute figure to whom meanings could be imputed.

Most of Googoosh's new postmigration repertoire has stuck to sentimental or romantic midtempo pop, but she has also performed pieces that further develop the link between her exceptional celebrity, the Pahlavi past, and her national symbolism. These themes marked her first foray into the Tehrangeles culture industries: a song of epic proportions called "QQ Bang Bang" (Taraneh Enterprises, 2003). In terms of ambition and scope, this collaboration between Googoosh, Zakarian, and songwriter Mehrdad Asemani was much grander than typical Tehrangeles productions. Over the song's ten minutes, Googoosh recites and sings over sixty lines of rhyming lyrics chronicling the hopes of a generation that came of age under Mohammad Reza Pahlavi, experienced a political awakening in the 1970s, and was disillusioned and displaced following the revolution. Everything about the production is on a grand scale: in addition to the length of the poem and song, the accompanying Los Angeles Philharmonic orchestra plays multiple melodic themes and modulations underscoring the shifting narrative, while the video includes a cast of eighteen credited individuals acting out the various scenarios described, along with 360-degree shots of Googoosh on a craggy cliff overlooking the ocean, and numerous excerpts from 1970s Iranian feature films—including footage of Googoosh herself—to conjure the prerevolutionary past. Zakarian's lengthy poem, discussed in detail by Nasrin Rahimieh (2016), references many cultural hallmarks of the eras evoked and conveys a complicated ambivalence regarding the path to the revolution as well as its outcome. Asemani's highly varied composition sets each of the poem's stanzas to a distinct theme. The packaging is also unusually elaborate for a Los Angeles Iranian production. Tehrangeles label Taraneh Enterprises released "QQ Bang Bang" in an instrumental version, and as a video along with a version subtitled in English and scenes from the making of the video, including hair-raising footage of a cameraman hanging out of a helicopter to get an aerial shot of the singer.[27] Also included are a booklet of lyrics and an autographed picture postcard of Googoosh with a handwritten line employing the political voice: "In the hope of singing the song of freedom in Iran together" (see Hemmasi 2017a; Rahimieh 2016, 52).

For all these distinctive features, the song is in step with the majority of popular music produced in the expatriate music industry, in which prerevolutionary Iran is nostalgically recalled and postrevolutionary Iran is either absent or portrayed as in a state of ruin. The song narrates the story of Googoosh's (and most of the song's cocreators') generation, from

FIGURE 4.2 A page from the lyrics booklet accompanying the DVD for *QQ Bang Bang* contrasts the somber Googoosh of 2003 with a prerevolutionary image of a smiling Googoosh, blissfully ignorant of the revolution to come. *QQ Bang Bang*, Taraneh Records, 2003.

the heady, hopeful days of their youth to the "winter" of revolution and, ultimately, the "false paradise" of exile. As Zakarian told me in 2007, the title "QQ Bang Bang" represents children making the sounds of gunshots; she intended the refrain to invoke a cycle of violence running throughout Iranian history. The song also indexes collective memory, signaled in the refrain "Brother, do you remember?" and its exclusive use of first-person plural pronouns. The singer asks listeners if they remember their ("our") childhood games of "cowboys and Indians" inspired by the Western film genre, outings to the movies as teenagers, and the "stolen kisses" of their adolescence when "Western stars" like Elvis Presley and James Dean were their "guiding lights." The next verses introduce the growing polarization and ideological experimentation preceding the revolution, in which some were "intoxicated with [Friedrich] Engels" while others "followed Buddha," and the "confusion" (*sargijeh*) of "leftist poets in the mosques / drunken puritans in the bars." The revolution tragically marks the era's conclusion, an innocent childhood game suddenly transformed into "real guns" as the lyrics ask listeners to observe how history "repeats itself." Exile does not offer a new beginning or new hope but the continuation of violence: in this "false paradise," "two immigrant kids" play with toy guns hooked up to a video game, shooting at a screen. Googoosh repeats the sounds of gunshots into the fade-out: "QQ bang bang . . . one more time—QQ bang bang . . ."

Like Zamani's experimental documentary, the song and video "QQ Bang Bang" is a meditation on Googoosh's iconic and indexical relationships to prerevolutionary Iran, interweaving her biography, cinematic portrayals, and a particular version of national history whose glory days end with the revolution.[28] The viewer is invited to remember "our youth" through Googoosh, who is a part of the generation whose experience the song depicts, and whose films, television programs, and songs embodied and propagated important aspects of the era's aspirations. The booklet containing the lyrics repeats this theme: each section of the poem is titled with an age ("At Seven Years Old") and features a photograph of Googoosh as background to the relevant lines of the poem. Each page of prerevolutionary stanzas also includes images of a semitransparent, ghostlike Googoosh from the period under discussion, a literal superimposition of her persona onto history. Yet unlike Zakarian and many others involved in the Los Angeles music industry who left Iran in the years immediately surrounding the revolution and have never or rarely returned, Googoosh's life story includes twenty years living in the Islamic Republic and, at least in her first statements after leaving Iran, an optimism about postrevolutionary Iran that is altogether missing from "QQ Bang Bang." She did not flee Iran under duress, nor did she arrive in the diaspora destitute and under pressure to perform shesh-o-hasht dance songs at weddings. Instead, she arrived in the diaspora with great fanfare, full stadiums of paying concertgoers, a sensational mainstream press reception, and tens of thousands of fans who eagerly embraced her. Within the song and its collective address, therefore, she is not relating her own biography but voicing the perspectives and experiences of others in the diaspora with whom she has worked and, perhaps, of imagined diaspora audiences to whom she hoped to appeal.

As much as "QQ Bang Bang" is a "Googoosh vehicle" that trades on resonances between the star and the prerevolutionary era, Googoosh's persona also overwhelms the contributions and perspectives of those who originated the content she animates in performance. The lyrics to "QQ Bang Bang" predate Googoosh's arrival in Los Angeles. Lyricist Zakarian told me in 2007 that she "needed to write [the lyrics] for [her]self," yet, once produced, the poem became associated with Googoosh. During my telephone call with Zakarian in 2016, she questioned whether I or other scholars would have paid any attention to her poem had it not been sung by this most influential of Iranian pop celebrities. She also noted that neither I nor others had grasped what was for her the central point of the song: that "Iranian intellectuals, confused and not so knowledgeable," pursued Islam, Eastern philosophy, and socialism without fully understanding them. Unlike "European intellectuals, who tried to enlighten their people, Iranian intellectuals only wanted people to follow them. Well, they were successful. What's the result?" she asked, rhetorically suggesting that the role-playing of the revolution had gone awry. Meanwhile, composer Mehrdad Asemani, who is too young to remember most of the events depicted in the lyrics, noted that it was his experience fighting at the front of the Iran-Iraq War in the 1980s that gave him the emotional reservoir needed to write the song.[29] While the very nature of celebrity is its intense focus on the star to the exclusion of the behind-the-scenes work and workers who make a star what she or he appears, it is also ironic that Googoosh, whose postrevolutionary silencing has been so critical to her fame, may have also occluded her collaborators with her larger-than-life presence.

PERFORMING SILENCE

The songbird would find new obstacles in Tehrangeles, particularly in the industry's notorious professional rivalries, business disputes, and litigiousness. Like most singers in Tehrangeles, Googoosh has worked with many artistic and business partners over the years, switching among them numerous times over the course of her postmigration career. Not infrequently, the dissolution of professional and other collaborative relationships becomes fodder for expatriate television and media as different parties present their grudges and discontents for transnational audiences. Googoosh's participation in these public scraps is notable because of how she has used metaphors of voice and silence in relation to her business disputes.

Googoosh performed a new set of political allegiances amid a publicized professional conflict in 2004. Googoosh had a contract dispute with Nederlander concert production company and Tehrangeles media entrepreneurs Alireza Amir Ghassemi and Masoud Jamali. In response, Nederlander, Amir Ghassemi, and Jamali filed a court injunction to prevent the vocalist from singing at a large December 25, 2004, concert in Las Vegas. This was a potential public relations disaster: Googoosh's inability to perform was announced before the concert but after many audience members had booked and paid for their concert and plane tickets. Leading up to and after the fateful concert, Googoosh took steps to present herself in a sympathetic light. In an advertisement preceding the concert, Googoosh asked her television audience, "Who among you wishes that I not sing—either at home nor in exile? Say to those nobodies (*hichkasān*) that I will sing for my people until my last breath!"[30] Deploying the language of silencing that connected her victimization in Iran with her mistreatment in the diaspora, Googoosh transformed a contractual dispute into the most recent battle in her lifelong struggle to sing "for her people." During the ill-fated concert itself, Googoosh performed her silence from a seat in the crowd. While her then-partner Asemani sang the concert program in her place, a camera filming the event focused on Googoosh's smiling face, the action on-stage, and her adoring fans, many of whom were waving photographs of her as they danced and sang along with Asemani. The concert concluded with a surprise: Googoosh took to the stage, held up a prerevolutionary flag, cloaked herself in it, and wept, all while the prerevolutionary patriotic anthem "Ey Iran" ("Oh Iran") played and the audience sang along. Placing the flag around her shoulders like a shield, Googoosh added another layer to her victimization and national metaphorization: to attack her was to attack Iran itself; to silence her was to silence Iran.

Why did Googoosh choose this moment to embrace the prerevolutionary flag, the quintessential symbol of the Pahlavi era but also of Tehrangeles's counterstate nationalism? Googoosh was asked just this question in 2005 by the sympathetic Tehrangeles journalist Homa Ehsan. With the prerevolutionary flag perched above them on the television sound stage, Ehsan delicately addressed Googoosh's patriotic gesture during the 2004 Las Vegas concert while also mentioning that some audience members doubted the sincerity of her actions. Would she explain why she had chosen this moment to identify herself with this potent political symbol? Googoosh answered slowly, her speech full of pauses: "For a very long time I have wanted to find some way of proclaiming our nation's identity (*hovveiyat-e melli-mun o faryād bezanam*). But I never found the right time or right place. On the 25th of December, we [Googoosh and her collaborators] decided that—because the flag bearing the lion and sun is a symbol of our national identity—we thought that in that concert, I could employ the flag to shout (*faryād*) this identity in a loud voice." Ehsan replied that people had said that Googoosh had to "resort" (*motevasel*) to using the flag because she had had so many problems with the concert. Googoosh denied this and asserted the sincerity of the gesture, saying that it was preplanned. The interview was then interrupted by a split-second black screen, the usually hidden work of editing suddenly visible, highlighting the staged nature of the conversation. After this almost imperceptible break, Googoosh concluded with a dramatically delivered declaration, emotionally hesitating between phrases and skillfully transitioning to a discussion of her soon-to-be-released nationalist song about the Persian Gulf: "My identity is Iranian [pause], my identity [pause] is the flag bearing the lion and sun; my identity [she looks into the camera and points her finger to emphasize] is the Persian Gulf (*khalij-e fārs*)."[31] Ehsan picked up the cue and moved the conversation to a discussion of Googoosh's forthcoming duet with Asemani. This song, "Shenāsnāmeh-ye man" ("My Birth Certificate"), supports the retention of the name "Persian Gulf" over the encroaching popularity of "Arabian Gulf" among Westerners and Arabs, a hot topic in diasporic debates for several years in the 1990s and 2000s.[32]

Linking legally mandated abstention from singing, metaphors of voice, political expression, and contested national identity into a single performative gesture, Googoosh took the moment to tell a new narrative about herself: "for a long time" she had wanted to display her allegiance to the prerevolutionary flag, the one that symbolized the true Iran. In the context of the Southern Californian Iranian diaspora, where affection for the Pahlavi era and animosity toward the Islamic Republic of Iran are givens, embracing the prerevolutionary flag is utterly unremarkable. Likewise, Googoosh's reference to the Persian Gulf was perhaps less a statement of bold opinion and more an iteration of the dominant trends in a diasporic nationalism that is hostile to Arab influence and zealously defends the nation against any perceived slights to the region's "Persian" past. Googoosh's explanation links the prerevolutionary flag with "our national identity"—the "our" here might be all Iranians everywhere, or it might be the diasporic public to which she, Ehsan, and many of their viewers belong. In any case, the identification is more with diasporic nationalism and participation in Tehrangeles political currents than a transcendent Iranian nation.

Throughout this extended episode, Googoosh showed herself to be a skillful performer, even when prevented from singing. My decision to call Googoosh a "performer" is not to question her intentions or assert a disconnect between her external actions and internal beliefs—intentions to which I would never presume to have access. Rather, within the context of postrevolutionary expatriate media and the tropes of victimization and national metaphorization to which Googoosh has been subjected, she can draw on an established repertoire of tropes relating to voice and nation and employ them in the service of her own projects. One of these is maintaining the sympathies of her diasporic audiences and recruiting them to her cause. In the Las Vegas concert, they sang for her as she had sung for them, and the people and Googoosh became one.

BECOMING "MOTHER IRAN"

The 2009 protests in Iran following the contested reelection of President Mahmoud Ahmadinejad were deeply felt in the diaspora. In cities worldwide, Iranians took to the streets to shout slogans, sing songs, and express their support for the protesters and deride the state's violent response. Los Angeles was no exception. For several days in June 2009, Iranians protested in front of the Los Angeles Federal Building on Wilshire Boulevard. Some Tehrangeles artists also participated in the demonstrations, among them Shohreh Solati, one of Googoosh's prerevolutionary peers who had moved from Iran to Los Angeles decades earlier. Around this time, Solati phoned Tehrangeles media personality Shahram Homayun's live satellite television broadcast. Her aim was to discuss the demonstrations and to call out prominent expatriate musicians who did not make an appearance at the protests—especially Googoosh. During her nine-minute-long diatribe, Solati became hoarse and eventually broke down in tears:

> Madame Googoosh, you stay sitting in your house. . . . In our country, children are [dying]. Can't you see? And you're going to wait to sing an anthem (*sorud*)? You're going to wait to send a message to the Iranian people? . . . Shame on you! [People are going to say] Shohreh is jealous. Not at all. We know you are a wonderful singer. . . . We grew up with you. I remember you as a child, I had your pictures in my room as a child. This isn't right! Get up, come out with your people, most importantly so that the people inside Iran can see you! You know what you can do, you know what you can do with a sorud! . . . You can bring about a revolution! . . . Googoosh is like a child of Iran (*mesl-e bacheh-ye Iran-e*), we grew up with her, she is a symbol of Iran. [She begins to sob.] Dariush, Googoosh—where are you? Your concert halls are full! [But y]ou don't even release a statement! You are the *heart* of the people of Iran![33]

Solati's impassioned accusation is another example of the very public intradiasporic feuds that are integral to Tehrangeles television. But it is more interesting for its clear articulation of expatriate contestation over their political responses and responsibilities in relation to "the Iranian people" (*mellat-e Iran*, translatable as both "the Iranian people" and "the Iranian nation"). As she acknowledges Googoosh's superior fame and talents, Solati also calls attention to Googoosh's unique national symbolism. While Solati is also a prerevolutionary female vocalist whose career in Iran ended with the revolution, she is not eligible to perform the same role. That is Googoosh's position, and with this privilege, Solati insists, comes the responsibility to act.

Solati needed to wait only a few weeks for the icon to offer herself once more as a representative of the voiceless within Iran. In July 2009 Googoosh joined a group of activists in a three-day hunger strike to draw attention to the plight of individuals killed or believed to be imprisoned in Iran for their participation in the 2009 protests. In a speech delivered in front of the United Nations building in New York City, she declared that her intention was to "be the voice of the suffering, bereaved, and concerned mothers" whose children had been harmed or had perished in their political quests. She had come to "be the voice of the intellectuals, writers, artists, and sexual, ethnic, and religious minorities" who, "like me, have been forced into silence." She had come "to send Iranians' grievances to the ears of the world," because "people are looking to us Iranians outside of the country to be the voice of those within the country."[34]

Later that year, she went even further by enacting the role of the Motherland in "Man hamun Iranam" ("I Am Iran Itself"), discussed in the opening of this chapter. The song lyrics depict the Motherland ruined (*virān*) at the hands of her ostensible stewards and protectors—implicitly, the Islamic state. Singing in the first person, Googoosh expresses the nation's plight while pleading with her dispersed "children" to come to her aid:

> *When you all left, I cried*
> *But you promised you would be back*
> *That was the only hope I had*
> *You promised, so I waited with sleepless eyes*
> *My dearest children, what happened to our promise*
> *To see each other again?*

"Man hamun Iranam" draws on a preexisting "matriotic" (as opposed to "patriotic") trope that first became prominent in secular Iranian counterofficial nationalist discourse and imagery in the late nineteenth and early twentieth centuries (Amin 2001; Kashani-Sabet 2011; Kia, Najmabadi, and Shakhsari 2009; Najmabadi 1997, 2005; Tavakoli-Targhi 2000, 2001).

This discourse, which appeared in periodicals, poetry, cartoons, and other popular genres, depicted a helpless, forsaken Motherland—the *mām-e vatan*—who calls to her wayward citizen-children to defend her from domestic threats and foreign incursions. Tracing the trope's relation to early twentieth-century political transformations, historian Mohamad Tavakoli-Targhi has argued that imagining Iran as a woman "symbolically eliminated" the official depiction of the nation as "the home headed by the crowned father" while it also contributed to "the development of a public sphere and popular sovereignty . . . [and] the participation of the 'nation's children' (both male and female) in determining the future of the 'motherland'" (2001, 218).[35] However, while the Motherland may be a female figure of self-determination, here Iran "herself" is portrayed as enfeebled, under attack, and requiring her guardians' intervention. Googoosh's transformation into Mother Iran reinscribes her as victim as it uses victimhood to invigorate her audiences' protective impulses.

"Man hamun Iranam" represents an expression of contemporary expatriate nationalism as much as the revival of a historically relevant national trope, and as such marks Googoosh's further association with the diaspora. The principal tragedy the song describes is the Motherland's abandonment by those who have emigrated—if they had kept their promise to visit Iran and were responsive to her needs, perhaps she would not suffer so. Performed by Googoosh in exile, the song imagines Iranian migrants as more crucial to the nation than its "faithful" citizen-children who stayed in Iran. In this sense, the song reads as migrant self-aggrandizement or a reassurance of relevance to the Iranian nation. At the same time, the song is rather ironic and even hypocritical: it would not be unreasonable to view Googoosh as a deserter who left the country to its fate—precisely the kind of irresponsible "child" the song decries—while in the space of the song, she not only audaciously claims to represent the homeland but calls on other Iranians in the diaspora to engage.[36] The video, directed by Los Angeles–based expatriate Sirous Kerdouni, further manifests this tension. In some scenes, Googoosh addresses the camera plaintively as Mother Iran, while in others she is a distant observer of Iranians' suffering: she sits alone in a movie theater gazing sadly upon a map of the Persian Empire, then strolls through an empty art gallery hung with photographs of bloodied protesters in Tehran's streets and a veiled woman buried up to her neck as if being stoned to death. As the Motherland, Googoosh is imperiled, but as Googoosh "herself," she is safe from physical harm. To refer back to one of the chapter's opening questions—"which Iran" and "whose Iran" Googoosh represents—the an-

FIGURE 4.3 Googoosh portraying the anguished Motherland in the video for "Man hamun Iranam" ("I Am Iran Itself"). Screen grab from "Man Hamoon Iranam," YouTube video, posted by Googoosh, June 22, 2009, https://youtu.be/9cBwT3H9Wlg.

swer is, here, the imagined Iran of migrants materialized in exile through performance and transnational media. In this intramigrant dialogue, Iranians within Iran hardly figure at all.

"Man hamun Iranam" marked Googoosh's transformation into a new iteration of the female national icon. Iran's silenced, mistreated daughter became the Motherland herself, her voice echoing back from exile. This feminine national symbolism points to an extensive array of current and historical alternative nationalisms that build on past models while asserting difference in the diaspora. Most audaciously, Googoosh sings the demanding words of the Motherland, using her female voice, the very musical medium most restricted in Iran.

Audience reactions to Googoosh since her reemergence have been very mixed. In my survey of roughly six hundred comments responding to the "Man hamun Iranam" video on YouTube written over the past nine years, certain patterns emerge. Most of her supporters professed their love for the singer and her voice—"May you live long, beloved lady—we all love you!"[37] Others linked her song to political aims: "God bless you, Googoosh! The song moved me and I hope it sends shivers down the back of the regime . . ." and "Thank you, my dear Googoosh. In hopes of Iran's freedom from this fascist Islamic regime of Mullahs . . ."[38] Others invoke a conservative, anti-Islam, anti-Arab nationalist strain common in the diaspora: "Our Iran has not failed in the past 30 years [since the revolution] nor in the 1400 plus years ago when these barbarians [Arab Muslim invaders] fell upon our heads with swords . . . ! Does this mean there is hope? Can this eternal lion of ours, without its sword and radiant sun of freedom, return . . . ?"[39] Googoosh's detractors were just as strident and reached back to many years' worth of political intrigue and alliances for evidence of Googoosh's shrewdness and insincerity: "She never stood up for her Iranian brothers and sisters before. . . . When Googoosh arrived in the US, she refused to comment on the dictatorship a few years ago, and we were all really pissed off. . . . It's too late . . ."[40] Another commenter referred to the Las Vegas flag incident as an indication of Googoosh's untrustworthiness: "Get out of here, Ms. Googoosh. What you say doesn't carry any weight anymore (*hanā-ye shomā digeh rangi nadārad* [literally, "your henna has lost its color"]). First you came out on stage with the pre-revolutionary flag on you and selling $1000 concert tickets, and now . . . you come and remember Iran."[41] For all their vulgarity and unsubstantiated allegations, these comments demonstrate the circulation of tropes and repeated claims growing out of the long popular memory surrounding Googoosh. The soft glow of nostalgia is only one aspect of the memories surrounding this icon. A catalog of sins interpreted through a polarized postrevolutionary history is another unshakeable aura trailing her.

In 2010 Googoosh embarked on an even more ambitious venture that transported her well-established representational tropes from Tehrangeles and the medium of song to reality television in Great Britain. In partnership with the London-based Iranian satellite television channel Manoto 1, she became the namesake and judge of a talent competition called *Googoosh Music Academy*, in which the star provided young men and women with motherly guidance (and publicity) to help them become professional pop vocalists.[42] The televised talent show form was important at this moment for its political affordances as "democratainment" (Hartley 2004 in Meizel 2010) that blurred "distinctions between entertainment and politics" and was "grounded in an ideal of 'free and fair elections.'" One memorable participant in the first season was Forugh, a slight twenty-five-year-old graphic design student with a pixie haircut who grew up in Iran and was living in Sweden. In the series's very first episode, Forugh described the challenges she faced as a young girl who loved to sing: "Because women's singing is prohibited in Iran, I couldn't sing much [there]. And because my voice is loud, I had to find some way to stifle it. One way I found to do this was to put a pillow in front of my face to absorb the sound or to sing in the bathroom. It was hard, but I kept at it." As Forugh continued, she explained her participation in the competition in obviously political terms: "Really, [the Googoosh Music Academy] is the opposite of the frustrations of mass suf-

FIGURE 4.4 Forugh, a contestant on the first season
of the television talent competition *Googoosh Music
Academy*, performs for Googoosh and the other judges.
Screen grab from "Googoosh Music Academy EII,P3,"
YouTube video, posted by manototv, November 12, 2010,
https://youtu.be/R5dhdZ_G3yw.

focation (*khofaqān*) in Iran, especially for women who want to sing. So [participating in this competition] is a really good feeling!"[43]

Forugh's comments follow the mold of Googoosh's own prior utterances by closely linking limits on her singing voice with the "mass suffocation" of Iranians within the country. *Googoosh Music Academy* is presented as an antidote, a much-needed avenue for the public expression of what otherwise should be private—in the bathroom—or stifled, as by the pillow. Forugh lauded Googoosh and her expatriate collaborators for creating opportunities for the public expression of their voices, and for stepping in where the state had failed them. While it is possible that Forugh came up with this statement on her own and that it accurately represents her feelings, it is also remarkably consonant with the larger claim of expatriate media, Tehrangeles song, and Googoosh's postmigration sung and spoken rhetoric. It falls neatly in line with the performance of voice.

In the final season of *Googoosh Music Academy* in 2013, the competition was won by Ermia, a young woman who grew up in Iran and lived in Germany, and who wore the veil out of religious observance (Hemmasi 2017c). Ermia was precisely the opposite kind of woman Iranians would expect to appear on a program with the "monarchist counterrevolutionary" Googoosh (as the conservative press sometimes characterizes her), much less competently sing pop songs in public. In the firestorm of reactions that swept across transnational Iranian media, blogs, and conversations in the

FIGURE 4.5 Googoosh gives Forugh comments on her Music Academy performance. Screen grab from "Googoosh Music Academy E11,P3," YouTube video, posted by manototv, November 12, 2010, https://youtu .be/R5dhdZ_G3yw.

wake of her win, Ermia's combination of solo pop singing and Muslim piety was treated, on the one hand, as bizarre and anomalous and, on the other hand, as potentially representative of a new generation of Iranian women for whom public singing and veiling are not mutually exclusive (see Hemmasi 2017c). It was profoundly ironic that Googoosh—the embodiment of the "Western doll" of the Pahlavi regime—would appear to support and nurture a veiled woman like Ermia, and yet Ermia's declarations of her long-standing affection for Googoosh's music indicated that reductionist binaries of religious versus secular, or modest versus corrupt, fell short in defining either woman—or their relationship to one another. Indeed, Googoosh's star power, and the regular repetition of young contestants seeking her attention, advice, and approval, was one of the foundations of *Googoosh Music Academy*, which brought together first- and second-generation Iranian youth in the diaspora in a celebration of pop music's pleasures and Googoosh fandom. Within the context of the program, loving Googoosh and wanting to be a pop star like her was a fragile strand of connective filament holding the diaspora together.

WHO IS GOOGOOSH?

Celebrities like Googoosh present a paradox in their simultaneous intimacy and publicity, a tension that results in fans feeling as if they know the star while hungering for more behind-the-scenes information to fill in the unavoidable gaps. A lifelong celebrity with a huge corpus of songs and films, Googoosh has lived much of her life in the public eye and has been a part of the lives of millions of Iranian listeners. Yet in spite of her omnipresence, the "real Googoosh" is out of reach, the subject of repeated rumors, conjecture, and conspiracy theories. Googoosh's voice is a privileged medium, and its sounded form indexes her unique identity, but it is not necessarily the vehicle of authentic, unmediated self-expression. In one-on-one interviews, she keeps to well-worn stories and anecdotes and reveals little of herself beyond her larger-than-life onstage and on-screen performances. Her 2004 interview with journalist Ehsan opened with just such an exchange: "Multiple generations of the nation have lived their lives with Googoosh. Fell in love, wept, laughed, had a good time (*shādmāni kardeh*), danced. They were silent with Googoosh, they cried out with Googoosh (*faryād zadeh*). But there's never been the chance for people to really know Googoosh. Tonight, [she] has given me the chance. . . . I know that all of you want to know, who is Googoosh. I will ask her. Googoosh dear, who is Googoosh?" Googoosh sighed. "Who is Googoosh . . ." she repeated and then paused, considering the question. "An artist. I think that Googoosh is clay (*khamir*) that takes shape onstage and comes out cemented as an artist. I am giving this opinion of Googoosh from the perspective of Faegheh Atashin."[44] Contrasting her given name with her lifelong stage name, the diva presented herself as a bifurcated being. The woman audiences see and hear onstage and on-screen has an undisclosed relationship to the being who coexists with Googoosh.

I understand Googoosh's response as both evasive and straight to the point: her persona is a substance that she is uniquely skilled at reshaping as needed. Throughout her life, this malleability has afforded her the ability to be many things to many people: an aspirational model of modern femininity, a pitiful child, a fashion plate, a sex symbol, a silenced woman, a freed woman, a counterrevolutionary, a corruptor, an entertainer whose sold-out performances attest to her continuing appeal, and "Iran herself." In the politically contentious landscape of Iranian expatriate media, performing a national voice has been one of her most recurrent roles. Not everyone accepts Googoosh's or her protégés' performances of the national voice, but she has been incontrovertibly successful in eliciting impassioned reactions from across the Iranian political spectrum.

It has been suggested to me by fans and those who know her personally that Googoosh is less interested in politics than relevance, and that to be relevant in the Iranian mediascape, one must be political. As she and her collaborators have incorporated the metaphorical language of voice, speech, and song into her sung performances to "sing the nation's tears" in "Zartosht," to sing the nation itself in "Man hamun Iranam," and, in her speech at the United Nations, to use her voice to "send the voices of Iranians . . . to the world's ears," they have linked voice, performance, and now political commitment to Googoosh's persona. These performances have generated controversy in the diaspora, where they touch on sensitive topics, particularly who has the right to perform the nation and who is most politically committed. Even if Googoosh's commitments to politics may be constructions or her preferred shape in the present moment, we need not therefore dismiss them as artificial, for "in more complex readings, the constructed is coterminous with the 'real'" (D. Taylor 2003, 8). Rather than cast her performances as antithetical to the authentic, we can also see Googoosh's silences and voice(s) alike as generating real meaning—however unstable and contested—for multiple generations of Iranians.

A NATION
IN RECOVERY

In the previous chapter, Tehrangeles pop singer Shohreh
Solati called Googoosh out on a television program, asking why she had not yet released a statement or song in support of the 2009 popular uprisings in Iran. If Googoosh would
make this gesture, Solati stated, she could "bring about a revolution"
in Iran. Solati's statement could be construed as sarcastic, but it also
links to a larger discourse among expatriate musical celebrities and satellite television producers about their potential to influence Iranian politics
from afar. Zia Atabay, for example, a prerevolutionary pop singer who began an expatriate television station in Los Angeles called National Iranian Television (NITV), claims to have successfully motivated his
Iran-based viewers to converge in public spaces and protest the
Islamic state.[1]

Not everyone buys these claims either in the diaspora
or in Iran. As one young Iranian man who had lived
in the United States since he was a child put it to
me, when he hears these kinds of exhortations

to protest by Iranians in Southern California, "I want to tell [satellite TV hosts], 'Go ahead and yell about how Iranians should rebel in the streets while you are in your air-conditioned TV studio in LA with your Benz parked outside! Why don't *you* go back and fight?'" Audiences are aware that though expatriate cultural figures assert their commitment to the nation while complaining bitterly of the pain of their separation from Iran, their separation also affords them the freedom to say and do whatever they wish (see also Alexanian 2009, 65–66).

And yet history shows that Iranian exiles have in fact been politically effective in their homeland. The paradigmatic example in Iranian history, and perhaps the world, is Ayatollah Ruhollah Khomeini's media-enabled reach into Iran from exile in France. Working with local supporters and networks within Iran, Khomeini and his allies recorded his revolutionary sermons onto cassette tapes, reproduced them in France and Iran, and disseminated them throughout the country. This "small medium" was crucial to inspiring and mobilizing Shiite revolutionaries and their sympathizers (Sreberny-Mohammadi and Mohammadi 1994). This incredible political success may be one of the reasons that the Islamic Republic of Iran and Tehrangeles media producers both take expatriate media activities so seriously.[2] But mere media distribution was not enough to catalyze broad-based change. Khomeini's charisma also played a role in motivating individuals to join and support revolution and then sustain the revolutionary state (see Byrd 2011; Sreberny-Mohammadi and Mohammadi 1994). The passion Khomeini inspired in his followers was unlike that surrounding any other modern cleric before or since. His devotees gave him heroic titles including the "savior of generations," "crusher of oppressors," "humbler of Satan," and "sole hope of the downtrodden." His charisma extended into death: millions of people attended his funeral, and in the chaos of his burial ten thousand were injured and eight trampled to death. On the fortieth-day commemoration of his death, another thirty thousand were injured (Sanasarian 1995, 189). Today several expatriates compete for the role of long-distance liberator of the Iranian people. These include Paris-based Maryam Rajavi, president-elect of the National Council of Resistance of Iran, and Reza Pahlavi, son of the deposed monarch Mohammad Reza Pahlavi, who lives in the Washington, DC, area. Though both have support from some other expatriates and even foreign governments, most Iranians with whom I have spoken agree that their prospects for mobilizing the masses are slim.

This chapter focuses on the individual in Tehrangeles who has invested the most in leadership from afar: Dariush Eghbali, a pop vocalist and, more recently, an activist and celebrity humanitarian whose music and media work in the space between political and personal transformation. Next to Googoosh, Dariush is the best-loved popular musician of his generation. He is exceptional among his Tehrangeles colleagues for several further reasons. First is his association with sadness. He specializes in morose, sentimental songs and inspires particularly passionate reactions in his fans. A second distinguishing feature is his critical stance toward both the Pahlavi and postrevolutionary governments: he was jailed under the Pahlavi government for singing leftist song lyrics, and since leaving Iran in 1978 has released many statements and songs decrying the Islamic Republic.

Dariush also differs from his peers in his very public struggles with drug addiction: his opium and heroin use have been common knowledge for decades. For some listeners this marks him as "a bad man." During my research, he was described to me several times as an untrustworthy addict whose performances of sincerity and political commitment I would be a fool to believe. Regarding Dariush's addiction history as a sign of his individual moral failing is at odds with both the contemporary conceptualization of addiction as disease and the historical prevalence of opium use among Iranian musicians and nonmusicians alike (Matthee 2005). Rather, what is exceptional is his decision to make addiction and recovery part of his public persona. Since entering recovery in 2000, Dariush has openly discussed his challenges with addiction and has encouraged others to do the same. Working with his Ayeneh (Mirror) Foundation in Southern California to address Iranians' "social maladies"—especially addiction—he and his foundation employ a diverse array of communications technologies to extend the message of recovery, and tools of personal and political transformation, to Iranians worldwide. His satellite television programs on addiction recovery attract callers from Iran and the diaspora, and the poems he has popularized through song have been taken up by Iran-based politicians and activists alike. Like Googoosh, Dariush has made it his business to "give voice" to Iranians with less audibility than himself, but he also reaches beyond representation of others to offer platforms for grappling with addiction, and to deliver what he hopes is an emancipatory, multivalent discourse of "cultural illness" and "recovery." Instead of attempting to distance himself from the depraved-musician stereotype, as Shahrzad Sepanlou and others in Tehrangeles have attempted to do, Dariush incorporates addiction and pain into his art and work and bases his connection to ordinary Iranians on shared suffering.

In this chapter, I argue that Dariush has attempted to hail dispersed Iranians into a change-oriented intimate public based on collective pain. This intimate public takes shape across various genres, discourses, and media technologies that are often considered separately but overlap in Dariush's output: sentimental popular music, expatriate nationalist anthems, and addiction recovery media with its internal genres of witnessing and testifying to personal transformation. What resonates throughout these genres, and over Dariush's decades of work, is a public intimacy based on the notion of shared suffering. Like the twentieth-century American women's popular culture described by Lauren Berlant, Dariush's music and recovery-oriented media have contributed to "an active and intimate public sphere . . . a culture of 'true feeling' . . . that sanctifies suffering as a relay to universality . . . , [through] commodities [that] help to distribute and to enable the building of this intimate public" (2008, 12). Where Berlant sees women's literature as occupying a "juxtapolitical" position or offering "relief from politics," Dariush has long understood his music and media productions to offer alternative modes of political engagement that begin with the individual and spread outward to the social, cultural, and (trans)national. Rather than leading toward a depoliticizing, neoliberal focus on the individual or privileged forms of complaint, Dariush and his colleagues at the Ayeneh Foundation hope that therapeutic discourse and practices will provide a road map for broad-based change. Working with the idea of Dariush's charisma in relation to Khomeini's superhuman endowments, in this chapter I refer to Dariush using a variety of titles inspired by the discourse surrounding him: the "sultan of sadness," "ever-faithful friend," "messenger," "fellow sufferer," and "cultural physician." Then, through an analysis of his nonprofit foundation Ayeneh's media communications, I show how Dariush and his partners have adapted concepts from the American recovery movement to encourage personal, cultural, and, ultimately, political transformation.

THE SULTAN OF SADNESS

Dariush is the quintessential "dark celebrity," one whose dramatic life story of "rebellion and redemption" played out on the public stage (Kitch 2007). Dariush was born in Tehran on February 4, 1951. Like Googoosh, he had a difficult childhood; his older sister died at the age of seven, and he spent his young life moving back and forth between his divorced parents' households and those of their families, spending a few years each in Tehran, Karaj, the Kurdish city Sanandaj, and a village in Iranian Azerbaijan. He has spoken of this period as a time of intense loneliness and, in a 2017 interview, attributed the sadness (*hozni*) listeners perceive in his voice to his difficult upbringing.[3] Dariush entered professional popular music in his teens; he also began smoking opium during this period. Like other singers in the urban cosmopolitan musiqi-ye pāp genre, his youth and fashionableness were important to his stardom. As a slight young man with large, doleful eyes and fashionably shaggy hair, attired in the latest formfitting European ensembles, he first became known as part of a pop vocal ensemble called Shesh-o-Hasht and turned to a solo career with the song "Be man nagu dustet dāram" ("Don't Tell Me You Love Me") at the age of nineteen. As the 1970s progressed, Dariush shed his innocent, cheery pop star image and transformed into a rebellious, troubled, and troubling figure. He recorded a dystopic corpus of songs on romantic themes that conveyed a depressed, despondent sensibility about the world. Hopelessness was a common theme in the songs of the 1970s, sometimes putatively in response to the disappointments of love and in other cases vaguer in its origin, which many listeners of the time understood as commenting on the mass dissatisfaction with life under the Pahlavi regime. Along with vocalists Farhad Mehrad and Fereydun Farrokhzad—and lyricists Shahyar Ghanbari and Iraj Jannati Attaie, and composers Esfandiar Monfaredzadeh and Farid Zoland, who wrote much of these artists' repertoire— these performers became associated with the coded expression of political disaffection and alienation (for specific examples, see Hemmasi 2013; Breyley and Fatemi 2016). Dariush's personal life also contributed to his bad-boy public image. Arrested and imprisoned in 1974 on charges of drug use and possession, Dariush was made to pose for a photograph in a prison uniform standing before a brazier and an array of opium pipes; the image was then published in *Ettelā'āt* (*Information*), the country's largest newspaper. A few months later, Dariush was arrested again along with Ghanbari, Jannati Attaie, and Masoud Amini.[4] Dariush made another appearance in the national news when he was badly burned on his face, neck, and torso after a female fan threw acid at him while he was onstage. He still bears the scars today.

While Dariush is particularly associated with scandal, his drug (ab)use is not unique. Plenty of other art and pop musicians, past and present, are rumored or known to (ab)use drugs and alcohol.[5] When Tehrangeles musicians have an off performance, the whispered explanation is sometimes that they are too drunk or high to manage themselves. Prerevolutionary vocalist–turned–Tehrangeles star Hayedeh is said to have died by accidental overdose (though others deny this as well). One night at an Iranian cabaret in Southern California, an obviously intoxicated mardomi singer reflected that when he had performed in Tehran before the revolution, he would "smoke anything anyone put in front of him." The idea that drugs and alcohol enhance musical performance and experience is also not uncommon. My father recalls that during his childhood in 1940s Kashan, the motreb who served at gatherings in his area was paid in opium, which he required to achieve the right *hāl* (mental/spiritual condition) to perform. Khomeini's revolution-era pronouncement of music as the opiate of the people draws on a long-standing comparison of music with intoxicants' pleasurable, disorienting effects. The connection between drugs, music, and passivity also appears in early twentieth-century musical reformers' dismissals of "morose" traditional Iranian music as appropriate only for opium smoking and lacking the vigor needed to march Iranians into the modern era (see Chehabi 1999; Meftahi 2016b, 153). Dariush's addiction history, his "sad" repertoire, and others' statements about him can thus be understood within Iranian aesthetics and ethics connecting drug (ab)use and music.

Dariush left Iran in the late 1970s during the unrest that preceded the revolution. His 1978 single "Vatan" was the first of his many songs developing the trope of ruined and/or lost Iran; others include "Kohan diyārā" ("Ancient Lands"), "Bā man az Iran begu" ("Speak with Me of Iran"), "Salām ey khāk-e khub-e mehrabāni" ("Greetings, Oh Good, Kind Earth"), and "Marā be khāneh-am bebar" ("Take Me to My Home"). Some of his songs present a bleak picture of the present and the future: "Āyeneh" ("Mirror") depicts a man whose identity falls to pieces in front of his own reflection, while his "Sāl-e do hezār" ("Year 2000") describes the millennial turning point as "a bitter autumn with no spring—a black year." Throughout this period, Dariush's addiction grew more severe. In Los Angeles he switched from opium to heroin; he is thin and sallow in photos and videos from the 1980s and 1990s.

Not everyone likes Dariush—in fact, many people dislike him and his music intensely. As a child and teenager, I never cared for him, probably because of a combination of what I had heard about him and what I felt when I listened to his music. He was a drug addict, I was told by family and friends, someone whose music was dangerously dark, whose politics were too extreme, and who was therefore best avoided. Both his pre- and post-revolutionary songs were too depressed, too sad, just too much, with a powerful melancholy that lingered long after I had finished listening. The first time I remember connecting Dariush's face to his voice was watching his 1995 Tehrangeles-produced "Bacheh-hā-ye Iran" ("Children of Iran") music video at a cousin's house in the Midwest.[6] A sunken-eyed, ashen Dariush sat

FIGURE 5.1 Dariush as a "dark celebrity" whose attentions are directed toward the homeland. The cover of his 2001 album *Salaam ey khāk-e khub-e mehrabāni* (*Greetings, Oh Good, Kind Earth*; Pars Video) features a somber Dariush superimposed over the pre-Islamic ruins of Persepolis.

in front of a classroom full of Iranian American children, a map of Asia on the wall behind him. He asked the class if they could recognize Iran on the map. After they replied affirmatively, he said in rhyming verse:

> *Children, this is the home of [our] ancestors*
> *A destroyed, thirsty land*
> *Wounded by the whips of despotism*
> *In need of a salve called . . . [a girl in the class raises her hand to supply the rhyming word]*
> *. . . Freedom*

As the Iranian American daughter of an expatriate geographer, I had been through the exercise of identifying Iran on a world map many times, but never with so much bitterness. I remember being confused and uncomfortable with Dariush's bleak description of Iran. The place he described bore no resemblance to what I remembered or heard of Iran. It was as if he had blotted out all the life in the country and was guiding impressionable children in the diaspora to do the same. I also couldn't comprehend how either the drug-addled Dariush or a bunch of kids could possibly be qualified to aid Iranians within the country. I chalked the whole thing up to aspects of Iranian popular culture I just didn't understand.

I was not alone. More than one person has told me they "can't stand Dariush"—that he is "too much," that "if you start listening to him, you might never stop." In discussions of Dariush's prerevolutionary music,

Mehran, whose older sister loved to listen to Dariush in Tehran during her "teenage angst years" in the 1990s, described the singer as sounding *tariyāki* (a word meaning "relating to opium and/or opium users"). Dariush was "downer" music that inspired and was inspired by opiate-induced lethargy, passivity, and depression. An apocryphal statement by the poet Ahmad Shamlu from the 1970s describes Dariush as a "modern Shiite panegyrist of the cabaret" (*nowheh-khun-e modern-e kābāreh*)—surely intended as an insult to both Dariush and Shiite vocalists, but also a direct link to the professional performer of lamentations whose artistry is directed toward bringing audiences to weep (Hemmasi 2013, 73–75).

THE EVER-FAITHFUL FRIEND

Many others find Dariush's music profoundly moving. In my conversations with Dariush fans, they have almost universally described his voice and music as "sad" and "beautiful," and explained that they listened to his music when they wanted to hear music that reflected or intensified their own feelings of sadness and depression. One individual fitting this description is Shobeir, who was born in 1979, grew up in Isfahan, and has lived in the United States since the 2000s. Shobeir knew not everyone shared his high opinion of Dariush. "People either love [Dariush] or hate him. A lot of people don't like [him] because they don't want to hear songs about disappointment, death, heartbreak, and so on," but the singer's seriousness and rebellious spirit were just what Shobeir and his friends were looking for in their teens. As a teenager in Iran, he listened to Dariush "constantly." Shobeir's access to large quantities of Dariush's music at age thirteen came from his aunt and uncle, who gave him their personal collection of pop music cassettes when they moved to Sweden. "That collection was a big deal" to Shobeir, especially considering the relative scarcity of Iranian pop music recordings in the country after the revolution. Though prerevolutionary and expatriate popular music were not officially permitted in Iran, the vast interpersonal circulation of cassettes meant that many of Shobeir's friends also had access to Dariush. Like him, Shobeir's male classmates were "obsessed" with the singer; he remembered them writing "Dariush" on their arms, notebooks, and desks and intensely discussing his lyrics during breaks at school. Shobeir also spent time deciphering the meanings of the singer's metaphor-laden songs with the uncle who had given him the cassette collection.

Shobeir's favorite song by Dariush was the prerevolutionary classic "Yāvar-e hamisheh mo'men," or "Ever-Faithful Friend," which describes a passionate friendship between the singer and his distant *yāvar* (friend, companion, or helper). In the song, Dariush thanks his yāvar for "responding to [his] cries" and being his "support" in his state of alienation (*gharib*). It was as if Dariush was Shobeir's yāvar, giving voice to his teenage fan's painful emotions while providing comfort and companionship from a distance. But Dariush was not the kind of friend Shobeir's father wanted him to have. "My dad didn't think it was good for me to listen to so much sad music, so he took the tape player and cassettes away," laughed Shobeir. He soon got his tapes back and returned to intensive audio communion with his distant idol.

According to my conversations with Shobeir's contemporaries, Dariush seems to have served a similar function for many young people in Iran during the 1980s and 1990s. In their discussion of Dariush's cultural relevance, G. J. Breyley and Sasan Fatemi note the artist's popularity with postrevolutionary youth and the "association with weeping audiences [that] has followed [Dariush] throughout his career" (2016, 126). I have observed this at Dariush's live shows as well. One memorable instance took place at Dariush's 2015 concert at the Sony Centre for the Performing Arts in Toronto. I sat near a woman in her thirties clad in a skintight forest-green cocktail dress who had been singing Dariush's songs at the top of her lungs the whole night. Along with others in the audience, she periodically yelled out "Shaghāyegh" ("Anemone," also a woman's name) requesting one of Dariush's best-loved prerevolutionary romantic songs, which was almost certainly released before she was born. When Dariush finally acquiesced and sang "Shaghāyegh," the woman crumpled to the floor and began to sob, her shuddering cries audible over the sound system and collective singing of a three-thousand-person music hall. Though I will never know what precisely moved her to tears—too much alcohol? exhaustion? nostalgia? a personal hurt that the song recalled?—I was struck by her rapturous release into grief in a highly public arena and through the public form of a celebrity vocalist's well-known song.

A recent short online film called *Didār dar ghorbat* (*Seeing One Another in Exile*) further underscores the passionate, tearful affection of Dariush's fans for him, and his for them. The film follows Dariush's interactions with fans during his 2014 visit to Antalya, Turkey, a resort town popular with Iranians that has become a regular stop on Dariush's and other Tehrangeles musicians' tours. In one scene, we see a young woman wearing a white sundress, a garland of white flowers in her hair, and bright pink lipstick waiting in line for her turn to greet Dariush. Dariush stands patiently waiting for her and other fans, a benevolent smile on his face as he graciously accepts their outpourings of praise and emotion, their embraces and kisses. Though Dariush has never met these individuals before, there is a sense of longed-for reunion, the meeting of old friends, expressed in the passion of their interactions. The young woman's turn finally comes. She moves toward Dariush, and sobbing overtakes her, her meticulous self-presentation crumbling. She weeps deeply into his shoulder. "Don't cry, my dear!" says Dariush, partly laughing as he places his arms around her in fatherly concern. "You'll see the pictures later and be so upset with yourself!" Everyone is wiping tears from their eyes.[7]

Like the motreb and their los ānjelesi dance music producer counterparts, Dariush is a specialist in affective labor: here, the labor of inciting audiences to sorrow and weeping rather than joy and its expression in dance. This kind of emotional work is not typically tarred with the brush of degeneration or Tehrangeles's frivolity. Though Dariush works out of Los Angeles, no one I spoke with used the term los ānjelesi to describe him because his music's sadness doesn't fit the stereotype. Instead, Dariush fits rather well with the "culture of sadness" that characterized domestic popular culture in the 1980s and 1990s, and with the larger Shiite veneration of sadness—hence Shamlu's designation of Dariush as a religious panegyrist. The projection of an empty, baseless happiness onto Iranian Los Angeles following the revolution not only is reductive but also overlooks the contributions of Dariush and a host of other Tehrangeles performers whose music tapped into the depression and hopelessness many Iranians experienced during this period.[8]

Dariush also inspires an intense identification and intimacy in his fans. Intimacy with celebrities is a contradictory yet commonplace phenomenon. The fan-celebrity relationship is defined by distance and unattainability; they are called "stars" because these exceptional humans are way up in the sky where we ordinary folks can never go (Dyer 1986). Yet celebrities' appeal also pulls from their familiarity through repeated media exposure, their relatability as the girl or boy next door, and the sense that celebrities are more famous, perhaps more beautiful, or just "more" than what we could ever be (Schickel 1986). The identification with celebrity vocalists seems to be particularly intense. Star vocalists perform first-person lyrics expressing longing, heartbreak, regret, and loss, mobilizing through mass media a sentimental, clichéd language affectively communicated through poetry, the musical arrangement, and the texture and feel of the star's voice (Fox 2004; Gray 2013; Stokes 2010; Yano 2002). The sentiments and sentimentality expressed in the songs are cyclical and pedagogical: the celebrity singer gives voice to emotional expressions that "everyone understands" and at the same time teaches audiences both how to feel and how to express these feelings. The impassioned identification, affective power, and language about how to feel are elements that Dariush transfers to his postrecovery activism.

THE MESSENGER

The dystopian future imagined in Dariush's song "Year 2000" was never realized. Instead, this was the year he entered recovery. After this turning point, his life and works oriented away from the despondency that he symbolized for so many years and toward hope and positive change. Dariush's appearance altered for the better: he gained weight and he looked healthier than he had since his early twenties. His first postrecovery album, *Rumi* (*The Beloved Is Here*) (DBF Records, 2003), was made up of jazzy pop settings of the ghazals of Rumi, one of the most important medieval Iranian mystic poets.[9] He began appearing in all-white outfits, a sartorial choice that seemed to underscore his "clean" status while also invoking the pure-white outfits some Sufis wear. Recovery translated to a more positive patriotic repertoire, like his album *Dobāreh misāzamet vatan* (*I Will Rebuild You Homeland*) (DBF Records, 2005), a collection of upbeat, marchlike songs with inspirational lyrics. While the prerecovery Dariush may have been imagined as a friend, he was also potentially a bad influence—a reaction evinced in Shobeir's father's and my own family members' appraisals of his works. Now Dariush began conceiving of himself as a messenger—a positive influence who could lead by example.

Dariush's 2005 song "Dobāreh misāzamet vatan" (from the album of the same name) represents his transformed sense of self and the relationship he hoped to facilitate between individuals and the homeland. It also reiterates the long-standing expatriate conceptualization of the homeland in need. Based on a poem of the same name written in 1982 by Simin Behbahani (1927–2014) during the Iran-Iraq War, the text speaks of self-sacrifice in service of reconstructing a destroyed homeland, using the very stuff of one's body to rebuild the nation. It has an exhortative tone—recognizing the challenges of the moment while proclaiming determination to work for a better future. In Dariush's composition, the instrumental opening quotes the first lines of "Ey Iran," a well-known prerevolutionary patriotic anthem, which serves to immediately position it in the lineage of nationalistic song.[10] Dariush then enters with the vocal melody and the first two couplets of Behbahani's poem:

> *I will rebuild you my homeland, even with bricks of my soul;*
> *I erect pillars to hold your roof, with my very bones*
> *I smell the scents of your flowers, for desire of your youth;*
> *I wash blood from you, with the flood of my flowing tears* (Behbahani 1999, 191)

When the poem was originally written, during the first years of the Iran-Iraq War, the nation was literally bloodied and destroyed, with millions of Iranian casualties and demolished cities and infrastructure. The expatriate appropriation changes its meaning. By 2005 Iran's postwar reconstruction and economic recovery had been well underway for over a decade, and the country had not seen war since the late 1980s: the song thus becomes a declaration that Iran is *still* in ruins. The original music video adds historical footage and photographs to support this interpretation, including men's and women's crying faces interspersed with images of dead and wounded soldiers from the Iran-Iraq War, followed by images of bloody postrevolutionary citizen clashes with the state. For whatever postwar rebuilding Iran has seen, the video showed a country full of strife and conflict still reeling from generations of political disappointment and violence.

As the vocalist enunciating his intention to rebuild the homeland in a heroic musical setting, Dariush is positioned as the messenger of transformation from exile. Though the poem never shifts from the first person, his invitation to his audiences to join him in rebuilding Iran is represented sonically by a mixed adult and children's chorus. In the first half of the song, the chorus enters after Dariush's full statement of the two opening couplets to repeat the opening melodic lines. At the piece's conclusion, Dariush sings the song's opening lines and is echoed by the choir, as if he is teaching them the song. Dariush then drops out altogether, and the chorus takes over his call—"I will rebuild you, homeland"—and repeats it until the track fades out. This moment marks the piece's transformation from a "presentational" pop song in which inexpert audiences merely observe a star at work to a "participatory" anthem in which all are invited to join (Turino 2008). It is as if "the people" have taken on the mission of rebuilding Iran individually and collectively, an "aspirational performance" that models audience inspiration and mobilization.[11]

As it turned out, "Dobāreh misāzamet vatan" was taken up in Iran, but not as Dariush had expected. The poem's opening lines became the centerpiece of presidential candidate Mostafa Mo'in's 2005 campaign slogan. Mo'in's campaign claimed that they selected the poem because it was well liked among young people, but Dariush and others maintain that his song was responsible for the popularity of Behbahani's decades-old poem. Dariush understands the poem's appearance in Iran as evidence of his transnational influence—even among state officials who decry him and his fellow Tehrangeles cultural producers. His message had been received in Iran, where it was shrewdly adapted in service of retaining power in the Islamic Republican system (Hemmasi 2017d).

I had heard the story of this song's domestic appearance before I arrived in Southern California, and I dreamed of interviewing Dariush about it. But he was such a big star that I thought he would be off-limits to me, the way people in Los Angeles told me that Googoosh was. I was delighted to learn from Pardis Mahdavi, then a fellow Iranian American doctoral student, that she might be able to arrange a meeting with Dariush through a friend. This friend then agreed to put me in touch with Dr. Abbasseh Towfigh, secretary of the Ayeneh Foundation and a podiatrist with an active medical practice in Southern California.[12] I was thrilled at the opportunity, but this feeling was combined with interest and incredulity. I knew I didn't understand Dariush's musical ethos, and I was suspicious of expatriates who painted a picture of a weak homeland and its desperate citizens. At the same time, I was aware of the seriousness of Iran's drug problem and was curious to see how he and his partners might address it. Dariush was also the only Tehrangeles musician I had encountered who was not just talking about the homeland but apparently doing something about it. I tried to keep an open mind.

I then met Dariush by accident. I was interviewing the editor of the Tehrangeles periodical *Javanan* (*Youth*) when our conversation was interrupted by a phone call: Dariush was on his way to meet the editor, so our interview would have to end early. I was surprised, not yet used to the idea that in Los Angeles one could run into famous Iranian actors and musicians almost any time or any place. I mentioned that I was hoping to interview Dariush for my project, and the editor suggested I introduce myself to him. I walked out to say hello, but upon seeing Dariush, I was unexpectedly starstruck. His large, sad eyes, silvery hair and beard, and husky voice—even his way of standing—were so familiar to me from all the music and videos I'd been exposed to over the years that it felt as though I already knew him and yet, of course, I didn't know him at all. I couldn't get over the fact that it was him—*him!*—talking to *me!* What was it about Dariush, or me, that had produced this reaction? I somehow managed to ask Dariush for his cell phone number—which I never called—and hoped that I hadn't embarrassed myself.

Weeks later, I arranged an interview with Dariush through Abbasseh. She wanted to meet me ahead of time to discuss my project and questions, so we made an appointment to see each other at the Coffee Bean and Tea Leaf coffee shop in Westwood, an American franchise typically packed with Iranians because of its proximity to the "Persian Square" business district at the intersection of Westwood and Ohio. Once again, my reactions caught me off guard. Abbasseh was a statuesque woman with long, dark hair, perfect makeup, and elegant clothing under her spotless white doctor's coat. She had lived in the United States since her late teens and spoke perfect English. Abbasseh listened to me explain my project and interest in Dariush's music, especially his songs that had sparked political reactions inside Iran. She then began talking about her work with Dariush on the addiction recovery television program and websites, and the Ayeneh Foundation's work with domestic addiction treatment centers. The addiction recovery mission was her reason for working with Dariush; I sensed she wanted me to focus on this as well.

Talking about Ayeneh, Abbasseh became electric. Dariush was the initiator of Ayeneh, she said; it was his concept, his passion, his mission, that motivated and inspired her to help him to help others. She told me story after story of Dariush and Ayeneh reaching addiction sufferers in Iran. Despite my foregoing skepticism and attempts at objective distance, I felt overwhelmed by her passion for Dariush's mission and the urgent necessity of "saving Iran." At one point, I felt the hair on my arms stand on end, an experience I had never had in an interview before. As I listened in rapt attention, I noticed a disheveled elderly Iranian woman seated a few tables away looking at Abbasseh with interest. After about fifteen minutes, she shuffled over and grasped Abbasseh's hand, thanking her earnestly for something—I couldn't make out what. When the woman moved away, Abbasseh leaned in and said in a low voice, "She knows me from the *Ayeneh Program* [on television]. It's amazing how often I meet people it has helped."[13]

A few weeks later, the long-awaited interview with Dariush took place in a dingy diner in the San Fernando Valley, in the very same shopping plaza where the headquarters of *Javanan* were located. I wondered if I would once again be swept away into the passion of the encounter, but I found the interview more awkward than awe-inspiring. This was probably at least partially because of my limited language skills. I couldn't read Dariush's reactions quickly enough to try different questions or approaches to elicit answers that touched on topics that interested me. Abbasseh was in the middle, translating as quickly as she could between Persian and English, trying to help me get the information she knew I wanted while editorializing a bit and endeavoring to keep the interview on track. Dariush told me he "had been asked these questions by many other people," and some of his recollections had a rehearsed quality.

The takeaway of the meeting was this: Dariush was now, and had always been, an artist with a sociopolitical consciousness, whose music delivered a "message" (*payām*) to the people. If he could be praised for anything, he said humbly, it was not his voice but his taste in poetry and music. Since before the revolution, he had sung political song lyrics based on works by famous poets and activists such as Ahmad Shamlu, Khosrow Golsorkhi, and Simin Behbahani, as well as the more literary-leaning lyricists in the pre-revolutionary and Tehrangeles music industries. He was not just a single-issue activist—he was against oppression, intolerance, and denial and was for freedom, democracy, and tolerance. His current work with the Ayeneh Foundation was an outgrowth of what he had already been doing through his music for years: delivering hope and encouragement to the people. He was now focused on addiction recovery and was working through many mass media and interactive platforms. Ayeneh was doing good work, making a difference, and regularly receiving responses that encouraged Dariush and Abbasseh to keep finding new ways to help and support their compatriots. His intention was to use his voice and his celebrity to perform, communicate, and reinforce these values among any who might be inspired to join him. The message of the interview was that Dariush was a messenger.

One moment in the interview stands out. Dariush had transitioned to talking about the power of collective action—the potential if people actually came together to work on the homeland, as he had sung about in his songs. He then smiled, looked me in the eyes, and said, "They say the revolution started with cassette tapes. We have so many weblogs, videos, and television stations—so where's our problem (*moshgel-e mā kojāst*)?" I felt a shiver of recognition. Dariush was referring to Khomeini's cassette sermons recorded in France, and was comparing the work he and other expatriate activists were undertaking to the late ayatollah's revolutionary mobilization from afar. I understood his point about the tremendous media resources he had at his disposal, but was he suggesting that he and his colleagues had the authority and the influence to make a revolution in Iran? When taken with his self-designation as a "messenger," a title that recalls the Prophet Mohammad's epithet *payghambar* (sacred "message-bearer"), Dariush's mission and self-conception took on a messianic tone.

THE RECOVERED CELEBRITY

What I did not fully comprehend at the time of the interview was how central the principles of Narcotics Anonymous (NA) are to Dariush's and Ayeneh's understanding of social change. As I came to learn, Dariush and the Ayeneh Foundation have transposed tenets and methods of the American recovery movement into the transnational Iranian public sphere, and mapped the language of denial, admission, acceptance, and proactivity onto their efforts in recovery, politics, and human rights. Programs such as NA hold that maintaining one's sobriety depends on being in regular contact with and assisting other individuals going through the recovery process: the ability to give those in need "the gift of recovery" is "the mark of true sobriety" (Travis 2009, 29). Driven by this mission, Dariush formed the Ayeneh Foundation in 2003 to deliver the message of recovery and the trinity of "education, awareness, and prevention" to as many individuals as possible. In what follows, I limit myself to two aspects of the recovery movement as they play out in Dariush's postrecovery career and activism. The first is the notion of addiction as a disease with sociocultural roots that links the personal to the political and the individual body to the national body. The second is Dariush's and Ayeneh's deployment of "alcoholic [addict] equalitarianism," which holds that all individuals are equals in the face of their addictions. This ethos of horizontality is consonant with Dariush's interest in promoting recovery and democratic behavior; it also exists in some tension with the fan-celebrity hierarchy. Like his music, Dariush's activism relies on public intimacy, but in a slightly different sense than the sentimental and affective experiences of popular music. Here, shared suffering, self-narration, witnessing, and the authenticity of experience are critical.

Citing figures provided by Iran's Drug Control Organization, a 2017 report in the *Independent* puts the number of Iranians "regularly using drugs" at 2.8 million.[14] Iranians generally perceive the rates of opiate and synthetic drug use to be higher—anywhere from 3 million to 10 million drug (ab)users out of an overall population of 80 million.[15] Opium has been used in Iran for centuries, while heroin use grew in the 1960s. Iranian *kerak* (crack) is a more recent opiate-based street drug on the market.[16] Recent studies suggest that drug use is expanding from the previously typical older male opiate users to young people and women, who favor cheaper synthetic drugs like methamphetamines (*shisheh*, or "glass") (Afkhami 2009; Figg-Franzoi 2011; Ghiabi 2015, 2017; Ghiabi et al. 2018; White 2015). It may not be an exaggeration to say that drug (ab)use touches every Iranian family in some way—my own included.

Since the revolution, Iranian state and civil society entities have made many, often contradictory, attempts to respond to the addiction crisis (for overviews, see Afkhami 2009; Figg-Franzoi 2011; Ghiabi 2015; White 2015). Following the revolution, drugs were treated as a moral problem and criminalized: drug users were jailed, forcibly enrolled in "detoxification camps" with prison-like conditions, and thousands have been executed. Iranian drug researcher Maziyar Ghiabi describes a three-pronged state strategy regarding drugs during the 1980s: "quarantining," or keeping drugs and addicts out of the public eye; propaganda presenting drugs and addiction as foreign conspiracies against the Iranian people; and a combination of "civic and military" efforts to combat drug distribution and addiction undertaken by paramilitary groups, parastatal organizations, and private charities (Ghiabi 2015, 145–158). By the early 1990s, it was clear that the state's punitive approach was not working: opium and heroin were increasingly cheap and ever more accessible, prisons were full of drug offenders, and intravenous drug use had increased, leading to the spread of HIV and other diseases (Afkhami 2009). This period began a gradual shift toward harm reduction through newly established state and private drug-cessation clinics, needle exchanges, and in- and outpatient facilities to support recovery. Progressive approaches have shown a stronger impact than prior methods, but drug use is still rampant and cannot be adequately combated with the measures and organizations currently in place (Ghiabi 2017; Himmich and Madani 2016).

Ayeneh's Iran-based endeavors therefore respond to what its participants perceive as an especially dire situation within their homeland. This was clearly represented in the Ayeneh Foundation's logo during my initial contact with the organization in 2007: the image of a white mask inside an outline of the Iranian borders, bloody tears streaming down from empty eyes. In Persian poetic discourse, "weeping blood" is an expression of extreme sadness, often inspired by romantic loss or religious feeling. If Ayeneh is a mirror, as its name implies, the image of Iran it reflects maps the suffering individual onto the nation, and the nation's woes onto the individual.

(Ayeneh's logo has since taken a more hopeful form: it is now the words "Ayeneh Foundation" in English, topped with a green leaf.)

Ayeneh's Persian-language radio and television programs, and Persian-language versions of NA-related materials, are directed toward the diaspora and Iran. Ayeneh also sponsors workshops on addiction in Persian in areas of diasporic concentration such as Southern California, Toronto, and Germany; and in locations without easily accessible resources, it connects people seeking recovery support with other individuals and groups in their area. Because of its associations with Dariush, Abbasseh told me, Ayeneh "cannot operate in Iran as much as we'd like." The foundation responds to this situation by sending cash and resources to individuals who then redirect donations to extant recovery programs and help establish new ones. Media are critical to this work. A network of websites—Ayeneh's own; a site called Behboudi (Recovery) with private chat rooms for addicts; Dariush's personal website and weblog; Ayeneh's dedicated pages and channels on streaming video platforms and social media sites like Vimeo, YouTube, Telegram, and Facebook—all provide access to interaction with other addicts, Ayeneh staff and partners, the addiction experts who periodically appear on Ayeneh programs, and Dariush himself. Dariush serves as the figurehead and public face of Ayeneh, but it is far from a solo venture. He works with a growing number of volunteers and paid staff members who contribute to Ayeneh media, provide on-the-ground services in Iran and the diaspora, organize and fund-raise, plan events, and work on other aspects of the organization. Day-to-day operations in Southern California, logistics, media production, website management, and countless other tasks are under Abbasseh's purview.[17] Abbasseh and Dariush coproduce the televised *Ayeneh Program*. While its content and format change, the program can include inspirational poetry and slogans, a dialogue with Dariush and invited Iranian experts on addiction or other social issues, and sometimes call-in segments in which viewers can speak with and ask questions of Dariush and/or the guest expert. Many of the programs also include footage of addicts and people in recovery whom the foundation claims to have helped; these are filmed clandestinely by Ayeneh partners within Iran. Testimony and self-narration are invariably a part of these segments, transposing the requisite confessional monologue to transnational Iranian television. For as much as it is a means of delivering hope, the program also focuses on the ugliness of addiction and therefore of Iran, stripping away the veneer of propriety and denial that might otherwise keep such unsettling images out of sight. One of the tactics of humanitarian media is to create an affective response in the receiver on the theory that feeling is a precursor to action (Chouliaraki 2006, 2013). Ideally, the representation of others' suffering, and the immediacy and intimacy of one-on-one dialogue and testimony, produces affective responses in viewers and spurs positive movement. Like the logo of an anthropomorphized Iran shedding tears of blood, Ayeneh intertwines Iran as suffering and Iranians who are suffering and posits an interrelation of self and society that is at the heart of Dariush's philosophy.

THE MIRROR

In May 2007 Abbasseh invited me to attend a live taping of *Ayeneh Program* at the studio of Iranian expatriate television station Omid-e Iran (Hope of Iran), which was in a small, unassuming office park in the San Fernando Valley town of Encino. The program was airing live during Iranian "prime time" evening hours. Since Tehran is eleven and a half hours ahead of Tehrangeles, I was asked to arrive at 8:45 a.m. to settle in before the three-hour-long show began. When I arrived Abbasseh was already in the dark, modest lobby, speaking with a woman seated behind a desk. She was a real estate agent by profession, but this morning she would serve as the telephone operator, answering calls to the live broadcast and patching them into the studio to speak directly with Dariush and Dr. Iraj Shamsian, a Los Angeles–based psychologist and addiction specialist who was this week's cohost. Beyond the lobby were the small control room and studio. An engineer (also Iranian) moved between these rooms, fixing camera angles, checking microphones in the studio, and tidying the control room. Abbasseh fulfilled virtually all other off-camera roles: she had brought a clean white dress shirt for Dariush in a dry-cleaning bag, set up the stage in front of the studio's green screen, supplied the video footage of addicts in Iran, and directed the timing of the encouraging slogans that ran along the bottom of the screen throughout the program.

The episode began with scenes of Ayeneh's work within Iran, which is accomplished through a network of mostly anonymous individuals whose faces do not typically appear on camera. This twenty-minute segment focused on a small family of women and children in an impoverished household in South Tehran. Those pictured included an older woman dressed in a black headscarf and coat, two women in their late teens or early twenties, and a boy who looked to be around six years old. All were regular drug users, including the child. The women sat on the bed or crouched on the

FIGURE 5.2 Dariush and addiction specialist Dr. Iraj Shamsian prepare to live-host the *Ayeneh Program* at Omid-e Iran's satellite television studios, Canoga Park, California, 2007. Photograph by the author.

ground of their dirty, sparsely furnished concrete cinderblock house, occasionally lighting their pipes on a brazier. Exhaled smoke clouded the air, illuminated by the wan light that streamed through a single small window. It was a grim scene of grays. The women described how they had started using drugs as children. The older woman wept openly and wiped her tears with her headscarf; she was so sorry her life had taken this turn, but she was unable to do anything about it. Her grief-stricken face filled the screen. She wanted to quit, but it was impossible in a house full of other addicts. The young boy looked on as his mother exhaled smoke into the air. Persian text running along the bottom of the screen read, "Kerak (crack) is the cheapest bullet for the youth." The scene went on and on. By the end of the segment, I felt that I, too, was trapped, suffocating under the horribleness of it all.

The program then switched to Dariush and Dr. Shamsian discussing the difficulty of achieving recovery in Iran. Throughout the program, the bottom of the screen showed the program's call-in number, the Ayeneh website address, and a rotating selection of slogans. Some of these were adapted from the addiction recovery discourse circulated through NA ("admit it,

FIGURE 5.3 Ayeneh's partners in Iran interview a woman who, along with her family, is addicted to the synthetic drug kerak. She is shown later in the program attending recovery meetings. Photograph by the author.

name it, and be free"), while another described Ayeneh's mission ("our goal is bringing awareness, education, and preventative measures with regard to social maladies"). Still another slogan indicted the Iranian state: "When the government addresses the people's cries by condemning and silencing them, it shows its true face to be violence."

In a later portion of the program, callers identifying themselves as based in Iran phoned in to speak with Dariush and Dr. Shamsian. Dariush greeted several of the male callers with great familiarity and warmth: "Hello, 'Ali dear! It has been a while since we've heard from you! How are you? How is your family?" 'Ali likewise greeted Dariush warmly and launched into a discussion of his recovery efforts as Dariush nodded and gave gentle affirmations. The suggestion that Dariush and 'Ali had developed a meaningful relationship realized the notion of the celebrity as the ever-faithful friend, now reconceptualized as remote recovery sponsor. The hopeful tenor of the program's last hour was underscored by a return to the women from the South Tehran household, now shown sitting on chairs in a tidy, bright private home where an Ayeneh-sponsored recovery meeting was being held.

The old woman who had wept in the earlier video was now smiling. Her daughter was, too; her makeup was done, and her face was rounder. With Ayeneh's help, they said, they had come off drugs and were ready to begin their new lives. (Some years later, I asked Abbasseh what had happened to the women after the program. They had relapsed. Synthetic drugs are harder to quit than opiates, she explained.)

When the taping was complete, my head was buzzing, and I felt emotionally exhausted. Dariush, Dr. Shamsian, and Abbasseh seemed unaffected: this was business as usual for them. Now that the program had aired, it was time to think of what was next. Dariush changed back into his street clothes and bid us goodbye; the other two men left the studio to drive off to whatever else their Sunday afternoon entailed. Abbasseh, the telephone operator, and I lingered for a bit longer in the studio's lobby. Abbasseh told me she was inspired by the explosion of Iranian weblogs: here was the voice of the Iranian people, enabled by technology and available in a new form. She hoped "she and Dariush" could find a way to "harness that power." It seemed within reach: on the program several weeks earlier, she and Dariush had asked bloggers watching the program to help Ayeneh with its cause. "The next day," she said, "I had 250 emails saying, 'We are ready—tell us what to write and we'll do it!'" While she was still working out precisely what to tell them, she perceived these responses as proof that their communications were reaching audiences and that this held great potential.

THE FELLOW SUFFERER

In Ayeneh programs and other media appearances, Dariush sometimes employs the term *hamdard* to unite himself with fellow addicts. The word is a combination of the words "same" (*ham*) and "pain" (*dard*); the word itself can be translated as "sympathizer," and suggests one who possesses or has experienced the same pain as another.[18] Dariush's discourse gives the term a different meaning: he uses *hamdardān* or *hamdard-hā* (both plural forms) to refer to addicts as a collectivity of which he is a part. This language choice emphasizes shared suffering, experience, and subjectivity as well as a horizontal relationship between himself and others as "fellow sufferers" of the same disease. This echoes the "alcoholic equalitarianism" of Alcoholics Anonymous (AA) and related recovery programs, which eschews a hierarchy between members through dialogue and self-disclosure, wherein "one-to-one conversation exemplifie[s its] democratic basis" (Travis 2009, 119). A 2007 interview posted on the website of Deutsche Welle's Persian-language news service is an example of Dariush's use of the term: "I am myself one of those hamdard-hā, I have also suffered a great deal from the disease of addiction. . . . I understand myself as one link in a chain of people seeking recovery. I am with them, and anywhere that there is need and I am present, I will be with them with love and interest, because I understand the pain of my fellow sufferers (*dard-e hamdardam o mifahmam*) and I deeply desire to be a messenger of hope for them."[19] At first glance, Dariush's self-identification as hamdard with other addicts may appear as a radical departure from the celebrity-fan, leader-follower relationship that many also have with him, but it also works in the same space as fans' perception of Dariush as the ever-faithful friend who understands and represents their emotional pain.

In keeping with NA philosophy, personal testimonies are a key genre of publicly intimate self-narration that evinces transformation. That they tend to follow a familiar trajectory—substance-use initiation, progression, hitting rock bottom, and transformation through commitment to the Twelve Steps (the "drunkologue")—confirms that what these narratives reveal is not merely individuals' experiences but something greater than them. The narratives are social, both in that they are taught by and learned from others and in that they are true for one and many (Burchardt 2016). In this sense, they resemble sentimental pop songs, which are at once personal, general, and generic, in the sense of being part of a genre.

An episode of the *Ayeneh Program* released in 2015 includes scenes of recovery-oriented personal narration and choreographed intimacy between Dariush and his hamdard-s in Iran through the immediacy of transnational testimony and sharing.[20] The episode opens on a young man inside the orange tent of a detoxification camp—temporary residences where addicts elect to go, or are sent by family or the police, to receive support in the difficult early stages of opiate withdrawal.[21] The man is hunched over in pain and clutches himself with his scabby forearms. A hand from an otherwise unseen body stretches a microphone to the young man's contorted face; its Persian logo reads "Ayeneh." In a barely intelligible slur, his eyes mere slits, the young man mutters, "I'm tired of living—I can't take it anymore."

The program cuts to a verdant rural landscape. A young man is walking down a gravel road. He turns his face, and we see it is the same person shown in the initial scene, now almost unrecognizable because he looks so healthy. He comes to a tall metal gate and knocks; it is opened by a middle-aged, white-haired man who warmly welcomes him inside. The older man, Hamid, addresses the camera directly. "This [program] is a gift from God to those who want to quit drugs and who are hopeless. Kami will show you that there is hope. It can happen." Hamid then passes the microphone to Kami, the young man whose transformation we have witnessed:

> I'm Kami, an addict. . . . I got involved with drugs when I was a child. . . . School, friends, fun . . . I thought my life was drugs, and drugs were my life. Nothing else interested me. I had big dreams . . . but none of them were possible. . . . No matter how much I thank God (*khodā*), it will never be enough. We have experienced another birth. We have understood that we have another chance. This is a miracle. . . . God didn't want me to die. God wanted me to live. Perhaps it was His wish that I could deliver this message today to my friends who are still suffering from addiction.

Kami performs the addict monologue genre to a T, introducing himself as an addict even in his recovery, giving us a curtailed version of his story and an acknowledgment of his relationship to a higher power (here the generic word for God rather than Allah, God's proper name in Islam). He is maintaining his recovery by sharing his recovery.

The program then cuts to an event Kami says he has "wanted for years": the chance to speak with Dariush. We see Dariush seated in Ayeneh's studio in Southern California. Hamid, Kami, and Kami's father, are shown sitting on a living-room couch in an undisclosed location in Iran. A phone call connects them.

"Hello, Dariush *jān* (dear)!" says Kami. "Hello, my dear! I'm so happy to hear your voice!"

"I'm also so happy to hear your voice!" replies Dariush warmly. ". . . You are a great message (*payām*) to the nation (*mamlekat*). We've shown your footage [on the *Ayeneh Program*] so many times that you yourself have become a message to young people!" Kami and Dariush address each other with deep affection and familiarity, and Dariush offers more encouragement to Kami as he continues with his recovery efforts.

Kami then makes a painful admission about the night he was filmed in the orange detox tent. He had willingly gone to the camp but then broke out before completing the program. "Dariush jān, I was in the meeting, but I escaped. I was hopeful that I could try again. I tried to get clean for years—

maybe ten years of trying. And I begged God to help me stay clean. . . . I am so thankful to God that I have a friend like you, and I thank you, because I receive such comfort from your words."

"May God protect you," Dariush responds. "Make arrangements . . . so that we can stay in touch. . . . Your presence [existence] is a message, Kami jān. You have worked so hard and endured so much to reach recovery. . . . Thank God you have [become clean]. Now you see how beautiful a life in recovery is. I kiss your beautiful face. I hope that one day we can see each other in person and that I can kiss your face."

Kami then hands the receiver to his frail, toothless father. Also in recovery, he is completely bald from the chemotherapy he is undergoing.

"I saw you on television five years into your recovery," Kami's father tells Dariush, slurring slightly. "I thought to myself—man, if Dariush can do it, I can, too! I received the message from you, and, thanks be to God, I've been clean for nine years."

Once again, the message has been received: if the notorious addict Dariush can get clean, anyone can. The program concluded with a scene of Kami and his father embracing and the text of a letter of condolence from the Ayeneh Foundation—Kami's father passed away shortly after the segment was released. As the images fade, we hear the opening lines of Dariush's 2015 dark, romantic song "Shekanjeh-gar" ("Torturer").

Public intimacy works on many levels in this program. Addiction is a family disease; as in the earlier *Ayeneh Program* discussed above, and in Dariush's own life, multiple immediate family members are drug (ab)users or even introduce one another to drugs. The national family is likewise riddled with disease.[22] If addiction can spread from one person to another, the program shows that recovery can also be contagious, a transformation accomplished through sharing stories, sharing pain, and providing mutual support. Ultimately, viewers are let into the "chain of people seeking recovery" via technological mediation, which brings the fellow sufferers onto the same screen and brings dispersed viewers into fellowship with them. Editing their physically distant yet simultaneous conversations produces a sense of intimacy and immediacy brought about by transnational communications media, but also through the emotional connection among these three hamdard-s whose shared experiences of addiction and recovery momentarily bridge the gap between fan and star, teacher and student, leader and follower, and exile and homeland.

Like the depictions of the addicted family's home or detox camp, many videos shot for Ayeneh show scenes of utter abjection—homeless children, disheveled, high, and huddled around an oil-barrel fire for warmth, their eyes half-shut from intoxication; worn, thin female prostitutes smoking kerak and crying openly about their children whom they've abandoned. These scenes of affective "stickiness" (Ahmed 2004) sadden, disgust, and enrage with the aim of making viewers hamdard with those depicted on-screen. As in the case of circulated imagery of mutilated and tortured male Sikh bodies in the Sikh diaspora, transnational media bear witness to the ravages of addiction on the national body (Axel 2002; see also Kolar-Panov 1996). "Because this story is rarely told [in such detail]" and because it is told by expatriates who are deeply critical of the Islamic Republic, "its narration becomes an explicitly political act" (Axel 2002, 412).

At the same time, Ayeneh works not only on the individual—the traditional focus of AA and other related recovery programs—but on the social and cultural patterns that contribute to addiction that predate and extend beyond today's political systems. The notion of a societal illness (*bimāri-ye ejtemāʿi*) transports the illness and addiction from the individual to Iranian society and culture. To address a person's illness is therefore to address the predispositions and symptoms that result from this "sick culture."[23] This is similar to the critique of postrevolutionary Iranian politics and society pervasive in Tehrangeles media, but Ayeneh combines critique with the classic American philosophy of addiction and recovery enshrined in AA and NA. In its early years, AA explicitly steered clear of politics and socioeconomic issues to reduce potential controversy and barriers to participation. Some feminists have criticized this aspect of AA as depoliticizing in its emphasis on a "personal language of pain, healing and individual responsibility rather than . . . a collective narrative of oppression and struggle" (Travis 2009, 219). Beginning in the 1970s, feminists', womanists', and people of color's adaptation of recovery philosophy and practices instead turned recovery into a practical plan to "recover" from culturally and socially grounded "psychological indoctrination. Far from being apolitical because it is *merely* about the self, for feminists invested in a vision of the psyche as a contested terrain," Trysh Travis writes, "recovery is political precisely *to the extent* that it is about the self" (2009, 227, emphasis in the original). In this view, self-care is a radical expression of the self-worth historically and systematically denied to people of color, women, LGBTQ+ people, and other marginalized groups (see hooks 1993, cited by Travis 2009, 227). One seeks recovery from addiction *and* from the experience of living in a denigrating, violent society.

In Iran, NA has been extremely successful, with an estimated 26 percent of the world's NA meetings taking place within the country—second only to the United States. Despite its American and Christian roots, NA has been able to acquire Iranian government support in part because its members strictly avoid politics.[24] This is different from Dariush's and Ayeneh's approach, which considers the staggering rates of drug use and addiction within Iran evidence of far-reaching, long-standing cultural and social maladies that have affected Iranians for generations, if not centuries. In the discourse of Dariush and Ayeneh, part of the responsibility for Iran's addiction problem is its "sick culture" (*farhang-e bimār*). While individuals posting on Ayeneh's websites or calling in to its television programs sometimes blame the Iranian state for the drug addiction epidemic (some assert, for instance, that certain government actors profit from drugs, and that other parties allow drugs to flourish because they prefer the populace incapacitated), Ayeneh communications and Dariush himself generally refrain from attributing Iran's "sick culture" to Islam, the revolution, the Islamic Republic, the shah, modernity, the West, or any other of the usual suspects of expatriate Iranian political polemics.[25] In this usage, "culture" and "illness" become something shared by all Iranians, something that both precedes and transcends the political: "we, the sufferers" are all a part of this constituency of the afflicted. Yet widespread drug addiction and the ineffectual official response make a personal, even "cultural" problem into one of national import that cannot be separated from society and politics, particularly given the shortcomings of official responses to drug consumption and trafficking.

Dariush regularly identifies Iranians' addiction problems as emerging from pervasive denial (*enkār*) that prevents the recognition of "unhealthy attachments" (*vābastegi-ye nāsālem*) to harmful substances, relationships, and ideas. This transforms the discourse of recovery into a mode of diagnosing not only addiction but all kinds of other interpersonal problems. This includes an unhealthy political culture. Encouraging individuals to become "healthy" is a means of empowering them; once healthy, confident, and part of a positive community, they can direct their efforts toward total health, which includes the environment, family life, society, and politics.

If individuals follow the NA/AA prescription to safeguard their recovery by helping others, then recovery spreads and instantiates the AA motto of "world-changing through life-changing." As Abbasseh explained to me:

> We [see that] we're helping one person at a time, and that person has the capability of helping another person. It's that pattern that just gives you hope that you can do the same thing with other issues, with human rights violations, because all of them are injured and diseased, because of . . . whatever it is individually that is hurting them. I think what Dariush has tried to do is look at it from that perspective. It's possible to help one person at a time. Like one of the mottos [people in recovery] believe in is, "Recovery step by step, day by day." It's also recovery one person at a time rather than saving the whole entire country.

Abbasseh's understanding of Ayeneh's mission and efficacy demonstrates dense interconnections between the language and philosophy of the American recovery movement and the foundation's work in Iran. She conceptualizes Iranians' social and political problems as "injury" and "disease" and has faith in the transferability of recovery between individuals and—ultimately—to culture and society. This gradual approach is on the surface more modest and less overtly political than Dariush's former calls to mobilize in service of a distant, "ruined Iran," but it is also more concrete. The individual addiction sufferers who use recovery chat rooms, show up in Ayeneh sponsored detox camps, comment on Dariush's blogs, send faxes and emails to Ayeneh, and are featured on Ayeneh's programs represent specific individuals who have received the "message of recovery" from Dariush and who now have the potential to spread that message and effect change in others.

Among the treatments for Iranians' "sick culture" that Dariush offers are the classic recovery creed "admit it, name it, and be free" and encouragement to learn respect for difference. In Dariush's thought, Iranians' historical and ongoing inability to respect and tolerate difference is one of the primary obstacles to (trans)national political health. He both calls on individuals to respect each other's beliefs and leads by example, incorporating on the same plane the statements of those who have commented on his weblog, reducing the difference between celebrity and fan, and between "enlightened" and ill. Dariush's post on his personal website from June 2013 deploys the cultural illness discourse and models respect for others' voices and opinions. Note his use of the first-person plural in establishing the collective: "Unfortunately, for generations we have deceived ourselves with denial and secretiveness (*panāhkāri*) and have filled society with something called 'fate' (*taghdir*, 'fatalism') . . . to such an extent that we have come to believe [this lie] ourselves. [These beliefs and practices] have silenced us so much that we don't even hear our own cries (faryād)."[26] Dariush then quotes commenters to his website by name, building his argument by including the voices of others who echo his calls to take responsibility for Iranians' sick culture of denial. "The place where [commenter] Ariobarzan writes, 'We are a sick people. Neither do we recognize our own sickness nor do we believe others who tell us we are sick'; . . . when [commenter] Fereshteh writes, 'The main reason for our backwardness is our people and not the regime,' [these comments indicate] that we know the problem, the reasons are clear." Dariush emphasizes that Iranians cannot simply blame the state or anyone else for their national travails but must instead take responsibility for transforming their lives. Deflecting attention from the state may resemble a predictable neoliberal strategy to hold individuals accountable for their recovery while abrogating the state's responsibility for tending to its people. But Dariush is instead calling for a different kind of collectivity—"we the fellow sufferers," which, like "we the people," is self-reflexive and performative, instantiating the collectivity it speaks (Lee and LiPuma 2002, 193–194).

Through quotation, Dariush enacts the larger goal of making individuals aware of their own perspectives and abilities while also confirming that he has read and processed his fans' posts. In a new medium, he acts again as the ever-faithful friend. He is a mirror, reflecting people's words back to them from the other side of the world. This technique resembles the participatory format of call-in television and radio programs like BBC Persian's *Nowbat-e shomā* (*Your Turn*), based on the BBC's *Have Your Say* program, and many other similar programs filmed in Los Angeles, including the call-in segments on the *Ayeneh Program* (Hemmasi 2017c; Voss and Asgari-Targhi 2015). It also performs the ethos of a philosophy of participatory, respectful, nonhierarchical political discourse. Dariush concludes this section of the post by linking illness to toxicity, thus relinking the discursive chain from democratic behavior to harmful substances and healing: "When will we reach a decisive cultural detoxification from this chronic cultural poisoning? . . . Let us depart from toleration, silence, and internalization of our problems, and let us move toward awakening (*bidāri*), effort (*talāsh*), and growth (*ruyesh*), let us break this rule of tolerance and patience [passivity] that this sick culture has issued us and let us join together to [overcome this] history of repetition and repetition of history. Let us write our futures with growth, ideas, and awareness."[27] Dariush moves from describing a pervasive social problem to calling on individuals to initiate change. He then shifts blame from the state to what he understands as the root causes of Iranian suffering and makes individuals responsible for change.

THE REVOLUTION WITHIN

I opened this chapter questioning the likelihood that an expatriate leader could effect change within Iran. The answer to this question depends in part on how one defines change. According to several of my sources (including drug researcher Maziyar Ghiabi), Dariush's televised messages helped move Iranian public opinion on drug (ab)users away from the previously dominant stigmatizing approach and toward a compassionate stance that now has many adherents in Iran. While individuals were holding NA meetings in Iran as early as the 1990s, Dariush and Ayeneh brought the tenets of NA—the Twelve Steps, the slogans, and the practice of witnessing recovery— into the Persian language and broadcast them on satellite television. This opened NA-style recovery discourse and methods to a much larger Persian-speaking audience than meetings alone could have. Finally, Dariush also serves as a rare example of an Iranian celebrity who openly discusses his addiction struggles and his path to recovery.

I had to see Dariush perform live something I did only after interviewing him and studying his music—to feel that I really experienced the charisma that draws in so many fans and followers. When he came to Toronto in 2015, I couldn't convince any of my Iranian friends to attend his concerts with me—Dariush wasn't their cup of tea. I went by myself and got an expensive orchestra seat. The three-thousand-seat auditorium was packed to the gills. Dariush's live repertoire stayed focused on his prerevolutionary hits, songs known to audiences of many generations. The show design was based on this familiarity and organized with the goal of engendering participation. During some of his very best-loved songs—"Yāvar-e hamisheh moʻmen" and "Cheshm-e man" ("My Eyes")—large screens positioned above and to the sides of the stage displayed the lyrics in time with the music. During these numbers, Dariush would look out into the crowd with a small smile of confident expectation on his face, secure in the knowledge, gleaned from years of performing for adoring audiences around the world, that he could rely on those present to take up singing for him: message received. Hearing everyone else around me and the full string section playing the songs' well-known introductions, and reading the lyrics as they help-fully appeared on the screen, I too was swept into the pleasure of participa-tion. When "Zendāni" ("Imprisoned"), one of my favorite Dariush songs, began, I added my voice to the thousands of others singing, together, about loneliness:

> *When missing someone, what's the use of freedom?*
> *Without love, life is a prison*
> *For a sorrowful person, life is a prison*
> *Even when with 100 million people*
> *We are still alone*[28]

We might be alone, but we were alone with him. As fellow sufferers, we were alone together. Dariush was making private pain beautiful, and he was making it social. After the intermission, a red carnation had been placed on my seat and all those in the rows in front of me leading up to the stage. I was unsure about the flowers' purpose, but at the curtain call, as the crowd demanded an encore, it became clear. Audience members got out of their seats, flowers in hand, and pushed toward the stage. Some brandished them in the air as they swayed to the gentle rhythms of Dariush's oldest songs, and others threw them onto the stage. A middle-aged woman made her way to the very front, grabbed Dariush's hand, and pressed it to her lips, holding it there for a moment with her eyes closed. As with the public weeping I de-scribed earlier, I can't say what moved this woman to perform her affection; I also don't know whether she or others would have gathered at Dariush's feet without the floral props that had appeared on their seats. But what I can say is that I felt the pleasure and sanctity of reciprocal devotion cours-ing through the crowd.

What is the political potential of this charisma? It seems that Dariush's thinking on this has changed over time. As the decades have passed, Dari-ush has begun singing and speaking less about the possibility of a physical return to Iran, or the massive, abstract goal of "healing the homeland" that once drove so much of his work. In an interview with an expatriate news outlet, Dariush signaled an even more profound shift regarding his concep-tualization of the homeland: "My vision for the song 'Dobāreh misāzamet vatan' was to invite everyone to build the nation, but lately I have become disappointed. . . . These days, I think more about *vatan-e asli* ('authentic' or 'original' homeland) than *vatan-e khāki* ('territorial' or 'earthly' Iran). . . . These days, I think we should first build the 'authentic vatan'—in other words, ourselves. I think that the nation within us has more shadows than

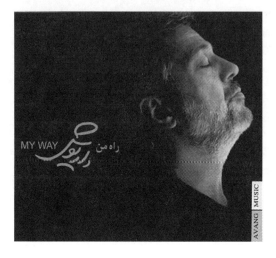

FIGURE 5.4 The cover of his postrecovery album *My Way* presents Dariush alone. The first-person title and image underscore his postrecovery focus on the individual. *Rāh-e man* (*My Way*), DFB Records, 2013.

those the Islamic Republic has created in our country. . . . Today, I think this song should be seen from this perspective."[29] The best way forward is to direct the intention inward, to work on what one can change: one's self.

In this intensified focus on the self, Dariush may appear to be moving away from the social change he has advocated and into the personal as outside of, or beyond, politics. I see this as distinct from the creep of neoliberal therapeutic discourse (see Foster 2015) or a slip from "political commitment" into the personal as "a relief from politics" (Berlant 2008). After years of trying to reach and change a place on the other side of the world, a place Dariush has not been in forty years, maybe another political revolution no longer seems possible, or even desirable. I wonder if acceptance isn't giving up so much as attempting an honest accounting of what can be done and what is within his power. In Dariush's career, he has been most efficacious in reaching into people's emotional lives, into their inner homelands. Maybe accepting this is also part of Dariush's journey. I am reminded of the Serenity Prayer common to the culture of addiction recovery:

> *God grant me the serenity to*
> *Accept the things I cannot change,*
> *Courage to change the things I can,*
> *And wisdom to know the difference.*

The Serenity Prayer is not a rallying cry like the revolutionary slogan "Death to the shah" or Iranian opposition groups' "Death to the Islamic Republic." It is not even so forceful as "Down with Addiction"—a futile statement since, in NA thought, addiction is a chronic condition. The prayer is an acknowledgment that not everything can be changed. Whether we take things as they are or keep working toward their transformation, we will inevitably suffer, and we will need that higher power and our fellow sufferers to make it through. But if someone receives Dariush's message and takes even one step toward healing the homeland within, then Dariush can claim victory.

CONCLUSION
FORTY YEARS

The year 2020 marks the fortieth anniversary of the Islamic Republic of Iran's establishment. This anniversary likewise marks four decades since the Tehrangeles culture industries' beginnings with Shahram Shabpareh's "Deyar." For forty years, individuals and groups holding opposing perspectives on the revolution and its outcomes have understood Iran's present, past, and future in starkly different yet intertwined ways. *Tehrangeles Dreaming* has attended to the work of the first generation of Iranian cultural producers in Southern California representing and circulating their imaginaries while claiming a transcendent, transformative intimacy with their distant compatriots. By way of conclusion, I assess the ongoing relationships between Tehran and Tehrangeles, look to future developments, and close with an examination of how Iranians from Iran and the diaspora negotiate their relationships in the present.

When one looks at some Tehrangeles productions today, it is remarkable how little has changed since the industries' inception. The 2018 song and video "Chehel sāl" ("Forty Years"), which refers to the fortieth anniversary of the Iranian Revolution, is a prime example.[1] Performed by Googoosh and fellow prerevolutionary-turned-Tehrangeles vocalist Siavash Ghomeishi, "Chehel sāl" designates the life span of the Islamic Republic as "a nightmare (*kāvus*) from which there is no awakening."[2] The chorus employs the vocal metaphors typical of Googoosh's "political" songs while speaking hopefully of a future-tense "freedom":

> *O thirstiest sea, we hear your cries, Iran . . .*
> *I believe in [the validity of] your resentments, [and] that one day you will be free*[3]

The accompanying video moves between footage of ordinary Iranians on the streets of Tehran and scenes of Googoosh and Ghomeishi emotively singing against a blank backdrop. Ghomeishi is attired in a close-fitting, sharply tailored black suit and shirt. A perfectly made-up Googoosh wears a floor-length gown with her blond hair in a chignon that shows off her dangling diamond earrings and necklace. Their glamorous appearance contrasts with the scenes of poverty and deprivation within Iran. A shabbily dressed man, either asleep or unconscious, is slumped on a concrete staircase, a pair of dirty crutches beside him. A woman gives money to a girl begging on the street. A man stares into the brightly lit window of a jewelry shop, its display case glittering with gold, as if he is contemplating what he wants but cannot afford. Video editing collapses the distance between Tehran and Tehrangeles: Googoosh's and Ghomeishi's bodies become silhouettes containing scenes of the homeland's pain.[4] Iran's suffering is their suffering. The revolution has failed to deliver on its promise to serve the *mostaza'fin* (oppressed masses). Its fortieth year is the anniversary of its people's ruin.

"Chehel sāl" recycles the dystopic postrevolutionary tropes and images that have characterized Tehrangeles productions over precisely the past forty years. Within Iran, the domestic press's response to "Chehel sāl" redeploys familiar accusations against Tehrangeles artists. A report in the semi-official newspaper *Kayhān* described Googoosh and Ghomeishi as escapees.[5] Googoosh was further described as immoral (*gheir-e akhlāq*) and idolatrous (*tāghuti*), the latter a revolution-era epithet for Pahlavi support-

FIGURE C.1 In the video "Chehel sāl" ("Forty Years"), Googoosh is depicted embodying Iranians' suffering. Screen grab from "Googoosh & Ghomayshi—40 saal Official Music Video," YouTube video, posted by Googoosh, July 31, 2018, https://youtu.be/mNGEwE4LpZQ.

ers. Ghomeishi was seemingly harder to defame: the only stain on his character mentioned in the article was that he had recently lip-synched to his own prerecorded voice during a concert. The report also incorporated familiar accusations against the lyricist, Raha Etemadi, calling him an agent of the "Baha'i-Zionist" expatriate Manoto 1 satellite television channel and stating that he was "wanted by the London police for child abuse." The report cast expatriate artists as depraved and dishonest, literal counterrevolutionaries who collaborated with the Islamic Republic of Iran's enemies to destabilize the state via music video. The artists, their music, their representations of Iran, and their expressions of care for the Iranian people were fundamentally false. What we have, then, is forty years of Tehran and Tehrangeles locked in a clash of mass-mediated imaginaries and counterimaginaries, each projecting its own legitimacy while attempting to delegitimize the other.

Given the repetitiveness of each side's claims to opposing truths, it is tempting to dismiss their perspectives as equally unreal and therefore irrelevant. What *Tehrangeles Dreaming* has argued instead is that we should respect these imaginaries, examine what gives rise to them in the first place, and attend to the conditions, beliefs, and experiences that grant them the "power to make a difference that calls for a response" (Bennett 2010, 32).[6] For all their differences, the various parties competing for Iranian hearts and minds also share a belief in the power of mass-mediated cultural products— especially popular music and musicians—to do things in the world, to reach or change or influence people's hearts, bodies, and minds. Dariush's music "sends a message of recovery," Googoosh "sings the nation's tears," and the Shabpareh brothers' dāmbuli pop makes "Persians' butts move." On the other side, Ayatollah Ruhollah Khomeini's revolutionary declaration likening music to opium also expressed a belief in music's influence over listeners, as did his allowances for patriotic music during wartime. The intervening decades of domestic policy treating music like a controlled substance that is permissible only under highly regulated circumstances further manifest its power.

I have also claimed that the fact that both sides' perspectives include elements of fantasy does not, therefore, make them false. With regard to *Kayhān*'s suggestion that expatriate artists have formed alliances with foreign governments, it is undeniable that the United States and the United Kingdom, among others, have invested tremendous resources in producing Persian-language media intended to attract Iran-based audiences, and that Tehrangeles and other expatriate musicians frequently appear in these media. It is also true that members of these and other governments have, at times, expressed interest in Iranian regime change. The persistent, unconfirmed rumors that Etemadi's and Googoosh's former employer, the Manoto 1 television network, is covertly funded by the United States, the British, or other governments may very well be untrue, but given the contested assemblage of which Iranian media are a part, the rumors are also not implausible. The millions of American dollars and British pounds, and the billions of Iranian tuman, poured into making Iran-directed music and media that assert an agenda, provide a perspective, offer a platform, or do some other kind of cultural-political work are evidence of a widespread belief that this investment is worthwhile.

As tattered from overuse as the "Iran-e virān" trope may be, here, too, there is truth to be told. Historically, Tehrangeles cultural producers have tended to identify the Islamic Republic and/or Islam as the root causes of Iran's postrevolutionary "ruin." Today expatriates, people within Iran, and external observers are increasingly attending to the very serious economic and environmental dangers Iran faces that extend far beyond the state. The long-term effects of US-led economic sanctions, coupled with domestic mismanagement and corruption, have crippled the country's economy and contributed to many other pressing issues. Sanctions cause tremendous collateral damage, for instance, making it difficult for Iranians to access medical treatments and prescription drugs (see Aloosh 2018). The line in "Chehel sāl" referring to Iran as the "thirstiest sea" strikes me as a reference to the appallingly rapid effects of desertification on the Iranian landscape, which has threatened to make large parts of the country uninhabitable.[7] Iran's crisis is incontrovertible—but attributing this primarily to the revolution collapses contemporary complexity and turns it into the same old conflict.

FORTY YEARS OF OVERLAP, ACCOMMODATION, AND CHANGE

An exclusive focus on conflict runs the risk of overlooking the synergistic, productive relationship between expatriates and Iranians inside the country that has also developed over the past forty years. Tehrangeles music's long-term, quotidian presence in Iran bubbles to the surface in a stream of domestic feature films that winkingly include direct references to Tehrangeles pop figures or songs or even incorporate Tehrangeles songs into their soundtracks. A domestic article titled "Los Ānjelesi Songs in Iranian Film" asserts that Tehrangeles pop "has always appealed [to audiences because] it is forbidden! . . . Los ānjelesi music is pervasive among ordinary people ('āmeh mardom). . . . Throughout the past decades, many generations have these songs in their audio-memories."[8] The author then notes that los ānjelesi pop has a longer history in Iran than (postrevolutionary) domestic pop; "pop of the homeland" (pāp-e vatani), as the author calls it, can't be used in films or anywhere else to recall the 1980s and 1990s because it wasn't available until around 1997. Iranian director Saman Moghaddam's *Nahang-e Anbar* (*Sperm Whale*; Seven Crystal Globe, 2015), for instance, is set during the Iran-Iraq War and incorporates snippets of songs by Shahram Shabpareh, Jalal Hemmati, and Shohreh Solati along with Michael Jackson, Modern Talking, and Boney M, all artists who were both officially prohibited and commonly listened to by many Iranians during this period. Cinema reveals the open secret of Tehrangeles pop in the Iranian collective memory.[9]

In the decades since domestic pop music's legalization, however, new generations of musicians at home have become increasingly productive and popular. These exclusively male pop star vocalists regularly hold concerts, release albums and videos, and have many domestic and diasporic fans. Official parameters of acceptability have pragmatically expanded to include many previously restricted cultural practices and forms. Shesh-o-hasht's exile is long over—now many domestic, officially approved songs build on this danceable rhythm, so it is no longer necessary to turn to Teh-

FIGURE C.2 A flyer advertising Iranian artist Ehsan Khajeh Amiri's Los Angeles concert represents the growing appeal of domestic pop in the North American diaspora.

rangeles to get in touch with this previously suppressed aspect of Iranian culture. Officially approved artists such as Benjamin Bardori and Ehsan Khajeh Amiri have toured North American cities with large Iranian populations, effectively reversing (though not ending) the trend of Tehrangeles artists traveling to countries near Iran. Even with the loosening of domestic restrictions on musical activity and the success of some stars, musicians who work within the official system often describe it as challenging, slow, and frustrating. This leads many individuals to make music on their own terms. Musicians lacking official permits record, disseminate, and perform their music via house concerts, private recording studios, the internet, and their domestic and international social networks. While individuals are occasionally arrested for participating in underground concerts or disseminating their music without official permission, many musicians are also adept at navigating local policies and law enforcement and regularly undertake these and other disapproved activities without issue (Niknafs 2016; Nooshin 2005b; Robertson 2012; Siamdoust 2017).

All the same, the challenges of working in Iran have contributed to a steady stream of musicians leaving the country and seeking opportunities abroad. Some musicians working in pop styles have joined forces with the Tehrangeles establishment. Shadmehr Aghili, one of the first official pop stars of the 1990s, left Iran for Canada and then landed in Los Angeles, where he has released a stream of albums. Shahbal Shabpareh's prerevolutionary-turned-Tehrangeles boy group Black Cats has taken in male pop vocalists from Iran and elsewhere in the diaspora; the newest front man, Edvin, grew up in Iran, lived in the United Arab Emirates, moved to Southern California as a young adult, and joined the Black Cats after trying his luck in the mainstream American music industry. Even as Tehrangeles's future as a center of Iranian popular music is called into question, pop musicians can still find opportunities there. Rock and hip-hop artists of the postrevolutionary generations, however, have tended to avoid working with Tehrangeles figures or institutions. In the mid-2000s, some unofficial rock bands like 127, TarantisT, Hypernova, and the Yellow Dogs, as well as a variety of solo artists, eventually immigrated to the United States, where they have been celebrated by diasporic audiences, the mainstream Western press, and Western government–sponsored Persian-language media. Many other musicians have immigrated to western Europe. Changes to the way music is made and disseminated mean that individuals can be physically separate and still create music together, so that satellite television, the internet, and social media are sites for media-enabled long-distance collaboration.

Even in the face of these differences, younger generations of postrevolutionary arrivals sometimes undertake similar activities and share perspectives with their Southern Californian elders. A recent example is the 2018 video "Shayād" ("Fraud"), a cover of prerevolutionary political singer Fereydun Foroughi's song of the same name, which is stitched together out of contributions by ten postrevolutionary first-generation artists from the United States, Germany, France, and the Netherlands (Shahrzad Sepanlou's participation in the project represents her move away from Tehrangeles and toward the "alternative" scene that did not yet exist in the diaspora when she was starting out). Released in response to a wave of urban Iranian protests in the winter of 2017–2018, the video opens with a dedication to "the oppressed people of Iran" (*mardom-e setamdideh-ye Iran*), while the song is a sarcastic rebuke of the state as a "fraud" that claims to represent the Iranian people.[10]

Also like their Tehrangeles counterparts, many of these recently arrived musicians avoid returning to Iran. Some have worked with Voice of America or Radio Farda, which, from the perspective of the Iranian state, makes them soldiers in the soft war. Expatriate musicians Mohsen Namjoo and Shahin Najafi have both been sentenced in absentia for insulting Islam through their musical works and cannot safely return to Iran. Ramin Seyed-Emami, an "unofficial" rock musician and former front man of the band Hypernova, went back to Iran after several years abroad and worked within the official music system. His father, the prominent environmental activist and professor of sociology Kavous Seyed-Emami, was arrested on espionage charges and died under mysterious circumstances while jailed in Evin Prison, prompting his sons to flee the country. While I am not aware of anyone suggesting that Kavous Seyed-Emami's death was related to his son's musical career, the tragic episode reveals the high stakes of working in Iran if things go terribly wrong.

Risk is also a reason that there are fewer women represented in the younger generation of popular music migrants from Iran. Despite all the official permissiveness toward popular music over the past decades, the public presence of the solo singing female voice and dancing body continues to be treated as a violation of public morality. The Iranian Islamic Penal Code makes women responsible to a more stringent set of standards than men; even if they undertake precisely the same activities as their male counterparts, they face harsher consequences for their online, on-screen, and offshore indiscretions. A particularly sensational example is Tehran teenager Maedeh Hojabri's 2018 arrest for posting Instagram videos of herself dancing at home to a mix of domestic and foreign pop music. Hojabri, who had an estimated 600,000 followers, weepingly confessed to her internet crimes on a nationally broadcast Iranian television program called *Birāheh* (*Wrong Path*).[11] The international media seized on Hojabri's case as the latest example of a cruel and out-of-touch Iranian government punishing young people for being young. Naturally, this attention massively increased the circulation of Hojabri's videos. It also spawned an internet campaign of Hojabri's supporters posting homemade videos of themselves dancing to highlight just how innocuous and common this activity is. Hojabri's story exemplifies the continuing sensitivities surrounding women, media, "moral corruption," and politics in the Islamic Republic's fourth decade. At the same time, individuals in and outside of Iran suggested that Hojabri's arrest and confession were strategically timed to distract from a domestic financial corruption scandal. Whether or not this is true, it is an important reminder that while the parameters of official moral acceptability can expand (as they did with music in the 1980s), they can also expediently contract.[12] The unpredictable outcomes associated with high-profile, morally transgressive participation in the transnational Iranian mediascape are, for many women, a deterrent—unless they have decided they do not want to return to Iran.

SECOND- AND THIRD-GENERATION
IRANIANS IN AMERICA

Overall, Iranians born and/or raised in America are not particularly active in the Persian-language mediascape. The perception among older Tehrangeles music and media producers is that these "hyphenated" individuals are less interested in Persian-language music than their parents or other first-generation Iranians. In 2007 Jam-e Jam satellite television channel operator Kourosh Bibiyan explained that Tehrangeles companies could not count on the second-generation Iranian Americans to sustain them in the future: "[Tehrangeles] record companies are making CDs for 70 million people [Iran's population], but they can only sell 200,000! Obviously, they cannot sell in Iran, and over here, everything is dissolving. My son is eighteen, and he doesn't know these singers anymore. . . . [The second generation] is not Iranian anymore. Maybe they speak Farsi, but they are not Iranian anymore. [To me:] You speak Farsi, but you're not Iranian. You eat *ghormeh sabzi* [an Iranian stew], see your parents. . . . [You] are Americans who happen to speak Farsi." Bibiyan's pessimism emerged from the entwined uncertainty of the music and media business and the transformations in the Iranian migrant population over time. At the time of our interview, the limited profitability of CD sales was hitting home, and Tehrangeles artists were increasingly producing their own music, both developments that called the Tehrangeles music companies' purpose into question. In terms of identification, Bibiyan and his generation had not been in Iran in decades; they might or might not relate to their compatriots who had spent those same decades in the Islamic Republic. They were also not "Americans" like their children. To whom would Bibiyan's productions appeal? Where and how would they be sold?

From another perspective, second-generation media business entrepreneurs have a leg up on their elders. Unlike the founding cohort of the Tehrangeles culture industries, who arrived in the United States as adults and, in many cases, have predominantly operated in diasporic social and professional circles for decades, second-generation Iranian music and media producers can function in mainstream American as well as Iranian diasporic environments. They enter what is called "the Iranian market" by choice, not out of necessity. In addition to being "native" to America, members of this group are also "digital natives": they were born in the internet age and do not have the same challenges adjusting to the fact that the sale of musical objects no longer drives the music and media business. Armin Hashemi, who has spent most of his life outside of Iran, now presides over longtime Tehrangeles music company Avang Records and has succeeded in taking the company into the age of social media. The triumph of pragmatism and profits over ideology is increasingly important to the next generation of expatriate media producers and distributors in terms of collaborations with Iran-based partners. Radio Javan (Radio "Youth") is a Persian-language media company based in northern Virginia that is operated by Iranian men, most of whom have lived in the United States since their teens. The site and mobile-device application feature artists from Tehrangeles, Iranian state-approved artists, and independent artists from inside and outside the country; the company has also expanded to a satellite television channel that broadcasts free to air in the Middle East. Radio Javan content avoids political opinions or allegiances; further, the conditions for entering this very popular site are not political but financial—it costs to be included. Radio Javan offers different pricing schemes for different levels of promotion, a model also followed by other expatriate media outlets.

Second-generation vocalists, songwriters, and lyricists do not have the same prominence in the transnational Iranian mediascape. Raha Etemadi is exceptional in this regard—he left Iran as an infant, grew up in Sweden, and went to university in Southern California, where he became involved in the Tehrangeles music industry before moving to London to be a host on Manoto 1; as of the time of writing, he has left Manoto 1 and is back in Los Angeles. Etemadi is also unlike many Iranians raised outside of the country in his ability to write lyrics and converse fluently in Persian. As evidenced in his lyrics for "Man hamun Iranam" and "Chehel sāl," despite having very little firsthand experience in Iran, he builds upon expatriate tropes that his Tehrangeles elders have been utilizing for years. Other second-generation artists appear in Tehrangeles pop productions from time to time, but comparatively few have become widely popular. Overall, they have different skills, genre preferences, and points of view than recent migrants of either pre- or postrevolutionary groups, who draw from the wellspring of Iranian language, music, culture, and history and are likewise often focused on Iran.[13]

TEHRAN MEETS TEHRANGELES
AT CABARET TEHRAN

Bibiyan's expectation of Tehrangeles's waning importance has been borne out in some regards. His father's pioneering Jam-e Jam cable and satellite television station closed in 2009, just two years after our interview. My visits to music shops on Westwood Boulevard's "Persian Square" have increasingly revealed dusty shelves and displays that change little from year to year. Ketab Corporation, an important book and music store in the heart of the neighborhood, closed in 2017. The action is online, on-screen, and elsewhere—other locations in North America, Iran, the United Arab Emirates, and Turkey. For some, however, Tehrangeles still holds allure, offers pleasures and potential professional opportunities and a chance to meet and work with some of the greats of Iranian popular music. To close *Tehrangeles Dreaming*, I turn to an episode I witnessed at a karaoke night at Cabaret Tehran, when an Iran-based artist came to perform in front of Shahbal Shabpareh, the evening's regular host.

Cabaret Tehran is one of the longest-operating Iranian night spots in Southern California. On Thursdays, Fridays, and Saturdays, the typical program includes several sets by Tehrangeles-based pop singers backed by a house band. Iranian DJs and usually non-Iranian belly dancers fill out the program. The space has a vaguely 1980s nautical theme—its polished wooden interior details resemble a boat's lower deck—while the narrow stage goes for more sparkle with tinsel garlands and a few flat-screen televisions showing music videos. On the five times or so I've visited Cabaret Tehran between 2007 and 2017, the crowd has been almost exclusively Iranian but otherwise diverse in terms of age and migration generation—some people who've been in Los Angeles for years, others who have just arrived from Iran, diasporic visitors from other locations, and everyone in between. The repertoire available on Cabaret Tehran's karaoke machine is a very Southern Californian Iranian mélange that emphasizes prerevolutionary and Tehrangeles pop with a handful of domestic Iranian pop selections and American hit songs thrown in. Shahbal Shabpareh is the regular host; on this night, he was joined by a cohost I will call Mani. The two of them work off each other to encourage participants, quiz them on Iranian music history, and rib them a little for the audience's amusement.

This episode took place in July 2015. The venue was packed with happy, boisterously chatting parties who drank beer or tea and egged each other on to take a turn at the microphone. Mani, a capable singer, warmed up the crowd with a rousing rendition of Elvis Presley's "It's Now or Never." A few other patrons sang prerevolutionary songs while the audience joined in on the choruses. The tone of the evening changed when a young man disrupted Shabpareh's usual routine of introducing each singer by name. After some off-mic exchanges, Shabpareh explained the situation to the crowd: "This [next singer] has just recently come from Iran. He's only arrived here one week ago. He's a singer from Iran, meaning . . . everyone knows him there. . . . He says we will recognize him not by his appearance, but by his name. . . . His name is 'Abdolreza.' He doesn't want to give his last name because there could be problems for him when he goes back."

"Abdolreza" had apparently described himself to Shabpareh as an officially approved singer who was well known in Iran and was visiting California for a short time. This night took place two years before the Trump travel ban, the series of executive orders and presidential proclamations limiting Iranians' and other foreign nationals' entrance into the United States. Restrictions on Iranian visitors are nothing new; since the revolution and the dissolution of Iranian-American diplomatic relations, few Iranians (other than students) have been granted visas to visit the United States. But it was not fear of Americans that led Abdolreza to hide his real name: it was the spectral presence of the Islamic Republic. A night of performing pop songs publicly alongside Tehrangeles figures in a venue in which men and unveiled women mixed freely and alcohol was served could damage Abdolreza's reputation and his career. Shabpareh had a patient demeanor when conveying this information to the crowd. Cohost Mani responded with rancor:

"Man, death to [current Supreme Leader Ali] Khamenei!" (*Yāru, marg bar Khamenei!*)

"No, no, don't say things like that here!" Shabpareh jumped in, attempting to diffuse the tension. Offhanded insults toward Iranian government officials are unremarkable in Southern California, but given Abdolreza's apparent sensitivity, attacking the religious and political head of the Iranian state could make him even more uncomfortable. Mani, however, wasn't done. As Shabpareh went through the karaoke machine lists searching for Abdolreza's selection, he questioned the singer again.

"So, you want to go back [to Iran]?" Mani said this as if it was a ridiculous idea.

Shabpareh jumped in once more: "Hey, leave him alone! Yes, he wants to make some music here and then go back!"

"But what about the internet?" Mani asked.

Even though he was halfway around the world from Iran, anyone in the audience could take a photo or video of Abdolreza, upload it to the internet, and expose his transgressions to the public. While that is perhaps not likely, "fear of the internet" is part of the larger phenomenon of Iranian celebrities and public figures taking great care to maintain a proper demeanor when they travel abroad because they assume they are under surveillance. For women, this self-monitoring includes wearing a veil in public—even if very small or made of sheer fabric—to perform their adherence to domestic Iranian modesty laws.

Ignoring Mani's impertinence, Abdolreza sang his selection with gusto. He had chosen prerevolutionary-turned-Tehrangeles star Ebi's song "Ghorbat" ("Estrangement"/"Exile"), which ends on a sustained high note. Abdolreza reached the dramatic conclusion and held the final note while the crowd clapped and hooted appreciatively. Now that he saw that Abdolreza could deliver, Mani became admiring.

"I swear to God, even Ebi can't sing that high! You sang at least two notes higher than him!" Mani said.

It was Shabpareh's turn to tease Abdolreza while complimenting his performance: "I hope you have somewhere to stay here [in Los Angeles], because now we are definitely not letting [you] go. Your name, again? Right—Abdolreza . . . because if you give us your real name they might [arrest] you."

"Shahbal," Mani quipped, "if they arrest him, he'll become famous!"[14]

Ignoring Mani's dark sarcasm, Shabpareh assessed Abdolreza's commercial prospects should he attempt to follow in so many others' footsteps and restart his career abroad.

"And *māshallāh*, he's good-looking, too! . . . But really, I'm telling you the truth. Don't leave Iran. I'm telling you, if you give a concert here, maybe these guys [he gestured to the audience] will buy some tickets at the last minute. They do that to all the singers. . . . The poor singer has been advertising the concert for six months, and people only buy tickets in the last hour. Buy the tickets, people!" Shabpareh wrapped up the theme of audiences' lack of support for Iranian music and asked the audience to applaud Abdolreza once more.

By making public his desire for his performance to remain private, or at least limited to the intimate gathering at Cabaret Tehran that night, Abdolreza showed how paranoid imaginaries coexist with the pleasures of performing collective memories through popular song. Abdolreza's aspiration to express himself abroad and still return to Iran is a deferred desire for many well-known Iranian musicians before him, who have instead made their music abroad and never gone back. Like the fictional Maxx, who warns his young fans in Iran not to follow him into the diaspora, Shabpareh cautions Abdolreza against the seductions of Tehrangeles dreams. For all the focus in Tehrangeles on what Iranians within Iran do not have, if Abdolreza can make a decent living under the current system, he might be better off staying put than placing himself at the whims of fickle diaspora audiences, who don't respect musicians much anyway. In addition to being unreliable, the number of Iranians in the diaspora is a small fraction of Abdolreza's millions of potential fans in Iran. Even as Shabpareh and Mani recognize Abdolreza's fears of exposure—a situation he could avoid if he remained in California—Shabpareh's directive that he should "stay in Iran" is also a rare Tehrangeles acknowledgment that Iran might not be completely "ruined" after all.

For decades, the dream of success on Southern California's sandy shores has borne seekers of all origins to Los Angeles. Powerful, transnational, media-enabled imaginaries have established it as a place of becoming, of possibility, where dreams can come true. In the case of the Tehrangeles culture industries' founders, the process of starting over and reinventing themselves in the aftermath of the revolution was an opportunity and, likewise, a tremendous loss. For this generation, California has also been a place to dream of Iran as they seek a role in the country's past, present, and future. The current dispersal of production and dissemination may mean that Tehrangeles's geographic concentration of artists, networks, and businesses is no longer necessary. Or, as Tehrangeles's founding cohort inevitably passes away, it may yet be replaced by more first-generation musical migrants who feel compelled to relocate abroad while pursuing connection and relevance to their compatriots at home. Whatever the case, Iranians—wherever they are—will be dreaming.

NOTES

INTRODUCTION

1 Sepideh, vocalist, "Kish," by Sepideh and Ramin Zamani, on *Girl in the Mirror* (*Dokhtar tu-ye āyeneh*), Caltex Records, 2004.

2 "Sepideh—Kish | Sepideh—Kish," YouTube video, posted by Persian Music Video, August 15, 2005, https://youtu.be/sfWXloPGs40.

3 Shahram Shabpareh, "Deyar (Folk Version)" ("Homeland"), by Shahram Shabpareh, on *Deyar* (*Country*), OF-OZ Record, 1980. Two versions of "Deyar" appear on this album: a "Disco Version" and a "Folk Version." I have most often heard the Folk Version at Iranian events; it is also the version Shabpareh used for the "Deyar" music video. When I discuss "Deyar" in the text, I am referring to the Folk Version. The Disco Version, created by established disco DJ and producer Farokh "Elton" Ahi, preceded the Folk Version and was played at mainstream European and American (non-Iranian) dance clubs in the 1980s and 1990s. According to Ahi, Shabpareh did not like the Disco Version; the Folk Version was made to suit his preferences. For more on Ahi's career, see Parham Nik-Eteghad, "Hit-Machine: Interview with Elton Farokh Ahi [*sic*]," Iranian.com, July 31, 2007, https://iranian.com/2007/07/31/hit-machine/.

4 Dariush, "Vatan" ("Homeland"), on *Sāl-e do hezār* (*Year 2000*), Caltex Records, 1991. "Vatan" fits new words by expatriate Iranian lyricist Iraj Jannatie Ataie to the melody and arrangement of José Feliciano's 1974 song "Gypsy" (on *For My Love...Mother Music*, RCA Victor). On all the recordings of "Vatan" I have seen, Feliciano is listed as the song's composer.

5 Reza Gholami (2015, 109) discusses the use of "pure Persian" on expatriate television in the context of anti-Arab Iranian nationalism. See Naficy (1993, 125–165) on the "fetishization" of nation in Los Angeles Iranian television in the 1980s.

6 Sepideh Music, accessed March 18, 2019, https://www.sepidehmusic.com.

7 Pre Islamic Iran has a long life in Iranian political imaginaries, most prominently in the last Pahlavi monarch's self-coronation as heir to the throne of Cyrus the Great, and in the postrevolutionary search for a non-Islamic Iranian identity.

8 See Gahan (2017, 106–119) for an extensive discussion of the history of public morality laws in Iran. Early twentieth-century laws were explicitly protective of women's honor (*nāmus*), but they did not require veiling. In 1936 Reza Khan issued his famous unveiling decree that forced women to appear in public without hijab.

9 The postrevolutionary Iranian Islamic Penal Code is a novel combination of Islamic law (*shar'ia*), modern law, local custom, and long-standing and newly developed Shiite jurisprudential notions of justice, property, propriety, and other issues. Public morality crimes and their punishments are detailed in Iranian Islamic Penal Code, bk. 5, ch. 18, articles 638–640. Available in translation from "Islamic Penal Code of the Islamic Republic of Iran—Book Five," Iran Human Rights Documentation Center, June 15, 2013, https://iranhrdc.org/islamic-penal-code-of-the-islamic-republic-of-iran-book-five/.

10 Iranian Islamic Penal Code, bk. 1, ch. 1, art. 7. For an English translation, see "English Translation of Books I & II of the New Islamic Penal Code," Iran Human Rights Documentation Center, April 4, 2014, https://iranhrdc.org/english-translation-of-books-i-ii-of-the-new-islamic-penal-code/.

11 Khomeini's proclamation appeared in "Ezhārāt-e emām dar mored-e barnāmeh-hā-ye musiqi-ye radio-television" [The Imam's statements on music programming on radio and television], *E'telā'āt* (Information), Mordad 1, 1358/July 23, 1979. On this pronouncement, see also Youssefzadeh (2000, 38).

12 Thanks to Jairan Gahan for insights regarding the language of this fatwa.

13 On expediency in relation to women's rights, see Ghamari-Tabrizi (2013); on drug policy, see Ghiabi (2015); and on food, see Chehabi (2007).

14 See Frishkopf (2010, 33) on a similar dynamic in commercial Arab satellite television.

15 On Cubans in Miami, see Johnson (2010); Laguna (2014); and Mirabal (2003). On Vietnamese in Orange County, see Aguilar-San Juan (2009); Cunningham and Nguyen (2003); and Adelaida Reyes (1999). On Taiwan, see Guy (2005); and Shiau (2009).

16 For more on prerevolutionary popular music, see Breyley (2010); Hemmasi (2013); Shay (2000); and especially Breyley and Fatemi (2016).

17 Kurzman compares this 10 percent participation in the Iranian Revolution with the French Revolution (estimated 2 percent of the populace) and the movement to overthrow Soviet rule (approximately 1 percent).

18 "Pishnehād-e hākem-e shar'-e Tehran barāyeh eshteqāl-e honarpisheh-hā" [A Tehran religious scholar's recommendations regarding the occupation of actors], *Kayhān*, Farvardin, 14, 1359/April 3, 1980. At the time of this interview, Gilani was a judge in the revolutionary courts. On the revolutionary courts' agenda, Gilani continues, "Our motive for summoning [popular vocalists] was public decency (*'effat-e 'omumi*) in a Muslim society. This means that in an Islamic government, state institutions prevent that which contradicts Islamic morality."

19 Songwriter Babak Bayat is an exception in that he left Iran for Los Angeles in the 1980s but then returned to Iran and became active in officially approved music productions.

20 I did not focus on second-generation Iranian Americans and therefore cannot be sure what accounts for their lower levels of participation. My guess is a combination of more opportunity and less skill: 1.5- and second-generation individuals had more non-Iranian avenues open to them than their parents' generation, while they also lacked the language and cultural knowledge needed to successfully perform or operate in the predominantly Persian-language music business. Iranian Swedish lyricist and media personality Raha Etemadi is a notable exception, as is the internet radio company Radio Javan (based in the Washington, DC, area), both of which I describe in the conclusion. Iranian Americans do make popular culture, but it tends to be more oriented toward their experience as minorities in the United States, while the first generation is more oriented toward Iran. For more on Iranian American diasporic media and cultural production, see, among others, Alinejad (2017), Maghbouleh (2017), and Malek (2015).

21 Decades of tense relationships between Iran and many other states have radically curtailed Iranian citizens' mobility. The process of acquiring a visa to enter western Europe or North America is typically expensive, lengthy, and uncertain. Those who wish to visit the United States or Canada, which do not have embassies in Iran, must take the additional step of traveling to a consulate in a third country. Since Donald J. Trump took office as the president of the United States, it has been virtually impossible for Iranians to enter the United States. Under the June 26, 2018, Supreme Court decision on Presidential Proclamation 9645, better known as the Trump travel ban, Iranians are prohibited from receiving all immigrant and almost all nonimmigrant visas. The proclamation also affects citizens of Libya, North Korea, Somalia, Syria, Venezuela, and Yemen. To my knowledge, most Tehrangeles artists have dual Iranian and American citizenship and are therefore not directly affected by the ban.

22 For more about BBC Persian and its mission, see Sreberny and Torfeh (2014); and Voss and Asgari-Targhi (2015). On the popular US-sponsored Radio Farda program *Parazit* (Static), see Semati (2012).

23 Soft war is an update of the 1990s rhetorical formulation of "cultural attack" (*tahajom-e farhangi*), which some commentators suggest was a cynical move to galvanize the population's nationalist impulses once the Iran-Iraq War was finished. See Kian (1995).

24 The same court gave a lesser sentence to Saeed Karimian, the founder of Dubai-based GEM TV, a satellite television company that dubs Western programming into Persian for Iranian audiences. The announcements of sentencing in absentia were reproduced on many websites in and outside of Iran, often titled with exclamation points and breathless commentary. See, for instance, the report "Googoosh be shānzdah sāl mahkum shod!" [Googoosh sentenced to 16 years in prison!], *Bahar News*, Esfand 16, 1395/March 5, 2017, http://www.bahar news.ir/news/126665/گوگوش-16-سال-زندان-محکوم.

25 A report on Googoosh's 2010 concert in Dubai appearing on the Radio Free Europe/Radio Liberty website identifies Radio Farda, a US government–supported media outlet directed at Iran-based audiences, as the concert's sponsor. "Googoosh Draws Thousands of Iranians in Dubai," *Radio Free Europe/Radio Liberty*, March 25, 2010, https://www.rferl.org/a/Googoosh_Draws_Thousands _Of_Iranians_In_Dubai/1993808.html.

26 Ardeshir Ahmadi's comic internet series *Az Vancouver tā Los Āngeles* (From Vancouver to Los Angeles) documents his adventures in Tehrangeles. Ardeshir Ahmadi, "Az Vancouver tā Los Āngeles ghesmat-e avval (From Vancouver to Los Angeles part one)," YouTube video, 8:51 mins., January 30, 2013, https://youtu. be/zHBK_68elDg. Arash Tebbi and Nima M.'s rap song "Kind of Persian" makes fun of "Persians" in Los Angeles; it features the video's director, Ahmad Kiarostami, asking Iranians in Southern California how they identify themselves. Most say "Persian." Much of the video is filmed at the annual Sizdah Be Dar festival at Balboa Park in the San Fernando Valley. "Kind of Persian," YouTube video, posted by Ahmad Kiarostami, October 12, 2009, https://youtu.be /OxBfJffCoAs.

27 Zed Bazi, "Iroonie LA," YouTube video, posted by Wig3n, December 1, 2009, https://youtu.be/510mQRIlj6w.

28 *Shahs of Sunset* participant, A$A Soltan released a single in 2012 called "Tehrangeles." However, neither the song nor the singer's other works are produced within the Tehrangeles music industry structure. See Maghbouleh (2017) on Los Angelenos' racist discrimination against Iranians.

29 "Un Cut with Mehrdad Asemani Part 5," YouTube video, posted by Tapesh TV Network, January 22, 2017, https://youtu.be/JjzPJoBaDoI.

30 Ida Meftahi's (2016b) prerevolutionary genealogy of artistic "degeneration" (*ebtezāl*) is critical to my understanding of the stigma surrounding Tehrangeles. I discuss the concept further in chapter 1.

31 Tehrangeles cultural producers' fears are grounded in uncertainty as well as the observed experience of their colleagues. As I discuss in chapter 3, in 2002 the Tehrangeles media personality, dancer, and aerobics instructor Mohammad Khordadian was imprisoned in the notorious Evin Prison for "spreading corruption" via his Los Angeles–produced aerobic dance instruction videotapes. See Papan-Matin (2009). In 2005 guitarist and composer Babak Amini was arrested and had his passport confiscated for collaborating with Googoosh. See Hemmasi (2011). Lyricists and musicians inside Iran who collaborate with Tehrangeles figures have also faced persecution at home: in 2013 well-known lyricist Roozbeh Bemani was arrested for writing lyrics for both Dariush and Googoosh. In chapter 3 I discuss the exceptional case of prerevolutionary-turned-Tehrangeles musician Habib Mohebbian (1947–2016), who made news as one of the only well-known members of the expatriate music industry to resettle in Iran.

32 The quintessential politically paranoid Iranian is Uncle Napoleon, the main character in Iraj Pezeshkzad's 1973 novel *Dāyi jān Nāpolon* (*Dear Uncle Napoleon*), whose belief in British-led plots against Iran is a humorous theme throughout the book. This novel was widely read and became a very popular television series in the 1970s; Iranians continue to reference Uncle Napoleon when poking fun at each other's paranoid tendencies. Dick Davis's 1996 English translation is titled *My Uncle Napoleon.*

33 For related scholarly takes on mass-mediated popular culture's potential blurring of postrevolutionary Iranian public and private spheres, see, among others, Amir-Ebrahimi (2008); Mozafari (2013); Nooshin (2018); and Siamdoust (2015).

34 The controversy raging around Azar Nafisi and her best-selling 2003 memoir *Reading Lolita in Tehran* is but one example of how diaspora portrayals of Iran become enmeshed in international and intradiasporic political contestation. See Hamid Dabashi, "Native Informers and the Making of the American Empire," *Al-Ahram Weekly Online*, June 1–7, 2006. On the question of what ethnographers make public about Muslims in America after 9/11, see Andrew Shryock's insightful 2004 essay.

35 See Ortner (2010) on the challenges of conducting fieldwork within the Hollywood movie industry, and the dynamics of "studying up" and "horizontally."

36 When used to describe people, *sonnati* (traditional) can mean religiously observant, employing *taʿārof* (Iranian etiquette), maintaining close extended-family relations, engaging in "traditional" professions (working as bazaar merchants, weaving carpets), and/or identifying with local, and specifically non-Western, aesthetics and ways of being. The conceptual opposite is *modern*, which typically refers to people who identify as secular and embrace technology, secular higher education, and "Western" ideals. This obviously reductive binary is part of common discourse.

37 My focus is less on revealing celebrities' "real selves" than attending to the labor

and strategy involved in constructing and managing celebrity personae. This approach is informed by P. David Marshall, Christopher Moore, and Kim Barbour's notes on "persona as method": "While the application of cultural studies to the media has led to a theorization of the collective agency of the audience, persona studies shifts to the study of the agency of the individual. . . . The focus of persona studies is thus on how the individual 'publicizes,' 'presents' and strategically 'enacts' their persona. Likewise, the study of the celebrity 'persona' is therefore trying to work out what are the strategies of foregrounding versions of public and private presentations and how these relate to the individual celebrity negotiating his/her persona within institutions and the broader culture" (Marshall, Moore, and Barbour 2015, 290).

1. THE CAPITAL OF 6/8

1 To my knowledge, there are no publicly circulating documents or decrees formalizing the ban. This is not unusual with regard to restrictions on cultural production. Rarely do strict policies come to light—the parameters are often divined via interpretation, some of which is inherent in the religious texts on which the policies build. See Siamdoust (2017, 28–30).

2 "Goftegu bā Shahyar Ghanbari, shā'er va tarāneh sarāi" [A conversation with poet and songwriter Shahyar Ghanbari], Tehran Review, October 23, 2012, http://tehranreview.net/articles/11696#.UIcUw1F_kR-.

3 Along with my own experiences dancing to shesh-o-hasht pop music with my family, Anthony Shay's (2000) "The 6/8 Beat Goes On: Persian Popular Music from Bazm-e Qajariyyeh to Beverly Hills Garden Parties" also inspired my documentation of this rhythmic figure's impressive historical continuity.

4 As Louise Meintjes puts it, "Musical style derives its meaning and affective power primarily through its association with the sociopolitical positioning and social values of music participants . . . and through the sensuous experience of those who encounter it" (2003, 9).

5 Compare the higher-status Qajar court musicians, who were Muslim. In a presentation at Columbia University in 2007, Houman Sarshar, who is carrying out an oral history of Jewish motreb in the United States, noted that low-status and negative associations with motreb are such that some former professional entertainers deny ever having served in the role, despite documentary evidence to the contrary.

6 The colloquial, folksy sung and chanted lyrics across these genres do not tend to follow the quantitative 'aruz metrical system of classical Arabic and Persian poetry but instead incline to trochees and iambs, which work well in the compound duple meter. See Breyley and Fatemi (2016, 33–62) on the motrebi repertoires, including a brief description of the rhythms of chanted rhyming poetry

in *charand-gui* ("nonsense"). Note the hemiolas in the charand-gui "Beshkan beshkaneh" ("Snap, Snap") (53). See also Fatemi (2003), a study of rhythm in children's nursery rhymes and games, which, he shows, are related to the motrebi repertoire.

7 The dance rhythm is associated with the Persian ethnic group, as opposed to Kurds, Azeris, or any number of other ethnolinguistic or regionally associated social groups in Iran. Shesh-o-hasht is also not only Persian. The same rhythmic groove—or something very similar—is also found in Tajik, Armenian, and Iraqi musical genres.

8 According to G. J. Breyley and Sasan Fatemi (2016, 106), from the mid-twentieth century, innovative performers and composers of tasnif sought to "liberate themselves from the yoke of these ternary rhythms, which were considered worn and banal, [and so] tended towards 4/4, 2/4 and 3/4 rhythms." Drummers were the lowest-status members of the ensemble, not even considered musicians but often insulted with the term *dombaki*.

9 In the 1950s, Iranians broadly used the term *jāz* to refer to new, locally produced, Western-influenced popular songs accompanied by guitar and drum kit. *Jāz* is also sometimes used to refer to a drum kit itself. Besides instrumentation, the Iranian jāz style of this period bears little similarity to American or European jazz.

10 In their extensive analysis of twentieth-century Iranian popular music, Breyley and Fatemi (2016) distinguish between motrebi, kāfe-i, and kucheh-bāzāri musical styles. Collectively, these are typically glossed as *mardomi* in popular parlance. Because *mardomi* was the term used in Tehrangeles and in conversations with Iranians elsewhere, I retain it here. Shay (2000, 344) describes mardomi music thus: "In the modernist/nationalist discourse mardomi popular music . . . occupies a negative space: its cheerfully vulgar lyrics and music represent the old, the traditional, the backward; and its consumption was associated in the public mind with the urban proletariat and professions such as taxi driving and trucking. It presented to both educated classes and government officialdom a subversive genre in which sexuality, gender, and sly political references created varying degrees of discomfort."

11 Sociologist Masoud Yazdi's (1978) article "Jā'meh-shenāsi-ye musiqi-ye tudeh-i dar Iran" [The sociology of popular music in Iran] is a fascinating example of a revolution-era Marxist intellectual's wholesale critique of virtually every genre of popular music in the 1970s. The piece was originally published in the periodical *Jadal* (*Controversy*) and was reproduced online. See "Jā'meh-shenāsi-ye musiqi-ye tudeh-i dar Iran—Masoud Yazdi" [The sociology of popular music in Iran—Masoud Yazdi], Mah Mag World Literature, accessed August 10, 2017, https://www.mahmag.org/farsi/mahmagfarsi.php?itemid=849.

12 This figure comes from a lecture delivered by Namjoo on Shahram Shabpareh's social influence and musical works. See Mohsen Namjoo, "Musical Talk: Shah-

ram Shabpareh: 'Honesty and Minor Scale,'" YouTube video, posted by Brown University, May 19, 2014, https://youtu.be/tKbimDu3-Ug.

13 The dotted eighth and sixteenth notes can also be rendered as straight eighth notes; in this case, the stress is typically on beats one and four, dividing the pattern evenly into two halves.

14 In the 1970s, Ahi DJ-ed at Studio 54, worked at legendary disco label Casablanca Records, and scored a hit dance single with Destination's "Move On Up / Dance Dance Dance / Destination Theme" (Butterfly Records), which spent four weeks in 1979 as the number one dance single on Billboard magazine's Hot Dance Club play list. He continues to write and produce music and is an active composer of Hollywood film scores. Ahi was also part of a team who won an Oscar for his work on sound editing and design for the 1992 film *The Last of the Mohicans*.

15 Ahi directed me to listen to Tehrangeles pop singer Siavash's 1985 hit "Dokhtar Iruni" ("Iranian Girl") from the album *Hamsāye-hā* (*Neighbors*, Caltex Records) to hear his most influential recording and a clear demonstration of his version of shesh-o-hasht.

16 In conversations with Iranian rock musicians, more than one has claimed difficulty in setting their Persian lyrics to rock's typical 4/4 meters because they understand Persian to incline toward 6/8.

17 "Arousak" is found on the album *Platinum* (Avang Music, 2004).

18 Meftahi (2016a) provides a fascinating genealogy of "national dance" and the chaste national dancer in twentieth-century Iran.

19 As demonstrated in Shay's 1999 ethnographic account of social and staged Iranian dance in Southern California, like shesh-o-hasht music, dance is both a prevalent activity and a source of ambivalence. Shay calls this "choreophobia."

20 Behrouz Bahmani, "Iranian Music, 6/8 Is Dead . . . Behrouz Bahmani," Iranian .com, April 22, 2005, http://www.iranian.com/BruceBahmani/2005/April/68 /index.html.

21 Breyley and Fatemi's definition of *khāltur* in *Iranian Music and Popular Entertainment* emphasizes the dāmbuli beat as a key musical characteristic: "Khālturi music is the most mediocre imaginable, with a very danceable 6/8 rhythm evoking scenes of debauchery, in brothels, a simple and extremely trite melody, and lyrics of meagre substance in colloquial language" (2016, 5). The term *khāltur* is also found in post-Soviet Azeri, Russian and Ukrainian, and other Slavic languages as халтура (*khaltura*). Thanks to Polina Dessianitchenko and Maria Sonevytsky for helping me confirm the connection to Russian, Azeri, and Ukrainian.

22 In order to avoid confusion with his brother, for the remainder of the chapter I refer to Shahbal Shabpareh using his first name.

23 In the 1990s Shahbal created the first Iranian girl group, called Silhouettt, a trio of young women in their twenties that made two albums and began the careers of Sepideh and Shahrzad Sepanlou. Other projects were a boy band of five

young second-generation male singers called Juniors 5, who performed R&B-inflected Persian pop, and an album by a young woman named Firoozeh, who also appears on the 2009 Black Cats album.

24 In not one but two songs called "Popfather," Shahbal has claimed to be the "father of pop" in Iran. These are found on the Black Cats' album *Popfather* (Caltex Records, 2003) and Shahbal's boy band Juniors 5's album *Popfather II* (Power Records, 2007).

25 In the 1960s the Rebels (the band out of which the Black Cats grew) also covered the Beatles song "(When I) Saw Her Standing There" and set it to a dāmbuli beat.

26 "In dāmbul o dimbol vel kon, bābā, mā nist / Tu khun o rag-e, Bābā Karam az mā jodā nist!" "Baba Karam" is the title of one of the best-known motrebi reng, or dance pieces, and is associated with the *jāhel* urban toughs of early to mid-twentieth-century Tehran. In Tehrangeles music videos and at parties, women sometimes don fedoras and hold canes to mimic jāhel dance styles. The song has been performed, covered, and reworked by many artists in Tehrangeles. See Naficy (1993, 178–187) for more discussion of the jāhel in Tehrangeles media.

27 This said, one of the most in-demand percussionists on the Tehrangeles touring set is the Lebanese American David Haddad, who has worked with Shahbal for years and is widely acknowledged for his skillful rendering of this beat.

28 After a conference presentation on this topic, I was approached by an anxious Iranian American scholar who chided me for using the term *dāmbuli*, saying, "Don't you know that this is only used as *dāmbuli kosak* [literally, 'pussy' dāmbuli or 'fucking' dāmbuli]?" I reassured the individual that I was aware of that usage but that Shahbal had purposefully employed the term to challenge its negative associations. The scholar was right to bring this to my attention, however. Plenty of references to dāmbuli kosak can be found in dismissive interpersonal and online discourse about this music, while rap group Zed Bazi's diss song "Iruni-ye LA" ("LA Iranian") refers to Tehrangeles pop as "dāmbuli kosak—all (*hamash*) dāmbuli kosak."

2. IRANIAN POPULAR MUSIC AND HISTORY

1 The Iranian Jewish History archives are at the University of California, Los Angeles; Harvard University has an Iranian oral history project; Zohreh T. Sullivan's *Exiled Memories: Stories of Iranian Diaspora* (2001) is a collection of oral historical accounts; and Ron Kelley, Jonathan Friedlander, and Anita Colby's edited volume *Irangeles: Iranians in Los Angeles* (1993) also contains oral histories with a diverse group of Iranians in Southern California. The flood of English-language Iranian American women's memoirs is another contentious arena of historical production. Some of the best known are Moaveni (2005); Nafisi (2003); and Satrapi (2003).

2　Jewish musicians have played crucial roles in developing, performing, and transmitting music in the Iranian cultural sphere, which extends from present-day territorial Iran into central Asia. For more on the roles of Iranian Jews in preserving and developing Iranian classical and secular entertainment genres, see Loeb (1972) and Sarshar (2012), who include biographies of key figures. Sarshar's entry on Iranian Jews in music ends with an extended description of Bibiyan's contributions to the prerevolutionary popular music industry. See Levin (1996) and Rapport (2014) on professional Jewish musicians in the related Uzbek Shash Maqam tradition.

3　Musiqi-ye pāp musicians Faramarz Aslani and Shahbal Shabpareh both told me they had traveled to England in the 1950s and described being impressed with American rock and roll and, later, with the Beatles. Both began their careers covering foreign songs but eventually turned to writing their own music, which blended Iranian and Western popular song styles.

4　Based on his interview with Bibiyan, Sarshar (2012) writes that Vigen's first song, "Khodā negahdār" ("May God Protect You"), was recorded in Bibiyan's home in 1956.

5　This song was re-released as "Dar mahd-e 'Ali" (A Eulogy of 'Ali) on Caltex Records' 2004 compilation album *Forty Hayedeh Golden Songs: Volume 1—Persian Music*.

6　The individuals Bibiyan listed that I had not included in my doctoral dissertation or 2013 publication were the composers Babak Bayat, Jahanbakhsh Pazouki, Anoushirvan Rouhani, and Javad Lashkari.

7　See lyricist Shahyar Ghanbari's 1995 *Daryā dar man* (*The Sea in Me*), a collection of poems, song lyrics, and recollections.

8　"Shabaneh: Shahram Shabpareh," YouTube video, posted by Shabakeh-ye jahāni-ye kānāl yek (Channel One Global Television), August 28, 2013, https://youtu.be/fVAP0YDcrqw.

9　Raha Etemadi began producing the *Dar Tab'id* program for Manoto 1 in 2013. Each episode is an interview between Etemadi and a well-known Iranian celebrity living outside the country. Many of the individuals featured work in the Tehrangeles cultural industries. "Shahram Shabpareh: Dar Tab'id" [Shahram Shabpareh: In exile], Manoto 1, reproduced by Iran Live-TV on Daily Motion, accessed August 12, 2016, http://www.dailymotion.com/video/x11qzs6_dar-tabeed-shahram-shabpare_shortfilms.

10　In "Iran Iran" and "Hich kojā Iran nemisheh" ("Nowhere Will Ever Become Iran"), both released in the early 1980s, Shabpareh uses the same formula of a "Western" section followed by an "Iranian" section.

11　Mohsen Namjoo, "Musical Talk: Shahram Shabpareh: 'Honesty and Minor Scale,'" YouTube video, posted by Brown University, May 19, 2014, https://youtu.be/tKbimDu3-Ug.

12　"Avang tā Taraneh bā Vartan Avanessian" [Avang to Taraneh with Vartan Avanessian], Manoto 1, YouTube video, posted by Saeid Music, August 21, 2017, https://youtu.be/HZBoYeWS460.

13 On the sensorium of South Asian grocery stores in the Bay Area, see Mankekar (2015, 71–107).

14 Taraneh Enterprises, "About Us," accessed June 11, 2016, http://www.taraneh records.com/aboutus.htm.

3. EXPATRIATE EROTICS, HOMELAND MORALITIES

1 "Shohreh Interview," Radio Javan podcast, December 17, 2008, https://www .radiojavan.com/podcasts/podcast/Shohreh-Interview-20081217.

2 "Andy-gole bandar High Quality," YouTube video, posted by toofan18, December 18, 2006, https://youtu.be/zVcbY64wFFM.

3 In twentieth-century political polemics and cartoons, the nation was conceptualized as a woman threatened by foreign invaders. I discuss Googoosh's adaptation of this role in chapter 4.

4 The history of blackface characters in Iranian theater and popular culture grows out of the history of African slavery and servitude in Iran. Manumission of slaves in Iran occurred only in 1929. Academic research on this important topic is just beginning (i.e., Baghoolizadeh 2018). For a comparative perspective on the international phenomenon of blackface minstrelsy, including in Iran, see Angelita Reyes (2019).

5 On Maxx in relation to repression, Rahimieh writes, "Zooming in on the diametrically opposed articulations of Iranianness (*iraniyat*) in Los Angeles and Tehran, Maxx deploys the genre of musical comedy to foreground the mechanisms by which each attempt at arriving at an 'authentic' Iranian identity necessarily rejects diversity and complexity. Ironically the very process of reconfiguring the self leads to repressions that undermine the stability of any given construct of the ideal Iranian. Mirroring this foreclosure of tidy resolutions, the film draws on the classical Hollywood model of musical comedy but stops short of offering a happy ending that would bring together the communities at home and abroad" (2016, 64).

6 Since the mid-2000s, Khordadian has publicly referred to himself using the English loanword "gay." For an English-language interview with Khordadian, see Negar Azimi, "Keeping Up with the Khordadian: The Life and Times of the Iranian King of Dance," *Bidoun* (Spring 2011), accessed December 3, 2013, https://www.bidoun.org/articles/keeping-up-with-the-khordadian. For discussion of contemporary and historical Iranian concepts and terminology for a range of sexual identifications, see, among others, Afary (2009); Babayan and Najmabadi (2008); Korycki and Nasirzadeh (2016); and Najmabadi (2005).

7 G. J. Breyley and Sasan Fatemi (2016, 93) include an undated (probably early

twentieth-century) motrebi tasnif containing barely veiled references to male sexual intercourse:

> *My dear beloved Soli, my dear Soli! [short for the male given name Soleiman]*
> *I have not yet been blessed by our union*
> *I have not yet dipped a plume in your inkwell . . .*
> *I beseech you, o my old lady!*
> *Fill the jug, for Soli has shat on me.*

8   On the 1970s television host and entertainer Fereydun Farrokhzad's ambiguous sexuality, see Najmabadi (2014, 120–144). For a different take on male dancers in Iran, see Shay 2006.

9   In Ottoman Turkey, professional, often young female-attired male dancers were called *zenne* (from the Persian *zan*, "woman") or *köçek* (from the Persian and Turkish words for "small"). An analysis of the twenty-first-century reclamation of this performance role in relation to contemporary discourses of LGBTQ+ sexualities in Turkey appears in Joanna Mansbridge's 2017 "The Zenne: Male Belly Dancers and Queer Modernity in Contemporary Turkey."

10 Sandra Marquez, "L.A. Dancer Arrested in Iran," APNews.com, July 25, 2002, https://www.apnews.com/f1dde45013e98ed809d62ba4f1915137.

11 Most recently, he was a judge on a televised talent competition called *Dance* (*Raqs*) in which mostly Iran-based contestants compete.

12 Papan-Matin (2009) discusses satirist Ebrahim Nabavi's fictional dialogue between Khordadian and an Iranian judge that portrays the dancer as so out of touch with postrevolutionary legal discourse and concepts that he cannot even understand the charges against him. In 2002 Peyvand Khorsandi wrote in an essay in support of Khordadian suggesting that his sexuality was behind his arrest: "His hip-rotations have also made him something of a revolutionary—one suspects that dance is only part of why he has been nabbed. Khordadian's distinctly camp and kitsch performances have led many to speculate about his sexuality and watching him may have prompted certain clerics to question their own. Latent sex appeal, I think it's called." "Dance for Khordadian," Iranian .com, June 1, 2001, https://iranian.com/2002/06/01/dance-for-khordadian/.

13 In a 2007 interview, prerevolutionary-turned-expatriate songwriter, multi-instrumentalist, and singer Hassan Shamaeizadeh commented that "Jalal Hemmati has sold more CDs than any other artist" but that people pretend not to listen to him because they want to "pretend [they] belong to a different class." See "Hich jā-ye donyā be andāzeh-ye Iran khānandeh-ye bad nadārad" [No place in the world has worse singers than Iran], *BBC Persian*, June 2, 2007, http://www.bbc.com/persian/arts/story/2007/06/070602_mf_shamaizadeh .shtml. In an article written in response to Hemmati's death in 2006, BBC journalist Behzad Bolour wrote that listening to Hemmati's music from Los Angeles during the Iran-Iraq War was one of the only beacons of happiness. It was from Hemmati that Bolour learned the motrebi reng "Baba Karam," which he

describes as "Iran's national anthem." See "Khāndan-e vājeb, tasliyyat-e lāzem" [Required reading, necessary condolences], *Ruz Haftom* (blog), BBC Persian, September 26, 2006, http://www.bbc.co.uk/blogs/r7/2006/09/post_88.html.

14 "Shahrzad Sepanlou Interview 2014 with Shahbal Shabpareh," YouTube video, posted by Ali Yazdanijoo, March 14, 2014, https://youtu.be/4rnRgWZKzMQ.

15 In his study of Iranian television in Los Angeles in the 1980s and early 1990s, Hamid Naficy (1993, 168–169) analyzes music videos that superimposed or blended images of expatriate singers with visual images of Iranian landscapes.

16 Indeed, the very act of standing on the street without hijab is grounds for arrest. In December 2017, Vida Movahed protested mandatory hijab by standing on a utility box on Tehran's Enghelāb (Revolution) Street with her head bare and with a white scarf hung on a stick like a flag. Throughout 2018 and into 2019, other women emulated her protest and were photographed or filmed in the act. Many of these women were subsequently identified and arrested for violating public morality laws.

17 Subtle or overt pressure to act seductively onstage, followed by regret and anger, is not an uncommon theme in prerevolutionary female performers' reflections on their past performances. See Talattof (2011) for interviews with Kobra Saidi (stage name Shahrzad), a prerevolutionary dancer and actress expressing this experience.

18 "Khānandegān-e los ānjelesi be Iran miyāyand?" [Are los ānjelesi singers coming to Iran?], *Farda News*, Esfand 27, 1391/March 17, 2013, https://www.farda news.com/fa/news/253193/-ایران-به-آنجلسی-لس-خوانندگانمی%8C%80%2Eآیند .

19 "Khānandegān-e los ānjelesi be Iran miyāyand?" Official statements claim that those artists abroad who had not been involved in crimes against the state or the "killing of Palestinians" could return to the country without fear of repercussions.

4. IRAN AS A SINGING WOMAN

1 "Man hamoon Iranam I Am Iran (Eng Subtitles)," YouTube video, posted by sedayehneda, June 22, 2009, https://youtu.be/SuBSrYEwN44.

2 The 2003 Danish documentary *The Voice of Iran*, for instance, is about classical male vocalist Mohammad-Reza Shajarian (b. 1940), a major postrevolutionary celebrity. The wildly popular Shajarian was one of the earliest singers to record following the revolution. He is known for his revolutionary ardor, virtuosic performances, and careful selection of poetic texts. His recorded rendition of the Ramadan prayer was played all over the country for years during that holy month. He eventually became disillusioned with the Islamic Republic after the 2009 election scandal and protests. Shajarian was barred from having his works played on state media after his 2009 songs protesting the state's response and subsequent instances of outspokenness. See *The Voice of Iran: Mohammad*

Reza Shajarian—the Copenhagen Concert, dir. Christian Braad Thomsen, Kollectiv Films, 2003.

3 For more on contemporary meanings and uses of the tasnif "Morgh-e sahar," see Siamdoust (2017, 37–39, 83–84).

4 See Simms and Koushkani (2012, 35–46) for an extensive analysis of Mohammad Reza Shajarian's revolution-era performance of "Bidād" ("Injustice") and a discussion of the term *dād*.

5 Many of these terms employ the diphthongized long ā sound special to Persian, the vowel sound vocalists most often use when performing the distinctive, yodel-like ornaments to melismatic passages called *tahrir*. The multivalent vocable *vāy* so common to Iranian speech and song is also important here. Depending on the context, *vāy* can mean "fie," "woe," "wow," or "oh," and it is a frequent inclusion and improvised interjection in songs of all kinds.

6 For analyses of "screams" and "silence" in twentieth-century Iranian poetry, see Jason Bahbak Mohaghegh's *The Writing of Violence in the Middle East: Inflictions* (2012) and *Silence in Middle Eastern and Western Thought: The Radical Unspoken* (2013).

7 Thanks to Mohammad Mehdi Khorrami for his comments on this topic and for bringing my attention to Shajarian's performance of "Faryād."

8 Claiming prerevolutionary imagery is common across the political spectrum, as evidenced by the opposition groups who employ much of the same nationalist terminology and imagery as monarchists while possessing a very different ideology. The logo of the National Council of Resistance of Iran's television station Simā-ye āzādi ("Image of Freedom") is the lion holding a sword in front of a rising sun—the same image as on the prerevolutionary flag.

9 Rereleased on the compilation album *The Best of Hayedeh*, vol. 4, Caltex Records, 1999.

10 Dariush, "Vatan," *Sāl-e do hezār (Year 2000)*, Caltex Records, 1991.

11 Randall Roberts, "Googoosh, Iran's Beyoncé before Revolution Halted Her Career, on Her Musical Exile and Grand Return," *Los Angeles Times*, May 11, 2018, https://www.latimes.com/entertainment/music/la-et-ms-googoosh-20180511 -story.html.

12 Robin Denselow, "The Iranian Madonna Breaks Her Silence," *Guardian* (London), January 7, 2001, https://www.theguardian.com/culture/2001/jan/08 /artsfeatures2.

13 Googoosh was only one of many female celebrities—mostly actresses, singers, and dancers—who pushed the boundaries of propriety with their performances. The male counterpart of the gharbzadeh woman was the *fokoli*, a faux collar–wearing dandy who lacked the manliness to protect Iranian women and Iran itself.

14 Zamani told me that when he was making his documentary, at least three different Tehrangeles music companies were selling Googoosh's prerevolutionary works in various guises. Unsure which, if any, of these companies had a legal

claim on this material, and unable to compensate Googoosh herself since she was still in Iran, Zamani decided to pay Googoosh's son, Kambiz Ghorbani, for the audiovisual rights since, at the time, he too had released her prerevolutionary works on CD.

15 Though Zamani's film was not widely distributed, he told me that he had heard that the film made its way to Iran through unofficial channels. The film also aired on a popular Iranian satellite television program based in Los Angeles.

16 *Fereshteh farāri* (*Runaway Angel*), dir. Gorji (George) Obadieh, Atlas Film Studio, 1961.

17 The documentary *Umm Kulthum: A Voice Like Egypt* (dir. Michael Goldman, Arab Film Distribution, 1996) is heavily based on Danielson's book and features interviews with Egyptian fans of Umm Kulthum.

18 In contrast, in Christopher Reed Stone's *Popular Culture and Nationalism in Lebanon: The Fairouz and Rahbani Nation* (2008), Lebanese superstar vocalist Fairouz appears virtually devoid of self-determination and dominated by her husband, his brother, and her son. See Frédéric Mitterand's documentary *Fairouz* (Arte France, 1998) for a related treatment.

19 This rendering of Iranian history strongly resembles Nima Naghibi's (2016) analysis of the revolution in Iranian American women's memoirs: it was a traumatic event that "happened to them," rather than a phenomenon in which these writers or their families had a role.

20 "Listen: Giving Voice to Iranian Women," Magnum Photos, accessed January 30, 2018, https://www.magnumphotos.com/arts-culture/newsha-tavakolian -listen/.

21 Laudan Nooshin (2018) discusses Iranian female vocalists' use of the internet to circulate their music.

22 Azadeh Moaveni, "Don't Cry for Me, Iran," *Time*, March 23, 2001.

23 Azadeh Moaveni, "Sing It Loud and Proud," *Time*, April 16, 2001, 92.

24 Ramin Tabib, "Romanticizing the Past: Googoosh Is No Feminist Heroine," Iranian.com, May 18, 2001, https://iranian.com/RaminTabib/2001/May/Googoosh /index.html.

25 "Googoosh, press conference in Toronto, part 2," YouTube video, posted by Nima Bigloo, May 4, 2012, https://youtu.be/Jf_kTEhcKFs.

26 See Chehabi (1999) for texts of patriotic art songs and anthems from the early and mid-twentieth century that also glorify pre-Islamic Iran. This stretches back to the poet Ferdowsi's celebrated and highly influential Iranian epic *Shāhnāmeh* (*Book of Kings*; 1010 CE), which chronicles ancient Iran's heroes, kings, and cultures prior to Islam.

27 In our 2017 phone conversation, Asemani suggested that the instrumental version was included because the composition was not mere accompaniment but rich enough to stand on its own. This is the only Los Angeles Iranian production that I am aware of being released in this way.

28 In general, younger artists who have come of age in postrevolutionary Iran do

not exhibit the same fixation on prerevolutionary Iran. Their gaze may be oriented toward a different past, as in Brooklyn-based avant-garde artist Mohsen Namjoo's "Daheh-ye shast" ("The Sixties"). "Daheh-ye shast" refers to the 1360s in the Iranian calendar, roughly equivalent to the 1980s in the Gregorian calendar. This is the first decade following the revolution. See Siamdoust (2017, 200–204) for a discussion of "Daheh-ye shast."

29 In our discussion, Asemani specified that he fought in the war for Iran's honor (*nāmus*), not the government (*dowlat*). The founding figures in the Los Angeles music industry left Iran before the war began; this may be why it is so unusual to hear mention of this seminal, traumatic moment in Iranian history in the music produced in Southern California.

30 "Googoosh Interview 2004," YouTube video, posted by Anjel gharakhani, March 9, 2012, https://youtu.be/NXGWTp_xuoE.

31 "Homa Ehsan Interview with Diva Googoosh, 2005 (Part 3)," YouTube video, posted by Nima Bigloo, December 11, 2015, https://youtu.be/F-3XFzcs6Lc.

32 Fellow Tehrangeles artist Ebi's song "Khalij-e fars" ("Persian Gulf," Taraneh, 1990) is the best-known expatriate pop song on this topic. See Akhavan (2013, 13–34) for a discussion of the Persian Gulf debates in Iranian diasporic internet communications.

33 "Shohreh vs. Googoosh," YouTube video, posted by Shahrokh2004, August 3, 2009, https://youtu.be/FzPzk3-sUyY. Note that Solati also calls on Dariush to make a statement. I discuss his political outspokenness in the following chapter.

34 "Googoosh Speaks at the UN," YouTube video, posted by Unite4Iran, July 25, 2009, https://youtu.be/njmL5X1t3zU.

35 Whether (or how) this trope related to actual shifts in men's attitudes toward women, women's attitudes toward themselves, or women's practical engagement in political affairs is a matter of historical debate.

36 Googoosh is not precisely a "runaway" (*farāri*), an epithet conservative news organizations sometimes apply to prominent prerevolutionary musicians who fled Iran during the revolution without appearing in court or serving their sentences. Her decision to remain in Iran even in the difficult decades following the revolution contributed to her integrity in some fans' eyes. Nevertheless, she left Iran voluntarily and has not returned.

37 Asghar Masoudi, 2010, comment on "Man Hamoon Iranam," posted by Googoosh, June 22, 2009, https://youtu.be/9cBwT3H9Wlg.

38 Salar Golestanian, 2010, comment on "Man Hamoon Iranam," posted by Googoosh; and Pedram Pasha, 2010, comment on "Man Hamoon Iranam," posted by Googoosh.

39 Kya KyaMehr, 2010, comment on "Man Hamoon Iranam," posted by Googoosh.

40 Daria Anvanian, 2010, comment on "Man Hamoon Iranam," posted by Googoosh.

41 Persian, 2010, comment on "Man Hamoon Iranam," posted by Googoosh.

42 Though located in London, Manoto 1 also has links to Tehrangeles. It was established by former Los Angeles residents Marjan and Kayvan Abbassi and hosted by "Man hamun Iranam" lyricist and fellow Los Angeles resident Raha Etemadi. Prior to opening Manoto, the Abbassis owned Bebin.tv, a media company in Los Angeles; Etemadi was working at Bebin.tv when I interviewed him in 2007. For more on Bebin.tv, see Rohani (2009).

43 "Googoosh Music Academy E1, P1," YouTube video, posted by manototv, October 29, 2010, https://youtu.be/6kuIIZvYqfg.

44 "Homa Ehsan Interview with Diva, Googoosh, 2005 (part 1)," YouTube video, posted by Nima Bigloo, November 30, 2015, https://youtu.be/4uj895XtG1A.

5. A NATION IN RECOVERY

1 For a behind-the-scenes look at Atabay's station in the early 2000s and some of his claims to have impacted events in Iran, see Michael Lewis, "The Satellite Subversives," *New York Times*, February 24, 2002, http://www.nytimes.com/2002/02/24/magazine/the-satellite-subversives.html.

2 See Mowlana (1991) for a discussion of expatriate news media in the late nineteenth and early twentieth centuries as motivating domestic political movements.

3 The most complete account of Dariush's life to date is his 2017 interview with the BBC, which is based on his forthcoming autobiography: "Be ebārat-e digar: Dariush- nāgofteh-hā: Bakhsh-e avval" [Stated another way: Dariush—Things unsaid: First part], YouTube video, posted by BBC Persian, March 22, 2017, https://youtu.be/8vK-MYyqAvg.

4 After his release, Dariush released the pro-regime song "Rasul-e rastakhiz" ("Messenger of the Resurgence"), whose title includes Rastakhiz (resurgence, resurrection), the name of the single party the shah introduced in 1971 in response to calls for democratic elections. Some have suggested that Dariush and the other musicians' release from prison was conditional on their creation and performance of such songs. Others instead suggest that Dariush didn't have any true political commitment and that he exaggerates even how conscious he was of the political implications of the material he sang. As discussed in chapter 2, many people in Tehrangeles contest their fellow expatriates' recollections and assertions of intent and influence.

5 Dariush Mehrjui's domestic Iranian feature film *Santouri* (Hedayat Film, 2007), about a young hammered dulcimer player's descent into addiction, explores the music-drug connection in contemporary Iran.

6 "Dariush—Bachehaye Iran," YouTube video, posted by caltexrecordsmusic, June 30, 2009, https://youtu.be/oN2kLafDvlg.

7 "Dariush—'Didar Dar Ghorbat (Documentary)' Official Video," YouTube video, posted by Radio Javan, September 2, 2014, https://youtu.be/yAR7BS4IuWM.

Directed by Ali Rafi'i, the film was produced by Radio Javan, a Washington, DC–area Iranian diaspora music and media company that has become the most popular North American Persian-language popular music streaming platform.

8 The Tehrangeles-based male vocalist Moein is another singer whose "sad voice" many fans prize.

9 Unusually for Dariush, this album was titled in English rather than Persian.

10 Written in 1944 by Ruhollah Khaleghi on a poem by Hossein Gol-e Golab during the occupation of Iran by the Allied Forces, "Ey Iran" is the best-known *sorud-e melli* (nationalist anthem) among Iranians in the diaspora.

11 In concerts Dariush sometimes performs teaching the audience to sing the song with him, engaging them in call-and-response in the song's first verses before completing the song on his own. More hopeful imagery now accompanies the live performances: green leaves, drops of water, tender shoots sprouting from seeds, and the faces of human rights heroes appear onstage behind Dariush and his accompanying orchestra. This strongly resembles Lilie Chouliaraki's (2013) observations on celebrity humanitarianism and "aspirational performances."

12 Since our first meeting, Abbasseh has been my main connection to Dariush and Ayeneh, patiently answering my many questions in lengthy interviews, helping me with translations, contacting Dariush directly with my questions, and allowing me to observe a live taping of the *Ayeneh Program*.

13 It was not until years later that I came to think of my affective response to Abbasseh in terms of witnessing and testifying, an experience familiar to me through years of attending Southern Baptist church services with my mother, where congregants' public witnessing to "the power of Jesus Christ working in [their] life" was a regular, moving occurrence. Witnessing and testifying are likewise fundamental to the American recovery movement as exemplified in Alcoholics Anonymous and Narcotics Anonymous, which, while agnostic, is deeply rooted in Protestant Christian thought and practice. I do not know if Abbasseh was consciously attempting to draw me in, or whether I was predisposed to react to her testimony because of my personal history—but it was not the last time I would have these experiences in her or Dariush's presence, or when working with Ayeneh media. See Susan Friend Harding's *The Book of Jerry Falwell: Fundamentalist Language and Politics* (2000) for beautiful descriptions of similar experiences while undertaking fieldwork with American evangelicals.

14 Bethan McKernan, "Number of Drug Addicts in Iran 'Doubles' in Six Years," *Independent*, June 26, 2017, https://www.independent.co.uk/news/world/middle-east/iran-tehran-drug-addiction-opium-heroin-afghanistan-taliban-a7809046.html.

15 See Nikpour (2018, 6n4) for an overview of sources for these varying estimates.

16 Ali Farhoudian and colleagues (2014) examined eighteen samples of Iranian kerak and found all to include heroin, codeine, morphine, and caffeine. See also Moghanibashi-Mansourieh and Deilamizade (2014).

17 Dariush2000.com, Dariush.net, DariushEghbali.com, Twitter feeds, Telegram channels, and other media are all ways that Ayeneh gets its message out.

18 *Hamdard* can be an adjective, where it means "sympathetic," or a noun, as Dariush uses it. As defined in Aryanpur-Kashani's *Concise Persian-English Dictionary*, the noun *hamdard* means "fellow sufferer, partner in pain, [and] sympathizer." Abbass and Manoochehr Aryanpur-Kashani, *The Concise Persian-English Dictionary*, 4th ed. (Tehran: Amir Kabir Publication Organization, 1986), 1408.

19 "Dariush Eghbali: Pishgiri az etiād mohemtar az darmān-e ān ast" [Preventing addiction is more important than its treatment], Deutsche Welle, November 11, 2007, https://www.dw.com/fa-ir/-از-اعتیاد-مهمتر-از-داریوش-اقبالی-پیشگیری /a-2974361.درمان-آن-است.

20 "Barnāmeh-ye āyeneh" [Ayeneh Program], YouTube video, posted by Ayeneh Foundation, March 15, 2015, https://youtu.be/EzE_2NGFdso.

21 As described by Ghiabi (2017), the camps are managed by a complicated array of state, private, legal, and illegal operators and range from therapeutic to near prison-like conditions.

22 Dariush has publicly spoken about his father's and two brothers' drug use.

23 There is a rich history of bodily and medical metaphors for "what's wrong with Iran," most famously "Occidentosis" (*gharbzadegi*), but also immorality as an illness. On the latter, see Gahan (2017).

24 John Lavitt, "The Crescent and the Needle: The Remarkable Rise of NA in Iran," The Fix, April 7, 2014, http://www.thefix.com/content/Iran-Narcotics -Anonymous-phonemoneon-Lavitt2099?pageDall.

25 According to Amir Arsalan Afkhami (2009, 204–205), this same period saw public "allegations of official involvement" in narcotics trafficking and rumors of official plots to keep Iranians drug addled and docile. I have heard similar statements in discussing the addiction epidemic in Iran. I understand these statements as representative of what Humeira Iqtidar (2014) calls "political skepticism" that is deeply distrustful of the state.

26 Dariush, "Ghodrat az nātavānā sarcheshmeh migirad" [Power can emerge from inability], blog post, Dariusheghbali.com, Khordad 14, 1392/June 4, 2006, http://www.dariusheghbali.com/archives/2013_06.php.

27 Dariush, "Ghodrat az nātavānā sarcheshmeh migirad."

28 "Zendāni" ("Imprisoned"), performed by Dariush, on the album *Salām ey khāk-e khub-e mehrabāni* (*Greetings, Oh Good, Kind Earth*), Pars Video, 2001.

29 "Bāyad be jā-ye vatan-e khāki vatan-e darun-e mān rā besāzim" [Instead of an earthly/territorial homeland we must build homelands inside of ourselves], Nedā-ye āzadi (Voice of Freedom), Mordad 13, 1393/August 4, 2007, http:// www.nedayeazadi.net/1393/05/10434.

1 "Googoosh & Ghomayshi—40 saal Official Music Video," YouTube video, posted by Googoosh, July 31, 2018, https://youtu.be/mNGEwE4LpZQ.

2 Ghomeishi is a well-known pop rock musician whose career began before the revolution and who, like Dariush, is admired by some for his serious lyrics and persona. See Breyley and Fatemi (2016, 141–151).

3 The lyricist, Raha Etemadi, inserted his own name into the second line of the chorus quoted here: "be boghzat e'temād darim / ye ruz ākhar rahā mishi."

4 See Naficy (1993, 161) on the use of this effect in 1980s Tehrangeles music videos. Many of Hamid Naficy's observations continue to accurately describe contemporary Tehrangeles tropes and aesthetics, especially among Tehrangeles's founding cohort.

5 As is typical of Kayhān's more sensational reporting, this report was reproduced on many Iranian news internet sites. For example, "Khabar-e Kayhān darbāreh-ye Googoosh, Ghomeishi, va Raha Etemadi" [Kayhān's news on Googoosh, Ghomeishi, and Raha Etemadi], Parsine.com, Mordad 14, 1397/July 11, 2018, https://www.parsine.com/fa/news/456284/خبر-کیهان-درباره-گوگوشقمیشی-و-رها-اعتمادی.

6 I am thinking of Jane Bennett's notion of "distributive agency" in assemblages. This notion "loosens the connections between efficacy and the moral subject, bringing efficacy closer to the idea of the power to make a difference that calls for a response" (2010, 32).

7 The Zāyandeh River, whose waters once flowed through the iconic arched bridges of Isfahan, now runs dry for much of the year. The northern Lake Urmia, once a giant inland salty sea, is now threatened because of climate change and illegal wells. Increasingly intense and frequent sandstorms have made some southern Iranian cities unlivable: the United Nations has recognized sand and dust storms as a major environmental issue and is beginning to address the problem.

8 "Tarāneh-hā-ye los ānjelesi dar film-hā-ye irani" [Los ānjelesi songs in Iranian film], Lahzeh Namā, Khordad 30, 1395/June 19, 2016, http://lahzehnama.ir/fa/news/23403/ترانه-های-لس-آنجلسی-در-فیلم-های-ایرانی.

9 The predominantly Persian-language nostalgic/fan Facebook group "Mā bā musiqi-ye los ānjelesi bozorg shodim" ("We Grew Up with Los Ānjelesi Music") is maintained by adults who grew up in Iran during the 1980s and 1990s. "Mā bā musiqi-ye los ānjelesi bozorg shodim" Facebook Group, accessed January 3, 2018, https://www.facebook.com/mabapopbozorgshodim/.

10 "Shayad (Music Video in Support of Uprising in Iran)," YouTube video, posted by Shahin Najafi, January 6, 2018, https://youtu.be/XWRtINNO1y8. The participating musicians were Shahin Najafi (residing in Germany), Hatef Pishdad (Germany), Melody Safavi (USA), Safoura Safavi (Sweden), Shahrzad Sepanlou (USA), Arash Sobhani (USA), Bardia Taghipoor (Germany), and Arash TarantisT (USA).

11 This confession was most likely involuntary. Forced confessions and recantations can be considered a postrevolutionary television genre in Iran. See Abrahamian (1999). On Hojabri's arrest, see Thomas Erdbrink, "Iran's Shaming of Young Dancer Draws Backlash," *New York Times*, July 9, 2018, https://www.nytimes.com/2018/07/09/world/middleeast/irans-instagram-dancer-teen.html.

12 On accusations that the Hojabri case was motivated by domestic politics, see "Posht-e pardeh-ye mājerā-ye Ma'edeh Hojabri az zabān-e vazir-e ertebātāt" [Behind the veil of the Maedeh Hojabri incident according to the minister of communications and technology], Entekhab.ir, July 11, 2018, http://www.entekhab.ir/fa/news/418387/-پشت-پرده-ماجرای-مانده-هژبری-از-زبان-وزیر-ارتباطات. هایی-بود-که-که-مدافعشان-از-موضوع-8C%80%2E%این-اتفاق-حاصل-تصمیم-اتاق-فکر سازی-ارزی-به-خطر-افتاده8C%80%2E%شفاف .

13 In *The Limits of Whiteness: Iranian Americans and the Everyday Politics of Race*, Neda Maghbouleh (2017, 74–75) describes a video called "King" by Amitis, a female Iranian American vocalist, which includes pre-Islamic Zoroastrian symbols, a heavy dose of Orientalist "ancient Egyptian" costumery, and a cameo appearance by American rapper Snoop Dogg.

14 Mani may have been thinking of Sasy Mankan or Amir Tataloo, two prominent domestic pop musicians who released songs and videos without the required permissions. When they were arrested, their popularity increased. Mankan eventually left Iran and moved to Los Angeles, where he has worked with Shabpareh. His 2019 song "Gentleman," which was recorded in Southern California, went viral in Iran. Cell phone footage of entire classrooms of Iranian schoolgirls singing and dancing to "Gentleman" that was posted to social media resulted in predictable cries for domestic vigilance against foreign plots. For a report and video, see Peter Stubley, "'An Enemy Plot': Iran Launches Crackdown after Videos Emerge of Iranian Schoolgirls Dancing," *Independent*, May 11, 2019, https://www.independent.co.uk/news/world/middle-east/iran-investigation-dancing-school children-video-sasy-mankan-a8909516.html. Tataloo went a different direction, publicly supporting hard-line political figures and, in a 2015 video, singing a song supporting the country's nuclear program from the deck of an Iranian warship. For the music video, see "Amir Tataloo—Energy Hasteei," YouTube video, posted by Amir Tataloo, July 12, 2015, https://youtu.be/VywTiTVMHts.

REFERENCES

Abrahamian, Ervand. 1993. *Khomeinism: Essays on the Islamic Republic.* Berkeley: University of California.

Abrahamian, Ervand. 1999. *Tortured Confessions: Prisons and Public Recantations in Modern Iran.* Berkeley: University of California Press.

Abrams, Lynn. 2010. *Oral History Theory.* London: Routledge.

Adelkhah, Fariba. 2001. "Les Iranienes de Californie: Si la République islamique n'existait pas . . ." *Les Etudes de CERI* 75. https://www.sciencespo.fr/ceri/sites/sciencespo.fr.ceri/files/etude75.pdf.

Afary, Janet. 2009. *Sexual Politics in Modern Iran.* Cambridge: Cambridge University Press.

Afkhami, Amir Arsalan. 2009. "From Punishment to Harm Reduction: The Resecularization of Addiction in Contemporary Iran." In *Contemporary Iran: Economy, Society, Politics*, edited by Ali Gheissari, 194–210. Online version. Oxford: Oxford University Press.

Aguilar-San Juan, Karin. 2009. *Little Saigons: Staying Vietnamese in America.* Minneapolis: University of Minnesota Press.

Ahmed, Sara. 2004. "Affective Economies." *Social Text* 22 (2): 117–139.

Akhavan, Niki. 2013. *Electronic Iran: The Cultural Politics of an Online Evolution.* New Brunswick, NJ: Rutgers University Press.

Alexanian, Janet. 2009. "Constructing Iran: Conflict, Community, and the Politics of Representation in the Digital Age." PhD diss., University of California, Irvine.

Alinejad, Donya. 2017. *The Internet and Formations of Iranian American-ness: Next Generation Diaspora.* Cham, Switzerland: Palgrave Macmillan.

Aloosh, Mehdi. 2018. "How Economic Sanctions Compromise Cancer Care in Iran." *The Lancet Oncology* 19 (7): e334.

Amin, Camron Michael. 2001. "Selling and Saving 'Mother Iran': Gender and the Iranian Press in the 1940s." *International Journal of Middle East Studies* 33 (3): 335–361.

Amir-Ebrahimi, Masserat. 2008. "Blogging from Qom, behind Walls and Veils." *Comparative Studies of South Asia, Africa, and the Middle East* 28 (2): 235–249.

Anderson, Benedict R. O'G. 1983. *Imagined Communities: Reflections on the Origin and Spread of Nationalism.* London: Verso.

Andsager, Julie L. 2006. "Seduction, Shock, and Sales: Research and Functions of Sex in Music Video." In *Sex in Consumer Culture: The Erotic Content of Media and Marketing,* edited by Tom Reichert and Jacqueline Lambiase, 31–50. Mahwah, NJ: L. Erlbaum.

Appadurai, Arjun. 1996. *Modernity at Large: Cultural Dimensions of Globalization.* Public Worlds 1. Minneapolis: University of Minnesota Press.

Apter, Emily S. 2006. "On Oneworldedness: Or Paranoia as a World System." *American Literary History* 18 (2): 365–389.

Axel, Brian Keith. 2002. "The Diasporic Imaginary." *Public Culture* 14 (2): 411–428.

Babayan, Kathryn, and Afsaneh Najmabadi. 2008. *Islamicate Sexualities: Translations across Temporal Geographies of Desire.* Cambridge, MA: Center for Middle Eastern Studies of Harvard University / Harvard University Press.

Baghoolizadeh, Beeta. 2018. "Seeing Race and Erasing Slavery: Media and the Construction of Blackness in Iran, 1830–1960." PhD diss., University of Pennsylvania.

Baron, Beth. 2005. *Egypt as a Woman: Nationalism, Gender, and Politics.* Berkeley: University of California Press.

Bayat, Asef. 2007. "Islamism and the Politics of Fun." *Public Culture* 19 (3): 433–459.

Behbahani, Simin. 1999. *A Cup of Sin: Selected Poems.* Edited and translated by Farzaneh Milani and Kaveh Safa. Syracuse, NY: Syracuse University Press.

Bennett, Jane. 2010. *Vibrant Matter: A Political Ecology of Things.* Durham, NC: Duke University Press.

Berdahl, Daphne. 1999. "(N)Ostalgie for the Present: Memory, Longing, and East German Things." *Ethnos* 64 (2): 192–211.

Berlant, Lauren. 2008. *The Female Complaint: The Unfinished Business of Sentimentality in American Culture.* Durham, NC: Duke University Press.

Berlant, Lauren, and Michael Warner. 1998. "Sex in Public." *Critical Inquiry* 24 (2): 547–566.

Bibiyan, Manouchehr. 2010. *Secrets of the Iranian Revolution: Jaam-e Jam Television's Open Forum.* Translated by Dokhi Bibiyan. Self-published, Xlibris.

Born, Georgina. 2011. "Music and the Materialization of Identities." *Journal of Material Cultures* 16 (4): 376–388.

Boym, Svetlana. 2001. *The Future of Nostalgia.* New York: Basic Books.

Bozorgmehr, Mehdi. 1997. "Internal Ethnicity: Iranians in Los Angeles." *Sociological Perspectives* 40 (3): 387–408.

Bozorgmehr, Mehdi. 2011. "The Iranian Diaspora." In *Encyclopaedia Iranica.* Ehsan Yarshater Center for Iranian Studies, Columbia University, 1982–. Article published December 15, 1995; last updated November 28, 2011. http://www.iranicaonline.org/articles/diaspora.

Bozorgmehr, Mehdi, and Daniel Douglas. 2011. "Success(ion): Second-Generation Iranian Americans." *Iranian Studies* 44 (1): 3–24.

Bozorgmehr, Mehdi, and George Sabagh. 1988. "High Status Immigrants: A Statistical Profile of Iranians in the United States." *Iranian Studies* 21 (3–4): 5–36.

Breyley, G. J. 2010. "Hope, Fear and Dance Dance Dance: Popular Music in 1960s Iran." *Musicology Australia* 32 (2): 203–226.

Breyley, G. J. 2013. "Sima's Choices: Negotiating Repertoires and Identities in Contemporary Iran." In *Women Singers in Global Contexts: Music, Biography, Identity,* edited by Ruth Hellier, 177–193. Urbana: University of Illinois Press.

Breyley, G. J., and Sasan Fatemi. 2016. *Iranian Music and Popular Entertainment: From Motrebi to Losānjelesi and Beyond.* Abingdon, UK: Routledge.

Brubaker, Rogers. 2005. "The 'Diaspora' Diaspora." *Ethnic and Racial Studies* 28 (1): 1–19.

Bryant, Lei Ouyang. 2005. "Music, Memory, and Nostalgia: Collective Memories of Cultural Revolution Songs in Contemporary China." *China Review* 5 (2): 151–175.

Burchardt, Marian. 2016. "The Self as Capital in the Narrative Economy: How Biographical Testimonies Move Activism in the Global South." *Sociology of Health and Illness* 38 (4): 592–609.

Byrd, Dustin. 2011. *Ayatollah Khomeini and the Anatomy of the Islamic Revolution in Iran: Toward a Theory of Prophetic Charisma.* Lanham, MD: University Press of America.

Chehabi, H. E. 1999. "From Revolutionary *Taṣnīf* to Patriotic *Surūd*: Music and Nation-Building in Pre–World War II Iran." *Iran* 37 (1): 143–154.

Chehabi, H. E. 2000. "Voices Unveiled: Women Singers in Iran." In *Iran and Beyond: Essays in Middle Eastern History in Honor of Nikki R. Keddie,* edited by Rudi Matthee and Beth Baron, 151–166. Costa Mesa, CA: Mazda.

Chehabi, H. E. 2007. "How Caviar Turned Out to Be *Halal.*" *Gastronomica* 7 (2): 17–23.

Chouliaraki, Lilie. 2006. *The Spectatorship of Suffering.* London: SAGE.

Chouliaraki, Lilie. 2013. *The Ironic Spectator: Solidarity in the Age of Post-humanitarianism.* Cambridge, UK: Polity.

Cunningham, Stuart, and Tina Nguyen. 2003. "Actually Existing Hybridity: Vietnamese Diasporic Music Video." In *The Media of Diaspora*, edited by Karim H. Karim, 119–134. London: Routledge.

Dadkhah, Kamran M. 1999. "Myths and Facts in Iranian Historiography." *CIRA Bulletin* 15 (1): 20–25.

Danielson, Virginia. 1997. *The Voice of Egypt: Umm Kulthum, Arabic Song, and Egyptian Society in the Twentieth Century*. Chicago: University of Chicago Press.

DeBano, Wendy S. 2005. "Enveloping Music in Gender, Nation and Islam: Women's Music Festivals in Post-revolutionary Iran." *Iranian Studies* 38 (3): 441–462.

DeBano, Wendy S. 2009. "Singing against Silence: Celebrating Women and Music at the Fourth Jasmine Festival." In *Music and the Play of Power in the Middle East, North Africa and Central Asia*, edited by Laudan Nooshin, 229–244. Farnham, UK: Ashgate.

Dueck, Byron. 2013. *Musical Intimacies and Indigenous Imaginaries: Aboriginal Music and Dance in Public Performance*. New York: Oxford University Press.

During, Jean. 2005. "Third Millennium Tehran: Music!" Translated by Rudy Steibel. *Iranian Studies* 38 (3): 373–398.

Dyer, Richard. 1986. *Heavenly Bodies: Film Stars and Society*. New York: St. Martin's.

Farhat, Hormoz. 1990. *The Dastgah Concept in Persian Music*. Cambridge Studies in Ethnomusicology. Cambridge: Cambridge University Press.

Farhoudian, Ali, Mandana Sadeghi, Hamid Reza Khoddami Vishteh, Babak Moazen, Monir Fekri, and Afarin Rahimi Movaghar. 2014. "Component Analysis of Iranian Crack: A Newly Abused Narcotic Substance in Iran." *Iranian Journal of Pharmaceutical Research* 13 (1): 337–344.

Fatemi, Sasan. 2003. *Ritm-e kudakāneh dar Iran* [Children's rhythms in Iran]. Tehran: Mahoor Institute of Culture and Art.

Feld, Steven. 1988. "Aesthetics as Iconicity of Style, or 'Lift-Up-over Sounding': Getting into the Kaluli Groove." *Yearbook for Traditional Music* 20:74–113.

Figg-Franzoi, Lillian. 2011. "Maslahat, the State and the People: Opium Use in the Islamic Republic of Iran." *Crime, Law and Social Change* 56 (4): 421–438.

Foster, Roger. 2015. "The Therapeutic Spirit of Neoliberalism." *Political Theory* 44 (1): 82–105.

Fox, Aaron A. 2004. *Real Country: Music and Language in Working-Class Culture*. Durham, NC: Duke University Press.

Frishkopf, Michael. 2010. "Introduction: Music and Media in the Arab World and *Music and Media in the Arab World* as Music and Media in the Arab World: A Metadiscourse." In *Media and Music in the Arab World*, edited by Michael Frishkopf, 1–66. Cairo: American University of Cairo Press.

Gahan, Jairan. 2017. "Red-Light Tehran: Prostitution, Intimately Public Islam, and the Rule of the Sovereign, 1910–1980." PhD diss., University of Toronto.

Ghamari-Tabrizi, Behrooz. 2013. "Women's Rights, Shari'a Law, and the Secularization of Islam in Iran." *International Journal of Politics, Culture, and Society* 26 (3): 237–253.

Ghanbari, Shahyar. 1995. *Daryā dar man: Quzinah-e tarāneh-hā, 1969–1995* [The Sea in Me: Selected Lyrics, 1969–1995]. Mountain View, CA: Nakisa.

Ghiabi, Maziyar. 2015. "Drugs and Revolution in Iran: Islamic Devotion, Revolutionary Zeal and Republican Means." *Iranian Studies* 48 (2): 139–163.

Ghiabi, Maziyar. 2017. "Maintaining Disorder: The Micropolitics of Drugs Policy in Iran." *Third World Quarterly* 39 (2): 277–297.

Ghiabi, Maziyar, Masoomeh Maarefvand, Hamed Bahari, and Zohreh Alavi. 2018. "Islam and Cannabis: Legalisation and Religious Debate in Iran." *International Journal on Drug Policy* 56:121–127.

Gholami, Reza. 2015. *Secularism and Identity: Non-Islamiosity in the Iranian Diaspora.* Farnham, UK: Ashgate.

Gray, Lila Ellen. 2013. *Fado Resounding: Affective Politics and Urban Life.* Durham, NC: Duke University Press.

Guy, Nancy. 2005. *Peking Opera and Politics in Taiwan.* Urbana: University of Illinois Press.

Harding, Susan Friend. 2000. *The Book of Jerry Falwell: Fundamentalist Language and Politics.* Princeton, NJ: Princeton University Press.

Hartley, John. 2004. "Democratainment." In *The Television Studies Reader*, edited by Robert Clyde Allen and Annette Hill, 524–533. London: Routledge.

Hemmasi, Farzaneh. 2010. "Iranian Popular Music in Los Angeles: Mobilizing Music, Media, and Nation." PhD diss., Columbia University.

Hemmasi, Farzaneh. 2011. "Iranian Popular Music in Los Angeles: A Transnational Public beyond the Islamic State." In *Muslim Soaps, Halal Rap, and Revolutionary Theater: Artistic Developments in the Muslim World*, edited by Karin Van Nieuwkerk, 85–111. Austin: University of Texas Press.

Hemmasi, Farzaneh. 2013. "Intimating Dissent: Popular Song, Poetry, and Politics in Pre-revolutionary Iran." *Ethnomusicology* 57 (1): 57–87.

Hemmasi, Farzaneh. 2017a. "Googoosh's Voice: An Iranian Icon in Silence and Song." In *Vamping the Stage: Female Voices of Asian Modernities*, edited by Andrew Weintraub and Bart Barendregt, 234–257. Honolulu: University of Hawai'i Press.

Hemmasi, Farzaneh. 2017b. "Iran's Daughter and Mother Iran: Googoosh and Diasporic Nostalgia for the Pahlavi Modern." *Popular Music* 36 (2): 157–177.

Hemmasi, Farzaneh. 2017c. "'One Can Veil and Be a Singer!': Performing Piety on an Iranian Talent Competition." *Journal of Middle East Women's Studies* 13 (3): 416–437.

Hemmasi, Farzaneh. 2017d. "Rebuilding the Homeland in Poetry and Song: Simin Behbahani, Dariush Eghbali, and the Making of a Transnational Anthem." *Popular Communication* 15 (3): 192–206.

Herzfeld, Michael. 2005. *Cultural Intimacy: Social Poetics in the Nation-State.* 2nd ed. New York: Routledge.

Himmich, Hakima, and Navid Madani. 2016. "The State of Harm Reduction in the Middle East and North Africa: A Focus on Iran and Morocco." *International Journal of Drug Policy* 31:184–189.

Hofman, Ana. 2015. "Music (as) Labour: Professional Musicianship, Affective Labour and Gender in Socialist Yugoslavia." *Ethnomusicology Forum* 24 (1): 28–50.

hooks, bell. 1993. *Sisters of the Yam: Black Women and Self-Recovery*. Cambridge, MA: South End.

Iqtidar, Humeira. 2014. "Conspiracy Theory as Political Imaginary: Blackwater in Pakistan." *Political Studies* 64 (1): 1–16.

Iyer, Vijay. 2002. "Embodied Mind, Situated Cognition, and Expressive Microtiming in African-American Music." *Music Perception* 19 (3): 387–414.

Johnson, Mariana. 2010. "Exporting Exile on TV Martí." *Television and New Media* 11 (4): 293–307.

Kashani-Sabet, Firoozeh. 2011. *Conceiving Citizens: Women and the Politics of Motherhood in Iran*. Oxford: Oxford University Press.

Keil, Charles. 1987. "Participatory Discrepancies and the Power of Music." *Cultural Anthropology* 2 (3): 275–283.

Keil, Charles. 1995. "The Theory of Participatory Discrepancies: A Progress Report." *Ethnomusicology* 39 (1): 1–19.

Kelley, Ron, Johnathan Friedlander, and Anita Colby, eds. 1993. *Irangeles: Iranians in Los Angeles*. Berkeley: University of California Press.

Khosravi, Shahram. 2008. *Young and Defiant in Tehran*. Contemporary Ethnography. Philadelphia: University of Pennsylvania Press.

Khosravi, Shahram, and Mark Graham. 1997. "Home Is Where You Make It: Repatriation and Diaspora Culture among Iranians in Sweden." *International Journal of Refugee Studies* 10 (2): 115–133.

Kia, Mana, Afsaneh Najmabadi, and Sima Shakhsari. 2009. "Women, Gender, and Sexuality in Historiography of Modern Iran." In *Iran in the 20th Century: Historiography and Political Culture*, edited by Touraj Atabaki, 177–197. London: I. B. Tauris.

Kian, Azadeh. 1995. "L'invasion culturelle: Myth ou realité?" *Cahiers d'études sur la Méditerranée orientale et le monde turco-iranien*, no. 20 (July–December): 73–90. https://www.persee.fr/doc/cemot_0764-9878_1995_num_20_1_1275.

Kitch, Carolyn. 2007. "'It Takes a Sinner to Appreciate the Blinding Glare of Grace': Rebellion and Redemption in the Life Story of the 'Dark' Celebrity." *Popular Communication* 5 (1): 37–56.

Kolar-Panov, Dona. 1996. *Video, War and the Diasporic Imagination*. Routledge Research in Cultural and Media Studies. London: Routledge.

Korycki, Katarzyna, and Abouzar Nasirzadeh. 2016. "Desire Recast: The Production of Gay Identity in Iran." *Journal of Gender Studies* 25 (1): 50–65.

Kurzman, Charles. 2004. *The Unthinkable Revolution in Iran*. Cambridge, MA: Harvard University Press.

Laguna, Albert Sergio. 2014. "Cuban Miami on the Air: Narratives of Cubanía." *Journal of Latin American Cultural Studies* 23 (1): 87–110.

Lee, Benjamin, and Edward LiPuma. 2002. "Cultures of Circulation: The Imaginations of Modernity." *Public Culture* 14 (1): 191–213.

Levin, Theodore Craig. 1996. *The Hundred Thousand Fools of God: Musical Travels in Central Asia (and Queens, New York)*. Bloomington: Indiana University Press.

Loeb, Laurence D. 1972. "The Jewish Musician and the Music of Fars." *Asian Music* 4 (1): 3–14.

Lohman, Laura. 2010. *Umm Kulthum: Artistic Agency and the Shaping of an Arab Legend, 1967–2007*. Middletown, CT: Wesleyan University Press.

Maghbouleh, Neda. 2010. "'Inherited Nostalgia' among Second-Generation Iranian Americans: A Case Study at a Southern California University." *Journal of Intercultural Studies* 31 (2): 199–218.

Maghbouleh, Neda. 2017. *The Limits of Whiteness: Iranian Americans and the Everyday Politics of Race*. Palo Alto, CA: Stanford University Press.

Malek, Amy. 2015. "Claiming Space: Documenting Second-Generation Iranian Americans in Los Angeles." *Anthropology of the Middle East* 10 (2): 16–45.

Mankekar, Purnima. 2015. *Unsettling India: Affect, Temporality, Transnationality*. Durham, NC: Duke University Press.

Mankekar, Purnima, and Louisa Schein. 2012. "Introduction. Mediations and Transmediations: Erotics, Sociality, and 'Asia.'" In *Media, Erotics, and Transnational Asia*, edited by Purnima Mankekar and Louisa Schein, 1–32. Durham, NC: Duke University Press.

Mansbridge, Joanna. 2017. "The Zenne: Male Belly Dancers and Queer Modernity in Contemporary Turkey." *Theatre Research International* 42 (1): 20–36.

Marshall, P. David, Christopher Moore, and Kim Barbour. 2015. "Persona as Method: Exploring Celebrity and the Public Self through Persona Studies." *Celebrity Studies* 6 (3): 288–305.

Matthee, Rudolph P. 2005. *The Pursuit of Pleasure: Drugs and Stimulants in Iranian History, 1500–1900*. Princeton, NJ: Princeton University Press.

Meftahi, Ida. 2016a. *Gender and Dance in Modern Iran: Biopolitics on Stage*. Iranian Studies. London: Routledge.

Meftahi, Ida. 2016b. "The Sounds and Moves of Ibtiẕāl in 20th-Century Iran." *International Journal of Middle East Studies* 48 (1): 151–155.

Meftahi, Ida. 2017. "Enlacer l'ajnabi: Une histoire politique de la danse de couple à Téhéran, 1920–1950." *Clio* 2 (46): 111–133.

Meintjes, Louise. 2003. *Sound of Africa! Making Music Zulu in a South African Studio*. Durham, NC: Duke University Press.

Meizel, Katherine. 2010. "Real-Politics: Televised Talent Competitions and Democracy Promotion in the Middle East." In *Music and Media in the Arab World*, edited by Michael Aaron Frishkopf, 291–308. Cairo: American University of Cairo Press.

Michaelsen, Marcus. 2018. "Exit and Voice in a Digital Age: Iran's Exiled Activists and the Authoritarian State." *Globalizations* 15 (2): 1–17.

Milanloo, Hadi. 2015. "Marginalized Agency: Women, Music, and Social Space in Iran." Paper presented at the Annual Meeting of the Society for Ethnomusicology, Austin, Texas, December 4, 2015.

Mirabal, Nancy Raquel. 2003. "'Ser de Aqui': Beyond the Cuban Exile Model." *Latino Studies* 1:366–382.

Mittermaier, Amira. 2011. *Dreams That Matter: Egyptian Landscapes of the Imagination*. Berkeley: University of California Press.

Moaveni, Azadeh. 2005. *Lipstick Jihad: A Memoir of Growing Up Iranian in America and American in Iran*. New York: Public Affairs.

Moghanibashi-Mansourieh, Amir, and Abbas Deilamizade. 2014. "The State of Data Collection on Addiction in Iran." *Addiction* 109 (5): 854.

Mohaghegh, Jason Bahbak. 2012. *The Writing of Violence in the Middle East: Inflictions*. New York: Continuum.

Mohaghegh, Jason Bahbak. 2013. *Silence in Middle Eastern and Western Thought: The Radical Unspoken*. London: Routledge/Taylor and Francis Group.

Mowlana, Hamid. 1991. "Iranian Exile Newspapers in the Nineteenth and Early Twentieth Centuries." In *Iranian Refugees and Exiles since Khomeini*, edited by Asghar Fathi, 37–54. Costa Mesa, CA: Mazda.

Mozafari, Parmis. 2012. "Carving a Space for Female Singing in Post-revolution Iran." In *Resistance in Contemporary Middle Eastern Cultures: Literature, Cinema and Music*, edited by Karima Laachir and Saeed Talajooy, 262–278. London: Routledge.

Mozafari, Parmis. 2013. "Dance and the Borders of Public and Private Life in Post-revolution Iran." In *Cultural Revolution in Iran: Contemporary Popular Culture in the Islamic Republic*, edited by Annabelle Sreberny and Massoumeh Torfeh, 95–108. London: I. B. Tauris.

Murphet, Julian. 2001. *Literature and Race in Los Angeles*. Cambridge: Cambridge University Press.

Naficy, Hamid. 1993. *The Making of Exile Cultures: Iranian Television in Los Angeles*. Minneapolis: University of Minnesota Press.

Naficy, Hamid. 2012. *A Social History of Iranian Cinema*. Vol. 3, *The Islamicate Period, 1978–1984*. Durham, NC: Duke University Press.

Nafisi, Azar. 2003. *Reading Lolita in Tehran: A Memoir in Books*. New York: Random House.

Naghibi, Nima. 2016. *Women Write Iran: Nostalgia and Human Rights from the Diaspora*. Minneapolis: University of Minnesota Press.

Najmabadi, Afsaneh. 1991. "Hazards of Modernity and Morality: Women, State, and Ideology in Contemporary Iran." In *Women, Islam and the State*, edited by Deniz Kadiyoti, 48–76. Philadelphia: Temple University Press.

Najmabadi, Afsaneh. 1997. "The Erotic Vatan [Homeland] as Beloved and Mother: To Love, to Possess, and to Protect." *Comparative Studies in Society and History* 39 (3): 442–467.

Najmabadi, Afsaneh. 2005. *Women with Mustaches and Men without Beards: Gender and Sexual Anxieties of Iranian Modernity*. Berkeley: University of California Press.

Najmabadi, Afsaneh. 2014. *Professing Selves: Transsexuality and Same-Sex Desire in Contemporary Iran*. Durham, NC: Duke University Press.

Niknafs, Nasim. 2016. "In a Box: A Narrative of a/n (Under)Grounded Iranian Musician." *Music Education Research* 18 (4): 1–13.

Nikpour, Golnar. 2018. "Drugs and Drug Policy in the Islamic Republic of Iran." *Middle East Brief*, June 2018, 1–7.

Nooshin, Laudan. 2005a. "Subversion and Counter-subversion: Power, Control, and Meaning in the New Iranian Pop Music." In *Music, Power, and Politics*, edited by Annie J. Randall, 231–272. New York: Routledge.

Nooshin, Laudan. 2005b. "Underground, Overground: Rock Music and Youth Discourses in Iran." *Iranian Studies* 38 (3): 463–494.

Nooshin, Laudan. 2011. "Hip-Hop Tehran: Migrating Styles, Musical Meanings, Marginalized Voices." In *Migrating Music*, edited by Jason Toynbee and Byron Dueck, 92–111. London: Routledge.

Nooshin, Laudan. 2017. "Whose Liberation? Iranian Popular Music and the Fetishization of Resistance." *Popular Communication* 15 (3): 163–191.

Nooshin, Laudan. 2018. "'Our Angel of Salvation': Toward an Understanding of Iranian Cyberspace as an Alternative Sphere of Musical Sociality." *Ethnomusicology* 62 (3): 341–374.

Ortner, Sherry B. 2010. "Access: Reflections on Studying Up in Hollywood." *Ethnography* 11 (2): 211–233.

Osanloo, Arzoo. 2009. *The Politics of Women's Rights in Iran*. Princeton, NJ: Princeton University Press.

Pak-Shiraz, Nacim. 2013. "Imagining the Diaspora in the New Millennium Comedies of Iranian Cinema." *Iranian Studies* 46 (2): 165–184.

Papan-Matin, Firoozeh. 2009. "The Case of Mohammad Khordadian, an Iranian Male Dancer." *Iranian Studies* 42 (1): 127–138.

Perks, Robert, and Alistair Thomson. 2006. *The Oral History Reader*. 2nd ed. London: Routledge.

Pezeshkzad, Iraj. (1973) 1996. *My Uncle Napoleon: A Novel*. Translated by Dick Davis. Washington, DC: Mage.

Price, Monroe. 2012. "Iran and the Soft War." *International Journal of Communication* 6:2397–2415.

Rahimi, Babak. 2015. "Satirical Cultures of Media Publics in Iran." *International Communication Gazette* 77 (3): 267–281.

Rahimieh, Nasrin. 2016. *Iranian Culture: Representation and Identity*. Abingdon, UK: Routledge.

Rapport, Evan. 2014. *Greeted with Smiles: Bukharian Jewish Music and Musicians in New York*. New York: Oxford University Press.

Rekabtalaei, Golbarg. 2018. *Iranian Cosmopolitanism: A Cinematic History*. Cambridge: Cambridge University Press.

Reyes, Adelaida. 1999. *Songs of the Caged, Songs of the Free: Music and the Vietnamese Refugee Experience*. Philadelphia: Temple University Press.

Reyes, Angelita D. 2019. "Performativity and Representation in Transnational

Blackface: Mammy (USA), Zwarte Piet (Netherlands), and Haji Firuz (Iran)."
Atlantic Studies 16 (4): 521–550.

Robertson, Bronwen. 2012. *Reverberations of Dissent: Identity and Expression in Iran's Illegal Music Scene.* New York: Continuum.

Rohani, Talieh. 2009. "Nostalgia without Memory: Iranian-Americans, Cultural Programming, and Internet Television." Master's thesis, Massachusetts Institute of Technology.

Sabety, Setareh. 2001. "Googoosh on Tour: Decoding a Popular Iranian Myth." *Journal of the International Institute (University of Michigan)* 8 (2). http://hdl .handle.net/2027/spo.4750978.0008.204.

Sanasarian, Eliz. 1995. "Ayatollah Khomeini and the Institutionalization of Charismatic Rule in Iran, 1979–1989." *Journal of Developing Societies* 11:189–205.

Sarshar, Houman. 2007. "The Role of Jews in the Preservation of Popular and Classical Persian Music." Paper presented in Columbia University's Iranian Studies University Seminar Series, New York, NY, October 9, 2007.

Sarshar, Houman. 2012. "Judeo-Persian Communities of Iran, XI. Music. (2) Specific Topics on the Jewish Contribution to Persian Music." In *Encyclopaedia Iranica.* Ehsan Yarshater Center for Iranian Studies, Columbia University, 1982–. Article published September 15, 2009; last updated April 17, 2012. http://www.iranicaonline.org/articles/judeo-persian-comms-xi-2 -specific-topics.

Satrapi, Marjane. 2003. *Persepolis.* New York: Pantheon Books.

Schein, Louisa. 2012. "Homeland Beauty: Transnational Longing and Hmong American Video." In *Media, Erotics, and Transnational Asia,* edited by Purnima Mankekar and Louisa Schein, 203–231. Durham, NC: Duke University Press.

Schickel, Richard. 1986. *Intimate Strangers: The Culture of Celebrity.* New York: Fromm International Publishing Corporation.

Semati, Mehdi. 2012. "The Geopolitics of Parazit, the Iranian Televisual Sphere, and the Global Infrastructure of Political Humor." *Popular Communication* 10 (1–2): 119–130.

Shannon, Matthew K. 2017. *Losing Hearts and Minds: American-Iranian Relations and International Education during the Cold War.* Ithaca, NY: Cornell University Press.

Shay, Anthony. 1999. *Choreophobia: Solo Improvised Dance in the Iranian World.* Costa Mesa, CA: Mazda.

Shay, Anthony. 2000. "The 6/8 Beat Goes On: Persian Popular Music from Bazm-e Qajariyyeh to Beverly Hills Garden Parties." In *Mass Mediations: New Approaches to Popular Culture in the Middle East and Beyond,* edited by Walter Armbrust, 61–87. Berkeley: University of California Press.

Shay, Anthony. 2006. "The Male Dancer in the Middle East and Central Asia." *Dance Research Journal* 38 (1–2): 137–162.

Shiau, Hong-Chi. 2009. "Migration, Nostalgia and Identity Negotiation: Teresa

Teng in the Chinese Diaspora." *International Journal of Chinese Culture and Management* 2 (3): 263–275.

Shryock, Andrew. 2004. "In the Double Remoteness of Arab Detroit: Reflections on Ethnography, Culture Work, and the Intimate Disciplines of Americanization." In *Off Stage/On Display: Intimacy and Ethnography in the Age of Public Culture*, edited by Andrew Shryock, 279–314. Stanford, CA: Stanford University Press.

Siamdoust, Nahid. 2015. "Tehran's Soundscape as a Contested Public Sphere: Blurring the Lines between Public and Private." In *Divercities: Competing Narratives and Urban Practices in Beirut, Cairo and Tehran*, edited by Nadia von Maltzahn and Monique Bellan. Oriental Insitut Studies 3. http://www.perspectivia.net/publikationen/orient-institut-studies/3-2015/siamdoust_soundscape.

Siamdoust, Nahid. 2017. *Soundtrack of the Revolution: The Politics of Music in Iran.* Stanford, CA: Stanford University Press.

Simms, Rob, and Amir Koushkani. 2012. *Mohammad Reza Shajarian's Avaz in Iran and Beyond, 1979–2000.* Lanham, MD: Lexington Books.

Sreberny, Annabelle. 2013. "Too Soft on 'Soft War': Commentary on Monroe Price's 'Iran and the Soft War.'" *International Journal of Communication* 7:801–804.

Sreberny, Annabelle, and Massoumeh Torfeh. 2014. *Persian Service: The BBC and British Interests in Iran.* London: I. B. Tauris.

Sreberny-Mohammadi, Annabelle, and Ali Mohammadi. 1994. *Small Media, Big Revolution: Communication, Culture, and the Iranian Revolution.* Minneapolis: University of Minnesota Press.

Steward, Theresa Parvin. 2017. "In between Home and Homeland: Diaspora Identity as a Cultural Hybrid in Mohsen Namjoo's 'Cielito Lindo.'" *Popular Communication* 15 (3): 207–220.

Stokes, Martin. 2010. *The Republic of Love: Cultural Intimacy in Turkish Popular Music.* Chicago: University of Chicago Press.

Stone, Christopher Reed. 2008. *Popular Culture and Nationalism in Lebanon: The Fairouz and Rahbani Nation.* London: Routledge.

Sullivan, Zohreh T. 2001. *Exiled Memories: Stories of Iranian Diaspora.* Philadelphia: Temple University Press.

Talattof, Kamran. 2011. *Modernity, Sexuality, and Ideology in Iran: The Life and Legacy of a Popular Female Artist.* Syracuse, NY: Syracuse University Press.

Tannock, Stuart. 1995. "Nostalgia Critique." *Cultural Studies* 9 (3): 453–464.

Tavakoli-Targhi, Mohamad. 2000. "Going Public: Patriotic and Matriotic Homeland in Iranian Nationalist Discourses." *Strategies: Journal of Theory, Culture and Politics* 13 (2): 175–200.

Tavakoli-Targhi, Mohamad. 2001. *Refashioning Iran: Orientalism, Occidentalism, and Historiography.* New York: Palgrave.

Taylor, Charles. 2002. "Modern Social Imaginaries." *Public Culture* 14 (1): 91–124.

Taylor, Diana. 2003. *The Archive and the Repertoire: Performing Cultural Memory in the Americas*. Durham, NC: Duke University Press.

Tölölyan, Kachig. 2007. "The Contemporary Discourse of Diaspora Studies." *Comparative Studies of South Asia, Africa and the Middle East* 27 (3): 647–655.

Travis, Trysh. 2009. *The Language of the Heart: A Cultural History of the Recovery Movement from Alcoholics Anonymous to Oprah Winfrey*. Chapel Hill: University of North Carolina Press.

Turino, Thomas. 2008. *Music as Social Life: The Politics of Participation*. Chicago: University of Chicago Press.

Voss, Alex, and Marzieh Asgari-Targhi. 2015. "The Inescapable History and Politics of Anglo-Iranian Relations: Audience Engagement at the BBC Persian Service during the London 2012 Olympics." *Participations: Journal of Audience and Reception Studies* 12 (1): 549–576.

Warner, Michael. 2002. *Publics and Counterpublics*. New York: Zone Books, distributed by MIT Press.

Washburne, Christopher, and Maiken Derno. 2004. *Bad Music: The Music We Love to Hate*. New York: Routledge.

Weidman, Amanda. 2014. "Anthropology and Voice." *Annual Review of Anthropology* 43 (1): 37–51.

White, William L. 2015. "Congress 60: An Addiction Recovery Community within the Islamic Republic of Iran." *Alcoholism Treatment Quarterly* 33 (3): 328–347.

Yano, Christine Reiko. 2002. *Tears of Longing: Nostalgia and the Nation in Japanese Popular Song*. Cambridge, MA: Harvard University Asia Center, distributed by Harvard University Press.

Youssefzadeh, Ameneh. 2000. "The Situation of Music in Iran since the Revolution: The Role of Official Organizations." *British Journal of Ethnomusicology* 9 (2): 35–61.

Youssefzadeh, Ameneh. 2004. "Singing in a Theocracy: Female Musicians in Iran." In *Shoot the Singer! Music Censorship Today*, edited by Marie Korpe, 129–134. London: Zed Books.

INDEX

Sousan, 12, 36, 45
Stokes, Martin, 29
Stone, Christopher Reed, 215n18
Sullivan, Zohreh T., 209n1

ta'ārof (Iranian etiquette), 205n36
Tabaraei, Jahangir, 30, 71, 89–93, 96
tab'id (political exile), 24–25
Taherzadeh, 93
tahrir poetry, 125, 214n5
Taraneh (Song) Enterprises, 71, 87–97;
  "QQ Bang Bang" production and,
  138–141
TarantisT (band), 192
tasnif (song), 38, 43, 125
Tataloo, Amir, 66, 221n14
Tavakolian Newsha, 134
Tavakoli-Targhi, Mohamad, 146
Tehrangeles cultural production: alternative histories of, 30; ambivalence
  about, 81–88; Bibiyan's influence in,
  71–80; current trends in, 187–199;
  declining influence of, 71; digital
  technology and, 90–92; drug abuse
  in, 157–158; expatriate community
  and influence of, 190–194; founding generation in America of, 11–14;
  geographic boundaries, 14–21; global
  reach of, 17–21, 94–97; Googoosh's association with, 134–141; Iranian audiences for, 19–21; Iranian politics and,
  124–127; laborers of joy, 55–58; longing
  for homeland in, 30, 98–121; in *Maxx*
  (film), 100–104; political potential
  of, 4–8, 30–31, 153–156; popular music
  and history and, 67–68; postrevolutionary Iranian politics and, 144–150,
  187–190; prerevolutionary Iran in,
  8–11, 71–80, 216n29; research meth-
  odology and, 34–37; resistance fetish
  and, 32–33; return to Iran of, 120–121;
  second- and third-generation Iranians
  and, 194–195; stereotypes of, 21–23,
  53–55; transnationality of, 2–3; uncer-

tainty and fear in, 205n31; in western
  Europe, 13; women in, 28–29, 69–71,
  109–120
Tehran Revolutionary Court, sentencing of Googoosh by, 21
television stations: Ayeneh addiction
  workshops and, 170–177; Taraneh
  presence on, 91; Tehrangeles cultural
  distribution through, 17–23, 68–71;
  unveiled women in, 109–110
tonbak goblet drum, 38, 46, 62, 75. See
  also *dombaki*
Towfigh, Abbasseh (Dr.), 164–167,
  171–174, 180–182, 218nn12–13
transnational media: drug addiction
  and recovery and, 178–182; Iranian
  women performers and erotics of,
  111–120; Tehrangeles cultural productions and, 99–121
Travis, Trysh, 178–182
Tribyun-e āzād (*Free Tribune*), 125–126
"Tu in zamuneh" ("In These Times")
  (song), 66
Turbulent (video installation), 133–134
TV Persia 1 television station, 94–95

Umm Kulthum, 132–133, 215n17
Uncle Napoleon (pop culture figure),
  205n32
United States, Iranian students in,
  11–14

Varuzhan, 75
"Vatan" ("Homeland") (song), 4,
  126–127, 158, 202n4
"Vāy vāy" ("Woe, Woe"), 82
veil, aural, 133; expatriate popular culture and, 117, 149–150; postrevolutionary Iranian law and, 6, 133, 213n16;
  prerevolutionary law and, 202n8. See
  also hijab
"velvet revolution" (*enghelāb-e makhmali*),
  popular culture distribution as,
  20–21

Voice of America, 68, 192
Voice of Iran, The (documentary), 213n2

websites: drug addiction and recovery
 and, 170–171; Taraneh Enterprises,
 91–92
women: as activists and political symbols, 124; exclusion from cultural
 production, 7–8; Iranian American
 memoirs by, 209n1, 215n19; matriotic
 discourse in postrevolutionary Iranian politics and, 145–150; migration
 of Iranian women artists, 193–194;
 modern gender systems and, 103–104;
 postrevolutionary Iran performances
 by, 122–124, 133–137; prerevolutionary
 Iranian music performed by, 128–133;
public solo singing prohibition for, 2,
 133–134; as Tehrangeles performers,
 28–29, 69–71, 109–120

"Yāvar-e hamisheh mo'men," or "Ever-
 Faithful Friend" (song), 161–163, 182
Yazdi, Masoud, 207n11
Yellow Dogs (band), 192

Zakarian, Zoya, 13, 115–116, 137–141
Zamani, Farhad, 130–132, 137, 140,
 214n14, 215n15
Zaresani, Sanaz, 112
"Zartosht" ("Zoroaster") (album),
 135–137, 153
"Zendāni" ("Imprisoned") (song), 183
Zoland, Farid, 13, 157